THE POLITICS OF WRITING

RURY CHR

^AY LOAN *

'This is an authoritative book with invitations to lecturers, researchers and students to resist the conformity of conventions, in the name of a more democratic world in which writers can be both creative and scholarly, original and disciplined.'

Jane Mace, *Goldsmiths College, University of London*

Writing matters: it plays a key role in the circulation of ideas in society and has a direct impact on the development of democracy. But only a few get to do the kind of writing that most influences this development.

The Politics of Writing examines writing as a social practice. The authors use examples from student writing, writing in the home and the media, and interviews with the playwright Trevor Griffiths. They draw on critical linguistics, cultural studies and literacy studies as they explore and analyse:

- the social context in which writing is embedded
- the processes and practices of writing
- the purposes for writing
- the reader–writer relationship
- issues of writer identity

They challenge current notions of 'correctness' and argue for a more democratic pedagogy as part of the answer to the inequitable distribution of the right to write.

Romy Clark coordinates the Academic Support Programme at Lancaster University. **Roz Ivanič** is a lecturer in linguistics at Lancaster University.

WITHDRAWN

THE POLITICS OF WRITING

Romy Clark and Roz Ivanič

London and New York

First published 1997
by Routledge
11 New Fetter Lane, London EC4P 4EE

Simultaneously published in the USA and Canada
by Routledge
29 West 35th Street, New York, NY 10001

© 1997 Romy Clark and Roz Ivanič

Typeset in Baskerville by Keystroke, Jacaranda Lodge, Wolverhampton
Printed and bound in Great Britain by Creative Print and Design
(Wales), Ebbw Vale

British Library Cataloguing in Publication Data
A catalogue record for this book is available from the British Library

Library of Congress Cataloging in Publication Data
A catalogue record for this book has been requested

ISBN 0–415–13482–X
0–415–13483–8 (pbk)

To all those – students, colleagues, friends and family – who have in various ways helped our understanding of writing.

CONTENTS

LIST OF FIGURES

ACKNOWLEDGEMENTS

Many of the ideas discussed in the book had their first airing at the Teaching of Writing Research Group at Lancaster University. We are grateful to all members of the group for their contributions to our thinking. We thank Jane Mace for her prompt and valuable feedback on the whole of an earlier draft of this book.

We also thank David Barton, Norman Fairclough, Nigel Hall and Catherine Macrae for helpful feedback on Chapters 2, 6 and 8.

Special thanks to Trevor Griffiths for the generous sharing of his thoughts about writing which have enhanced our understanding of the processes and practices of writing.

Thanks also to family, friends and colleagues for giving us the space to get on with this book when we most needed it.

We are grateful to the editor of *Prospect: The Australian Journal of TESOL* for permission to reprint an article that was originally published there in a revised form as Chapter 6 of this book. We are also grateful to *Changing English*, the *Guardian*, Macmillan and Faber & Faber for permission to reproduce extended extracts for commentary in the book

1

INTRODUCTION

A TASTE OF THE CONTENT OF THE BOOK

Some types of writing have more status than others:

> That's me, and this is me playing the 'I have an elaborated code' syndrome. Some of it I'm playing a game – playing a game with words really now . . . sometimes it's like the working class person trying to speak posh.
>
> It's one minute with the dinner jacket on and the next minute with the cleaning outfit. I know that that's what's happening, but I just think 'Oh get on with it, Rachel, get on with it'.
>
> (Rachel, 1991)

Writing is a struggle, even for the most experienced writers:

> In spite of what I've said about being extraordinarily familiar with my own way of writing plays, I still feel whenever I sit down to write . . . like I know nothing. I feel like an amnesiac on a diving-board, staring down at the pool, knowing I have to dive but not remembering that I can swim.
>
> (Trevor Griffiths, 1993)

Writing constructs identities for writers:

> Now if I've got access to new clothes, different clothes, I will make distinctions in which ones I'm going to buy . . . and it's the choice between the words that you use, between the clothes that you buy, says something about you, which is ever-changing as well, I think. It won't be static, it will be ever-changing . . .
>
> (Rachel, 1989)

1

Writing is a tool for thinking:

> You've got that many ideas rushing. You know what you want to say and then changing it into the words to put onto paper ... cos speaking is completely different from writing so you ... but I found it great.
>
> (Jay, 1983)

Writers can be constrained by the demands and expectations of their readers:

> Sometimes I feel they want you to do so much: you've got to present it in an academic way, write it with your ideas; you've got to argue both sides and see things on two sides, AND they want ethics. Now to try and bring those things together in one is not easy. Especially when a lot of the things which naturally arise are ethical like questions of resources and if you're talking about an Aids patient should get more or less money there's a tendency to think, well, it's an ethical issue, so ethics are in there, but I think what they want is to be clouted over the head.
>
> (John Simpson, 1991)

and writers can resist the pressures on them to write in a certain way:

> I think it's appalling, I really do. I will never submit to that. I think she can ask me to put quotations in, if these are the rules of the academic game ... I don't like them ... but my quotations are there for a reason.... the length of the quotation I feel will back up a point and I wouldn't have carried on writing if I didn't feel that it was all appropriate and I will never ever give in to someone telling me to shorten them.
>
> (John Simpson, 1991)

The conventions of written language are not all logical:

> It's carrying on: it's telling about the green. I've not changed dramatically. It was carrying on from 'the green' ... I could've swore blind it should've been a comma ... it's come as quite a shock!
>
> (Michael, 1983)

2

Written language is a web of intertextuality:

> I don't even know where my own words are coming from,
> Roz, any more.
>
> (Rachel, 1989)

WHY READ A BOOK ABOUT THE POLITICS OF WRITING?

Our aim in this book is to provide a synthesis of a range of perspectives on writing. As teachers of writing we have, over the years, come to realise how important it is to have a sophisticated, wide-ranging understanding of the nature of writing as a political, social, mental, physical and linguistic act. Our attempts to understand what is involved in writing took us on an unexpected journey way beyond the confines of any one discipline. In this book we present a genealogy of our understanding of writing, sharing with you the paths we have trod in developing a view of writing that can help us make principled decisions when we teach it.

We imagine you, the readers, to be interested in the politics of writing because you recognise that writing is more than just a mechanical skill. We imagine most of you to be interested in writing as part of a wider interest in how society works. We imagine many of you, like us, to be interested in writing because you teach it in school, in adult education, or in higher education. We hope you will also find that reading this book helps you to reflect on your own experience as a writer, and that this will enable you to bring fresh insights to the next piece of writing you undertake.

Our search for an understanding of what is involved in writing has taken us on a journey through a wide variety of fields of study, the main ones being social theory, cultural studies, media studies, semiotics, discourse analysis, linguistics, applied linguistics, literacy studies and composition studies. In our bibliography you are likely to find references with which you are familiar alongside others that may be new. We are not aiming to make a major contribution in any single one of these fields; rather, we aim to bring them together and make connections among them that will provide a more broadly based understanding of writing than can be offered from within any single discipline. Within the space constraints of the book we have not been able to deal with every field in great depth, but we have tried to provide at least one reference which will allow you to pursue an interest further.

We originally intended to focus mainly on academic writing, and many of our examples in Chapters 3–7 are of students writing for university courses. However, we believe that the way of thinking about writing we are presenting can be extended to all types of writing, and in many places we draw out the connections, similarities and contrasts among types of writing. We intend our comparisons to work in both directions: what we say about academic writing is intended to provide the grounds for thinking about writing of all types, and what we say about other types of writing is intended to shed new light on academic writing. The political issue of which members of a society become transmitters of meanings (which we discuss in Chapter 2) is an important starting point for thinking about any type of writing, and the aspects of writing that we use as headings for Chapters 3–8 apply to writing in general, not only to academic writing.

We devote most of the book to developing an understanding of writing as a social and political act, because this is, in our view, a prerequisite for making any pedagogic recommendations. Recognising the political nature of writing is what motivates us, and many other teachers of writing, to work with people who want to improve and extend their writing capabilities. Recognising the political nature of writing is what has led us to the pedagogic principles that guide our practice as teachers of writing, as we present them in Chapter 9. This is why we have chosen the title *The Politics of Writing*, and we have organised the book to reflect that priority.

WHO ARE WE TO WRITE ABOUT WRITING?

We have both been teaching writing for over twenty years in a variety of settings. This experience has stimulated a fascination with what is involved in learning to write, and given us experience, between us, of a wide variety of learner writers. Since 1982 we have both been engaged in research on writing and learning to write. In 1986 we founded the Teaching of Writing Research and Development Group at Lancaster University, and have been collaborating on various teaching and research projects to do with writing and learning to write since then. We have ourselves both struggled with writing throughout our lives, and still do. Each new writing task is a new threat and a new challenge, particularly (but not only) when it involves a new genre. Collaboratively writing a book is at this moment a new undertaking for us, facing us with the very difficulties and complexities we are writing about in it. All writing is still for us always also learning to write, as we gradually acquire new genres and new discourses. Our teaching, our research and our critical reflection on our own experiences as writers are central to this book, so here, first, is a sketch of each of our lives as teachers of writing, and an outline of the research projects in which we have been involved.

Teaching writing

Romy: I taught writing as part of my EFL work, mainly with adult learners, in Italy, Singapore, Venezuela and England. My real interest in writing developed in 1986 when I became responsible for the in-sessional provision of academic support for overseas students at Lancaster University. A large part of that work is focused on helping bilingual undergraduates and postgraduates from many different countries with academic writing. Since 1987 I have been providing the same support service for students whose first language is English who need help with writing. Trying to provide support for a wide range of students with differing backgrounds, discipline areas and learning needs has forced me to question the view of writing as a 'skill', as some sort of neutral technology that can be neatly packaged up and passed on to learners. I have learned that it is important to see writing as a social practice, embedded in social relations within a specific community, each with its own complex ideological and conventional practices within which individual students have to find identities as writers that they feel confident and comfortable with. So, central to my work has been trying to gain more understanding of the processes and practices of writing that people engage in and why, and to share that understanding with my students: this book is part of that attempt.

Roz: I taught English to children aged 10–17 in rural English secondary schools for five years. I had not intended to become an English teacher: the job I originally applied for was to teach Drama and Latin. However, day-to-day life in a secondary school gradually led me to what was to become my main professional interest: working with learners who found writing difficult. At first I saw this simplistically as a difficulty with spelling. This led me to find out more about 'dyslexia' and to start taking holiday jobs on summer schools for children aged 7–14 with specific language difficulties – work I continued to do intermittently for ten years. I learned a lot from the opportunity to talk individually with the children, learning to see 'writing' from their point of view. I ran the Language Support Service at what was then called Kingsway-Princeton College in London for eleven years, making special provision for students who needed extra help with literacy, aged 14–68. The variety in this job is an important source of my questioning about writing. It included a writing club for teenagers who had given up on school, evening classes for adults wanting help with writing, initial literacy for students who had left school and wanted a second chance, support for students on courses ranging from general vocational preparation, through 'O' Level as it was called in those days, now 'GCSE', to Access to Higher Education courses. I worked for a year in the writing lab at San Joaquin Delta College, California, where I met inspiring teachers and learner writers from very different backgrounds and educational cultures from Britain. One of the main questions that emerged from all that work was: Why write? Education itself provided the answer for some, but not for all. Since starting work at Lancaster University in 1986 my work as a writing teacher has been more sporadic: I have worked as a volunteer for the Lancaster College Adult Basic Education service, I have worked with Romy teaching academic writing to MA students in Linguistics, and I have responded to many knocks on my door.

Researching writing

The research we have undertaken individually and collaboratively has illuminated writing from various perspectives. Contrasting different writers and different types of writing has stimulated our thinking about the nature of writing. Both of us have been motivated mainly by a desire to understand writing better in order to teach it better, but some strands in our research have been less pedagogically oriented.

Research on adults' perceptions of punctuation

Roz worked with ten adults on a Basic Education programme, asking them their reasons for punctuating their writing as they did. The main finding of this project was that these learner writers always had good reasons for putting full stops and commas where they did, even though 23 per cent of these were wrong according to the standard conventions of written English. They were appealing mainly to the commonsense criteria of sound and meaning 'putting punctuation where you pause' and 'putting a full stop at the end of a complete idea' but these were not adequate guidelines all the time. (For more details see Ivanič 1996.)

Research on reader response to newspaper articles

Romy researched the effect of ideological presuppositions on readers of accounts of the miners' strike in that year. She found that most readers conform to the writer's representation of the world, but some resist it. Although this research was focused mainly on reading, it is the springboard of her understanding of the political nature of writing, as presented particularly in Chapters 2 and 7 of this book. (For further details see Clark 1984.)

Research on characteristics of writing across the curriculum

Roz researched the characteristics of words like 'purpose', 'factor' and 'effect', and the way in which such words pervade the discourse of secondary and higher education. On the basis of a small-scale study she found that those who use them successfully in their writing seem to do well in GCSE. (For further details see Ivanič 1983, 1991.)

Research on the nature of the writing process

Together with the Teaching of Writing Group at Lancaster University, we have evolved a list of the components of the writing process which includes affective and socio-political aspects of writing as well as cognitive. We have done this by running an exploratory activity with a variety of groups of participants: groups of learners from various countries, ages and backgrounds, groups of teachers and groups of researchers. We describe this work in Chapter 4, and give further details in Clark and Ivanič 1991.

7

Research on writer identity

Our work on the writing process led us to be particularly interested in challenging the convention that academic writing is
'impersonal', and revealing the ways in which the self is bound
up in all types of writing. Romy worked with students of several
nationalities on a Diploma in Politics and International Relations,
exploring the issues of identity that arose for them in their
writing, particularly the construction of authority. Roz worked
with mature students on a range of courses in the social sciences
and humanities, exploring how they were positioned by particular pieces of writing, and their reasons for identifying with or
distancing themselves from these positionings. We draw on this
work particularly in Chapter 6. (For further details see also Clark
and others 1990b; Ivanič and Roach 1990; Ivanič and Simpson
1992; Ivanič 1993, 1994a, forthcoming, Ivanič and others 1996.)

Research on Critical Language Awareness in relation to writing development

Critical Language Awareness (CLA) means explicit discussion
of issues of power and ideology underlying language use. It is a
term coined by a group of us at Lancaster University (Clark and
others 1990a and 1991; Fairclough 1992b) at the time when there
was considerable interest in increasing the amount of explicit
'Knowledge About Language' in the curriculum in British schools.
We were particularly interested in ways in which CLA-raising could
help students with their academic writing. This issue pervades the
whole of this book in that Chapters 2–8 are about the aspects of
writing that might be part of CLA in educational settings. Then
in Chapter 9 we summarise pedagogical issues associated with
CLA-raising. (For further details see Ivanič 1988 and 1990; Clark
and Ivanič 1991; Clark 1992; Janks and Ivanič 1992.)

Research at the Communication Skills Unit, University of Dar-es-salaam

Between 1988 and 1994 we worked closely with Martha Qorro at
the University of Dar-es-salaam on ways of developing the teaching
of writing to students entering the university who had to write their
coursework and exams in English. This involved considering the
multilingual and multiliterate nature of the student population,
the differing demands of the university lecturers in a variety of

faculties and departments, and the structuring of a communication skills programme to support writing in this context.

Research on writing demanded by local authorities (for the Citizens' Advice Bureaux)

In 1990 Romy was asked by the CAB to run a workshop for local authority revenue officers and CAB welfare rights workers to discuss how to improve written communication between local authorities and householders about the newly introduced 'Poll Tax'. Problems identified included multiple-address standard letters and forms, unexplained jargon, high numbers of nominalisations, long sentences, unclear agency (not enough 'I', 'we' or 'you'), and the type of font used.

Research on Trevor Griffiths as a writer

Romy has recently been examining the writing processes and practices of the British playwright Trevor Griffiths. She has done this by comparing what he said about his intentions with the impressions gained by different readers (see Clark 1993a), and through taped conversations about his working practices. Insights gained from talking to this professional writer have illuminated and furthered our understanding of the nature of writing which was previously based on work with learner writers.

A VIEW OF LANGUAGE AND LITERACY FOR UNDERSTANDING WRITING

In the central chapters of the book (Chapters 3–7) we discuss writing from the perspective of a social view of language and literacy. Here we outline the ways of thinking about language, literacy practices, discourse and genre on which we draw in those chapters.

Since writing is an aspect of language, discussing writing presupposes a view of language. We take as a starting point Halliday's view that language is the way it is because it serves three macro-functions: the 'ideational' function of representing the world, the 'interpersonal' function of conducting social relations, and the 'textual' function of organising the message (Halliday 1994). We explain and discuss these further below.

Writing is also an aspect of 'literacy': while 'language' is a semiotic system, 'literacy' is the ways of using, and ability to use, that semiotic system. This difference in emphasis between the words 'language' and 'literacy' can actually be applied to all semiotic systems, but the term 'literacy' is usually used to refer to the use of a specific semiotic system: *written* language, and this is our focus. A social view of language involves seeing the semiotic system embedded in the uses that are made of it, and these are in turn embedded in other aspects of social context, as we explain in this section and discuss in detail in Chapters 3 and 5. We are concentrating here on broad issues to do with the nature of language and literacy, including definitions of terms we use elsewhere in the book.

By describing language as a 'semiotic system' we are taking the Hallidayan view (1978, 1994) that the form of language is inextricable from its content. Fairclough (1992a) says that language conveys three types of content: 'social reality', 'social relations' and 'social identities'. 'Social reality' is what Halliday calls 'ideational meaning': the propositional content of language: the events, processes, objects, topics, concepts and ideas that are spoken or written about. 'Social relations' and 'social identities' are what Halliday calls 'interpersonal meaning': messages about the interlocutors themselves and the relationships between them. The function of language is to convey these three types of meaning simultaneously. These types of meaning are not just what people speak and write about, but they are actually part of the resources of language itself. In other words, it is not just *what* people say or write, but also *how* they word it that conveys meaning.

People do not make meanings in a vacuum: language use is embedded in social context. A framework for integrating a description of language with a description of its social context is provided by Fairclough (1989 and 1992a). In Figure 1.1 we have reproduced Fairclough's diagram as he presented it in *Language and Power* (1989), adding arrows.

One advantage of this diagram is that it illustrates graphically how the words themselves – 'text' – are embedded in the processes and social forces that produce them. Fairclough shows how a text (written or spoken) is inextricable from the processes of production and interpretation that create it, and that these processes are in turn inextricable from the local, institutional and sociohistorical conditions within which the participants are situated.

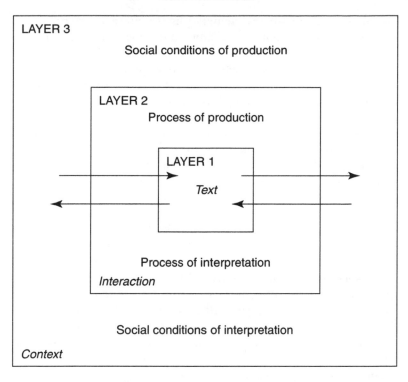

Figure 1.1 Discourse as text, interaction and context
Source: Fairclough 1989: 25

The outer layer of Fairclough's diagram is what distinguishes it from many other views of language. The 'social context' in his view contains not only the local circumstances in which people are communicating, but also the social, cultural and political climate within which this communication takes place. The most important aspects of social context are the relations of power that exist in it, and the interests (in both senses of the word), values and beliefs that maintain these relations of power. In most historical periods, interests, values and beliefs are not singular but multiple, and relations of power are open to contestation and change, as we discuss in more detail later in this chapter and also in Chapter 2. The arrows in Figure 1.1 show the role of language in this process: meaning-making in individual texts connects directly with the reproduction or contestation of values and beliefs about social reality (ideational meaning) and power relations (interpersonal meaning). This process is mediated by the literacy practices, discourses and genres that are available in the socio-cultural context, as we discuss next.

The interests, values, beliefs and sets of power relations in the social context as a whole are inscribed in the prototypical ways of doing things that people draw on in their day-to-day uses of language. Where writing is concerned, prototypical ways of doing things can be divided into, on the one hand, the physical, mental and interpersonal practices that constitute and surround the act of writing, and on the other hand, 'textual practices' or 'discourse conventions': conventions for using the semiotic system itself. These two aspects of writing are often so closely interrelated that it does not make theoretical sense to distinguish them: the term 'literacy practices' conveniently covers both. So, for example, the literacy practices associated with writing a phone message at home include, firstly, the social conditions in which telephones are established as a means of communication, the choice to use the phone rather than other means of communication, the types of social relations in which the call itself is embedded, the conventional ways of integrating telephones and message-taking into the physical layout of a room, the culturally recognisable ways of deploying paper and writing implements, the socio-culturally shaped mental processes of recall and selection of what to write, and the conventions for how to deliver the message, in addition to the conventions for wording the message. This example also demonstrates how spoken and written communication are often so interwoven that it does not make sense to separate them.

The term 'practices' refers to *prototypical* ways of doing things with language, but it often also refers to the *actual*, observable practices employed in a particular instance of language use. Gee (1990) distinguishes these two meanings by writing 'Practices' with a capital 'P' for the prototypical, and with a lower case 'p' for the actual. However, we are happy to live with the ambiguity of the single term, to capture the idea that the actual is always an instantiation of the prototypical. We discuss the use of the term 'practices' further in Chapter 4; see also Barton 1994.

There are many ways of talking about 'textual practices': the prototypical ways of doing things specifically with the semiotic system of language. Fairclough uses the term 'orders of discourse' to refer to conventions that are the product of the struggles over meaning that have taken place in the recent socio-political history of particular institutions, or the culture as a whole. Orders of discourse are resources for representing reality: the resources for 'ideational' meaning-making, to use the Hallidayan term. Orders of discourse are bound up with the values and beliefs that serve particular power relations in the social context: they have ideological underpinnings and ideological consequences. For example, the order of discourse within the institution of education in the UK has recently begun to represent education as a marketable commodity, using such words as 'deliver' to refer to the pedagogic process, and 'educational packages' as the entity delivered. These ways of thinking about education will serve the interests of those who stand to gain from 'marketing' education. Someone writing publicity material for a school or college, for example, is likely to have encountered this order of discourse, to be positioned into reproducing it in their own text, and thereby to maintain their own or someone else's interests in presenting education in this way.

Our example leads to an important element in our view of language: discoursal positioning. Orders of discourse affect writers by providing them with templates for appropriate ways of writing about particular topics. Fortunately, orders of discourse in most socio-political contexts are not unitary, as we argued in relation to power relations, values and beliefs: for any field of representation there are likely to be two or more competing orders of discourse on which to draw for the representation of a particular field of reality. Of these, one is likely to be dominant at any historical moment – as the order of discourse representing education as a marketable commodity is dominant in the early 1990s in the UK. Writers may be seduced into drawing on the dominant order of discourse, but they have the option, in principle, to do otherwise. The terms 'discourse', 'discourses', 'discoursal' and 'interdiscursivity' all concern 'orders of discourse', and are to do with the way in which language constructs the reality that is its content.

Genres are also abstract, socially legitimated ways of using language. They consist of norms and conventions for organising and presenting messages for particular social purposes. Genres are resources for language as social action: for conducting social relations and getting things done; genres are the resources for 'interpersonal' meaning-making, to use the Hallidayan term. (See especially Kress 1985 for this meaning of 'genre'.) In terms of Halliday's macro-functions of language, they combine the function of conveying 'interpersonal' meaning with the 'textual' function of organising and holding texts together. When people draw on particular genres they are taking up and hence reproducing particular social roles and relationships, and reproducing a particular, socially ratified way of communicating. For example, the same person writing publicity material for a school or college would draw on the genre of the advertisement and the genre of the information leaflet in order to decide what to write about, in what order, and how to set up the relationship with the reader. Some definitions of 'genre' maintain that the linguistic norms and conventions are the inevitable product of the purposes that they serve. However, in the chapters that follow, you will find us contesting this view, believing instead that these norms and conventions are the product of current relations of power and discourse practices in particular institutions, or the culture as a whole. The generic conventions for writing in response to a particular social need are therefore not singular and set in stone, but heterogeneous and open to contestation. As with orders of discourse, genres can be mixed and used strategically. Every instance of language use contributes to the possibilities of new genres, or generic variations emerging.

We use the terms 'discourse' and 'genre' contrastively when we want to make the distinction between the way in which reality is represented by language and the generic form in which it is represented. However, these two are often inextricably intertwined. For example, the order of discourse that represents education as a commodity almost certainly affects the genres in which this representation is ensconced. In this book we therefore often use the broader terms 'discourse' and 'discoursal' when we are referring to the whole discourse-and-genre complex as a social act, socially shaped and socially shaping.[1] When we do not need to distinguish between 'discourse' and 'genre', we use the term 'discourse type' as a catch-all term in much the same way as Fairclough does in *Language and Power* (1989).[2] One reason for wanting to use the term 'discourse type' rather than 'genre' is that the term 'discourse type' can encompass discourse *practices* beyond linguistic characteristics, as we discussed above. Another reason for not using 'genre' as an overarching term is that it has been used by some theorists in a rather simplistic way, not taking account of the ideological nature of linguistic resources that is central to our view of language.

14

As we emphasised above, these socially ratified, prototypical ways of doing things – literacy practices, discourses, genres, or 'discourse types' – are shaped by and carry with them particular interests, values, beliefs and sets of power relations in the social context as a whole: they have ideological underpinnings and their use has ideological consequences. In most social and historical contexts these communicative resources exist in a climate of multiplicity, contestation and change. There may be dominant practices and conventions, but there are usually alternatives. It would therefore be theoretically unsound to create a typology of discourse practices or discourse types, setting out their characteristics as if they could be learned and reproduced like a list of spellings. We eschew the 'typology' approach, preferring to think of many possibilities for the representation of social reality and the conducting of social relations through language, in which certain literacy practices and discourse types may be dominant, but not fixed.

So far we have discussed in detail the outer layer of Fairclough's diagram: the most important in relation to the politics of writing. The other two layers are more self-explanatory, and we deal with them more briefly here. Layer 2 of the diagram, labelled 'Interaction', represents the practices and processes of producing and receiving language. This layer contains both the 'actual' literacy practices in which people engage as they write and the cognitive processes going on in their heads: decisions about how to word a message, and acts of interpretation. These practices and processes are what mediate the outer and the inner layers – the prototypical and the actual. Depending on the access people have had to literacy practices and discourse types, their social, cultural and political allegiances, and their personal 'interests' in both senses, they will prefer certain practices and discourse types over others, and will reproduce them in their own practice. We discuss this process in detail throughout the book, but particularly in Chapter 4, and we discuss the take-up of written meanings through reading in Chapters 2 and 7. In the case of some uses of language, such as broadcasting and advertising, layer 2 of the diagram also contains the institutionalised and often technological processes of production, distribution and consumption, which we discuss further as part of our discussion of the press in Chapter 2. (See also Fairclough 1992a for further discussion of this aspect of language.)

15

Finally, the central box in Fairclough's diagram, labelled 'Text', refers to a stretch of actual spoken or written language that appears whole in some way. Developing the examples from earlier in this section, the actual school publicity leaflet, the telephone message and draft versions of them are 'texts'. We use the term 'linguistic characteristics' as an overarching term for referring to the language of a text. The connection between this central box of the diagram and the outer ones is that writers draw on 'literacy practices' and 'discourse types' in order to produce their texts. The arrows on the diagram represent the way in which the 'text' is shaped by and in turn shapes the social interaction and the social context within which it is embedded. In Chapters 3, 4, 5, 6 and 7 we discuss the way in which linguistic characteristics of texts are affected by the particular aspect of social context that is the focus of each chapter.

An important aspect of text which, for lack of space, we do not address in this book is the way in which its 'linguistic character-istics' are integrated with other visual means of representing meaning. This aspect of text is dealt with thoroughly by Kress and van Leeuwen (1996), and is one that we view as particularly relevant to thinking about writing in the future, as changing technology infuses the semiotic landscape with ever more inven-tive mixtures of the verbal and the visual. In addition, more and more people are becoming familiar with the use of hypertext – the technology for linking different elements together that is used in CD-ROM encyclopedias and on the World Wide Web – which means that messages no longer need to be structured in linear form. Literacy theorists (particularly The New London Group 1996) are predicting that in the twenty-first century people will be so used to receiving messages in non-linear, multi-modal forms that they will no longer think of writing continuous prose as the default means of conveying meaning. Although we do not discuss these interesting new developments in this book, we believe that a great deal of what we say about the politics of writing applies to communication through these modes and technologies too.

What we have presented here is a view of language and literacy based on Fairclough's diagram, but integrating insights from other sources. Many of the issues that we have introduced in general terms here we will revisit later in the book when we discuss them in more detail with specific reference to writing.

16

HOW DOES THIS BOOK WORK?

The chapters of the book work from the outer layer of Fairclough's diagram inwards towards the centre. We deal with what are sometimes known as 'the four Ps' of writing: product, process (including practices and participants), purpose and politics. These 'four Ps' map out the history of research on writing, but in line with our priorities we reverse this order. Our order reflects our view that there is no question of 'the politics of writing' being an optional extra, tagged on to the end of a view of writing: the political issues are integral to all other aspects of writing and learning to write. In Chapter 2 we start with the large-scale aspects of writing as a political act: the way in which power relations in society affect people's opportunities for writing and feelings about writing. This provides the guiding framework for our discussion of issues that come closer, as the book progresses, to the actual marks on the page. In Chapter 3 we examine what is meant by 'the social context for writing', expanding on some of the issues we introduced in the previous section. A central claim of this book is that the social context of any specific act of writing constructs both the way in which the writing is carried out and the written language of the text itself. In Chapters 4–7 we elaborate on this claim, discussing each aspect of writing as a social practice in detail: the processes and practices involved in writing (Chapter 4), purposes for writing and their relation to the content of writing (Chapter 5), and the participants in the process: writers and readers (Chapters 6 and 7). Chapters 4–7 span the outer layer and layer 2 of Fairclough's diagram, each dealing with both the effect of the broader social context on writing and the way in which writing is a form of social interaction. We set issues of 'text' in the context of social factors in two ways. Firstly, in each of Chapters 4–7 we comment on the way in which the linguistic characteristics of written language are shaped by the social factor under discussion. Secondly, we leave our chapter on the political issues of correctness and standardisation in written language (Chapter 8) until after we have discussed writing as a social practice (Chapters 3–7). Throughout the book we illustrate points we are making about the nature of writing with detailed examples of 'real writing' done by the writers we have taught and studied, as described earlier in this chapter.

Chapter 9 presents some implications of our view of writing for social and educational policy and practice. Picking up on the political issues we raised in Chapter 2, we do not see opportunities to write and be read as a matter of concern just in educational settings, but as a burning issue for everyone as they engage in social life. We do not separate 'writing' and 'learning to write', as we take the view that learning to write is never complete: new life experiences bring new demands that make all of us 'learner writers' throughout our lives. However, in the second half of Chapter 9 we focus on ways in which this life-process of developing writing can be supported in educational settings, and enhanced or accelerated by well-informed pedagogic practices.

Finally, we draw your attention to two issues that we take up across more than one chapter in the book:

1 *The relationships, similarities and differences between writing and speaking.*
   This issue is addressed in Chapters 3, 4 and 5.
2 *The ways in which writing is related intertextually to reading.*
   This issue is addressed in Chapter 6, where we discuss the way in which writers draw intertextually on discourse types that they have encountered in their reading, and in Chapter 7, where we discuss the way in which writers consider their readers.

WHY INCLUDE THE PLAYWRIGHT TREVOR GRIFFITHS IN OUR BOOK ON THE POLITICS OF WRITING?

In many chapters of the book we discuss the writing of Trevor Griffiths and include quotations from Romy's conversations with him. Trevor Griffiths has been writing plays for the stage, cinema and television for over thirty years and is one of Britain's major contemporary playwrights. His writing embodies many of the socio-political and cultural issues surrounding writing that we examine in this book: writing as a political act, writing in order to contribute to the (re)shaping of society, the complex role of people who write in society. He has been very generous in his willingness to talk about his writing and we are fortunate to be able to draw on several conversations with him about his writing practices and what writing means to him. These conversations have helped us to understand better what is involved in writing and we think these insights are worth sharing with others.

THE POLITICS OF WRITING COLLABORATIVELY

Throughout the book we have struggled over the use of the first person plural 'we', 'us', 'our'. We have avoided using it in the common academic way to mean 'you, we, and people in general', and tried to use it only as a simple plural expression of two people writing in partnership: 'the two of us'. This has led us to consider very carefully, sometimes painfully, what we can sincerely write as 'us'. Our personal histories are different and we are rooted in different political perspectives. This has sometimes made it hard for us to agree on the explanations for some of the practices and circumstances we describe in this book, and where we have been unable to reach agreement we have tried to make this clear to you. In most cases, however, we were able to reach agreement by talking through our differences. Although each chapter started off as the responsibility of one of us, in the end it is often difficult to say exactly who wrote what.

Our differing political stances have led to disagreements not only over content but also over some of the wording of the book. We have experienced for ourselves how closely our identities are bound up with the discourses we draw on as we write (the topic of Chapter 6). Lexical choices tie us into particular orders of discourse and associated ideologies. For example, Romy felt comfortable using the term 'bloc of alliances', Roz did not. Even such a few words can signal allegiance to a particular way of viewing the world. In such cases we had to find alternative wordings with which both of us could identify.

Despite these differences we are both strongly committed to the view of writing as a political act that we present here, and to a pedagogy that does not merely enable learner writers to take on the dominant practices of a discourse community but rather questions them and opens up the possibility for challenge. Arguing ideas out with each other has been an important and we think enriching part of the experience of writing this book and has, we hope, made it a better one.

2

WRITING, POLITICS AND POWER

PREFACE

This chapter focuses on the political context in which any public act of writing is embedded. As authors, we are not always in agreement on what, in the broader political sense, is in the best interests of the majority of people and what is said to be 'in the national interest'. We have therefore found it impossible to present this chapter in a way that represents both our political stances. The chapter is written mainly by Romy, and represents her positions on some issues which are not always shared by Roz. The main points of disagreement are over whether a liberal democracy and free market economy are or are not in the interests of the majority of the people and over whether the Falklands/Malvinas War and the Gulf War were or were not in the 'national interest', and we have not committed ourselves to a shared position when discussing these issues. However, this does not affect our shared conviction that writing is at the centre of political struggle, and in making this point we have been comfortable to write 'we'. The very fact that joint authorship is leading us into ideological struggles is part of the point we want to make about the place of writing in struggles over meaning.

INTRODUCTION

All writing is located within the wider socio-political context; this means that issues concerning writing, the values attached to it, and its distribution in society, are all essentially political and bound up with the way in which a social formation operates. In this chapter we first outline what are for us some key aspects of social theory, drawing in particular on the work of the Italian thinker Antonio Gramsci. We then discuss the way in which the press operates as one of the main institutions responsible for the distribution of meanings through writing. We take up the issues of what gets written and how, who gets to write, and the roles writers play or are not allowed to play. In the second half of the chapter we discuss the way in which education is responsible for the reproduction of social structures, and the particular role of writing and learning to write in this process.

Society is not homogeneous; it is made up of different social classes and groups with competing and often conflicting interests and ideologies operating, as we see it, in a hierarchy. The dominant ideologies are those that have the power to project particular meanings and practices as universal, as 'common sense'. This power operates either by winning the consent of others (hegemony, in Gramsci's terms) or, in moments of crisis and instability, by coercion, forcing others either to follow or to avoid certain practices; the ultimate coercion being the threat of imprisonment or death.

The dominant overarching ideology operating in Britain (and elsewhere in the West) at the moment is that of liberal democracy embodied in the representative state, based on economic liberalism (the market economy). This ideology is overarching in the sense that it permeates and defines all socio-economic relations in society. Alongside and frequently connected to this overarching ideology is a range of other dominant ideologies concerning patriarchy, race, the family and so on. These dominant ideologies and their accompanying practices coexist with other dominated or marginalised ideologies (e.g. socialist ideologies, feminist ideologies) that are struggling to become hegemonic.

Writing is of strategic importance to the outcome of these ideological struggles, as we discuss in relation to two significant sites: the press and schooling. We argue that the writing practices of these two institutions play a major role in the construction and maintenance of dominant ideologies and the related socio-economic order that these sustain. In order to understand the relationship between the modern representative state and institutions like the press and schooling, we first outline Gramsci's concept of 'hegemony' and the related concepts of 'civil society' and 'political society'.

21

SOCIAL THEORY

Hegemony: power and consent in liberal societies

Gramsci's concept of 'hegemony' is a key to understanding the way in which the modern representative state functions and how the dominant political forces build and maintain their power in modern liberal democratic societies such as Britain. For Gramsci, hegemony is essentially a relationship between social classes in which one class or section of a class exercises leadership over the other social classes by gaining their active consent for the policies and decisions they take. The notion of active consent is important, because it helps to explain how, for example in advanced capitalist societies such as Britain, many of the conflicting interests between social classes are resolved. For hegemony is not a relationship of domination by force or coercion but one of consent achieved by 'intellectual and moral leadership', which is exercised in what Gramsci calls 'civil society'.

The hegemony of a socio-economic group/class consists in its ability to re-present its own interests so that they appear to be the 'universal' interests of the whole society and to unite to itself and its goals a group of allies:

> bringing about not only a unison of economic and political aims, but also intellectual and moral unity, posing all the questions around which the struggle rages not on a corporate but on a 'universal' plane, and thus creating the hegemony of a fundamental [dominant] social group over a series of subordinate groups.
>
> (Gramsci 1971: 181–2)

The struggle for hegemony is ongoing and its outcome is not fixed for all time; the struggle for hegemony is also an emancipatory struggle, and we will be arguing that writing plays an important part in this. Before that we briefly explore Gramsci's view of the state.

The state: civil society and political society

The term 'the state' is a notoriously difficult one. We use the term, drawing on Gramsci, to mean the juridical political system which incorporates government and parliament and the public agencies that are part of the apparatus of government, such as ministries, and the political control over the police, the civil service and the armed forces (see also Fairclough 1989: 53). Gramsci's broad analysis is applicable to any modern state; it is an analysis, not a judgement as such, although it was prompted by the need to figure out how a communist state could be brought about in modern conditions.

Gramsci makes a fundamental distinction between civil society and political society. He says:

> We can . . . establish two major superstructural 'levels'; one we can call 'civil society', that is the group of organisms which are commonly called 'private', and the other which we can call 'political society or the State' and they correspond respectively to the function of hegemony which the dominant group exercises in the whole of society and to the function of 'direct domination' or command which is expressed in the State in the 'juridical' government.
>
> (Gramsci 1967: 836, Romy's translation)

Civil society, then, refers to the so-called 'private' institutions, such as schools, churches, political parties, trade unions and the press. It is the site of struggle, where the dominant class (and its allies) is constantly challenged and fights to maintain its hegemony. Political society refers to the government and its apparatuses. Although civil society is distinct from the 'public' apparatus of political society, the two are not completely separate and independent of one another. The distinction is a methodological one. In practice, they are intertwined in a dialectical relationship, influencing and shaping one another. This is specially true in advanced capitalist societies like the United Kingdom where the political and economic connections between government and publicly funded institutions, such as education, and quangos or even private enterprise are extremely complex and boundaries are often unclear. The press, which is technically independent of government in the United Kingdom but constrained by law, provides a good example of this complex relationship in three ways.

Firstly (as Herman and Chomsky [1994], argue), the mainstream press is crucial in constructing and maintaining consent around the interests, values and actions of the dominant socio-economic group whose interests are more or less directly represented by the

23

government. This can be seen from the coverage, for example, of the 1982 Falklands/Malvinas War in the United Kingdom, where there was a convergence between the majority of the press and the official government line, partly as a result of direct control over information by the government and the military (political society) and partly because of the particular ownership and interests of the press (civil society) – which we discuss further below.

Secondly, the non-mainstream press, such as the *Morning Star* newspaper in the UK, and oppositional bodies can exert some influence over the way in which events are represented and understood by circulating alternative information and interpretations of events. These alternative representations, however, have limited circulation and are not seen by the majority of the reading public. For example, *War Report* – an alternative view of the Gulf War – was produced by a group of journalists and available by subscription only.

Thirdly, sections of the press can enter into conflict with the government (representing the state), and this permits the (albeit limited) circulation of conflicting views of the 'national interest'. In the case of the UK coverage of the Falklands/Malvinas War, the government and the military intervened directly, using coercive force to impose censorship (see Glasgow University Media Group 1985a, and the Beach Report, Ministry of Defence 1983, set up to scrutinise the issues of war reporting after the Falklands/Malvinas conflict). The government used the courts to bring the press into line in the case of the information leaked about the arrival date of Cruise missiles in Britain.

There is no deterministic relationship between political society and civil society: in the modern liberal state the first does not have total control over the institutions of the second, but political society can and does intervene when it feels challenged; as Stuart Hall has put it, '"civil society" is no ideal realm of pure freedom' (1989: 130).

Commenting on different ways of analysing the relations between society and the state, Hall (1984) argues that Gramsci offers a subtle, non-reductionist approach. Summing up Gramsci's analysis of how the state functions, he says:

> We must see [i.e. understand] the state as having the specific role of creating the political and ideological conditions in which the whole society can be conformed to or brought

24

into line with fundamental trends or tendencies in the social formation. The conditions in which this 'reconstruction' can come about are, however, conditional on the effective mastery of the political and ideological, as well as the economic, terrain; also on the formation of a social bloc, comprising sections of different classes, which forms the necessary underpinning for the state; and on the winning over to this bloc of a significant section of the popular classes. . . . If and when conditions of political leadership in the state have been created (for there is, for Gramsci, no determining necessity about it), this represents a moment of what he calls 'hegemony'.

(Hall 1984: 11)

Clearly, public writing plays a crucial role in the 'ideological mastery' that Hall refers to, namely in the discursive construction and maintenance of the hegemony of the dominant class and its allies (the 'social bloc'). It is here that significant construction of consent around dominant ideologies takes place and where meanings are transmitted by few and received by many. For Althusser (1971) the press is one of the most important Ideological State Apparatuses (ISAs). Bell (1991) and, more recently, Green-slade, the ex-editor of the *Daily Mirror*, in an article in the *Observer* newspaper (1996), show that most news stories originate in the written press and are then taken up by the broadcast media. Over the centuries the recognition of the power to influence opinion has meant that newspapers and journals all over the world have been banned, journalists have been arrested, tortured and even killed; such is the power of the written word. The Egyptian government recently introduced a new law which, among other penalties, allows journalists to be imprisoned for up to fifteen years if they print 'false and subjective information and rumours, inflammable allegations with the aim of disrupting the public good and censuring state institutions and those who lead them' (reported in the *Guardian*, 7 June 1995).

It is important to note the stress laid here on written/printed media rather than audio, visual or electronic media. The power of the written word derives primarily from its permanence; written words can be kept, pored over again and again, passed from person to person intact and compared with other written words. Texts that are spoken on special occasions can also reach a much wider

25

audience by being printed in the press: speeches such as Nelson Mandela's first to the parliament of the UK in 1996 (printed in full in the *New Statesman and Society*, 19 July 1996). Despite the technical possibilities for recording electronic broadcasts, few people other than researchers ever record news and current affairs programmes. The written media also have the advantage that they can deal with issues in greater depth than television or radio, where time slots are carefully controlled. For example, news bulletins usually have to cover international and national news of all kinds within half an hour.

THE ROLE OF THE PRESS IN THE MAINTENANCE OF DOMINANT IDEOLOGIES

In this section we discuss the political significance of the press in more detail. This is bound up with writing in two ways. Firstly, the press operates through written language: writing is the discursive technology by which meanings are constructed and disseminated. Secondly, as a consequence of this, anyone writing anything will have a whole range of meanings (especially representations of the world) already privileged for them by what they have encountered in the press.[1] This is confirmed by our teaching experience, for example with students of Politics and International Relations. While discussing the importance of attribution and justifying evaluations and judgements, one student persistently commented: 'But it's in the news . . . it's in the press . . . everyone knows that.'

The discursive construction of consent through writing in the press

There is a commonly held view that the media in general are 'a mirror held up to society' (James Callaghan quoted in Bennett 1982: 287), that is that the media have a purely reflective role. This view has been contested in media and cultural studies by such people as Stuart Hall, Dave Morley and Tony Bennett (Centre for Contemporary Cultural Studies, Birmingham) and it is at some of their views that we now look briefly in order to show in outline how the press works and how this ties in with the concept of hegemony described earlier.

In his essay on how the concept of ideology re-entered discussions on the media, Hall says this. In a society that is *democratic* in its formal organisation, but committed at the same time by the concentration of economic capital and political power to a *massively unequal* distribution of wealth and authority, there is much to gain, for the dominant socio-economic group, from the continuous production of popular consent to the existing structure (Hall 1982: 63). He goes on to argue that the media (including the press), far from merely reinforcing an already achieved consensus, as earlier media studies had tended to assume, play an active role in the process of consensus formation. The media as he sees it do not simply reflect or reproduce reality; they define it, by selecting, structuring, shaping and re-presenting reality. This re-presentation implies an active process, a practice:

> a production of meaning: what subsequently came to be defined as a '*signifying* practice'. The media are signifying agents.
>
> (same book: 64)

Hall perceives meaning as a social production, and if meaning is not 'given' but socially produced this implies that different meanings can be ascribed to the same events (see Chapter 7 of this volume). This would further imply that he does not subscribe to the 'neutral reality' view, rather that the encodings of reality will differ according to the social ideologies underlying the different perceptions of reality; hence the 'struggle over meaning' (Vološinov 1973: 23).

Hall argues that what we need to explain is how one meaning wins credibility or legitimacy over other available meanings. As the mass media in modern society are the principal institutions for describing and explaining, i.e. defining, the world's events, how do they succeed in maintaining a preferred or delimited range of meanings in a society where opposing or conflicting interests are at stake? The power here is ideological; the power to signify events in a particular way:

> The signification of events is part of what has to be struggled over, for it is the means by which collective social understandings are created.
>
> (Hall 1982: 70)

We find Hall's concept of 'ideological grammaticality' useful in explaining how partial accounts of 'reality' appear as the 'truth'. Ideological presuppositions are what make a text cohere. Ideological propositions about the social world are based on premises and entail a framework of linked unstated propositions. Hall argues that these premises have to be assumed to be true for the propositions that depend on them to be taken as true (see also Fairclough's definition of presupposition, 1992a: 120). Hall gives an example:

> [a] statement like 'the strike of Leyland toolmakers today further weakened Britain's economic position' was premised on a whole set of taken-for-granted propositions about how the economy worked, what the national interest was and so on. For it to win credibility, the whole logic of capitalistic production had to be assumed to be true.
>
> (Hall 1982: 74)

It is obviously in the interest of the dominant economic and political groups to have as few contesting definitions of reality in the public domain as possible; hence the importance of the question: who owns the media?[2] Lack of access to alternative positive information about the Leyland toolmakers and to discussion of alternative economic models in the British media means that, for most people, the striking toolmakers of Leyland were the culprits for Britain's economic decline. Without any other version of reality, this one holds.

Hall argues that without a whole range of unstated premises or assumed shared views of the world 'each descriptive statement would be literally unintelligible'. But this deep structure of presuppositions which makes the statement ideologically 'grammatical' is rarely made explicit and is largely unconscious both to the encoder and the decoder. As he says:

> the very declarative and descriptive form rendered invisible the implied logic in which it was embedded. This gave the statement an unchallenged obviousness and obvious truth-value. What were in fact propositions about how things were, disappeared into and acquired the substantive affirmation of merely descriptive statements: 'facts of the case'.
>
> (same book: 74)

This concept of unstated, underlying presuppositions is, we believe, a very fruitful one in terms of being able to explain how

28

hegemony is discursively constructed and maintained and how difficult it is for oppositional definitions of socio-political reality to prevail in the struggle. (See Fairclough 1995 for a more comprehensive analysis of the representations, social relations and identities set up in the media.)

In his book, *Marxism and the philosophy of language*, Vološinov (1973) views language, the prime carrier of ideology, as 'an arena of struggle' over meaning. On the struggle over the signification of events and the multiple referentiality of language to the real world, Vološinov says:

> Existence reflected in the sign is not merely reflected but refracted. How is this refraction of existence in the ideological sign determined? By an intersecting of differently oriented social interests in every ideological sign. Sign becomes an arena of class struggle. This social multi-accentuality of the ideological sign is a very crucial aspect. ...A sign that has been withdrawn from the pressure of class struggle – which, so to speak, crosses beyond the whole of the class struggle – inevitably loses force, degenerates into allegory, becoming the object not of a live social intelligibility but of a philological comprehension.
>
> (Vološinov 1973: 23)

So the sign reflects social struggle – not just in class terms, we would add, but also in terms of gender, ethnicity and all contested areas of social life – and is itself a site of struggle. A good contemporary example of this struggle is the 1990s backlash, largely male and right wing, against attempts to challenge long-dominant negative labels of minority groups in society: the so-called 'politically correct' movement. It is clear that those who object to more positive labels being adopted for such groups implicitly recognise the power of words in categorising and constructing the world. (The significance of lexical choice – one set of signs – in labelling participants and events is well captured in the extract from the *Guardian* in Figure 2.1.) This is a more linguistically focused equivalent of Hall's concept of 'ideological grammaticality' and his notion of 'naturalisation' (1982: 74–5) and of Gramsci's insight that for a class (and its allies) to become hegemonic it has to re-present its own interests as the 'universal' interests of the whole society.

Mad dogs and Englishmen

We have	They have
Army, Navy and Air Force	A war machine
Reporting guidelines	Censorship
Press briefings	Propaganda

We	They
Take out	Destroy
Suppress	Destroy
Eliminate	Kill
Neutralise or decapitate	Kill
Decapitate	Kill
Dig in	Cower in their foxholes

We launch	They launch
First strikes	Sneak missile attacks
Pre-emptively	Without provocation

Our men are . . .	Their men are . . .
Boys	Troops
Lads	Hordes

Our boys are . . .	Theirs are . . .
Professional	Brainwashed
Lion-hearts	Paper tigers
Cautious	Cowardly
Confident	Desperate
Heroes	Cornered
Dare-devils	Cannon fodder
Young knights of the skies	Bastards of Baghdad
Loyal	Blindly obedient
Desert rats	Mad dogs
Resolute	Ruthless
Brave	Fanatical

Our boys are motivated by	Their boys are motivated by
An old fashioned sense of duty	Fear of Saddam

Our boys	Their boys
Fly into the jaws of hell	Cower in concrete bunkers

Our ships are . . .	Iraq ships are . . .
An armada	A navy

Israeli non-retaliation is	Iraqi non-retaliation is
An act of great statesmanship	Blundering/Cowardly

The Belgians are . . .	The Belgians are also . . .
Yellow	Two-faced

Our missiles are . . .	Their missiles are . . .
Like Luke Skywalker zapping Darth Vader	Ageing duds (*rhymes with Scuds*)

Our missiles cause . . .	Their missiles cause . . .
Collateral damage	Civilian casualties

We . . .	They . . .
Precision bomb	Fire wildly at anything in the skies

Our PoWs are . . .	Their PoWs are . . .
Gallant boys	Overgrown schoolchildren

George Bush is . . .	Saddam Hussein is . . .
At peace with himself	Demented
Resolute	Defiant
Statesmanlike	An evil tyrant
Assured	A crackpot monster

Our planes . . .	Their planes . . .
Suffer a high rate of attrition	Are shot out of the sky
Fail to return from missions	Are Zapped

- *All the expressions above have been used by the British press in the past week*

Figure 2.1 The significance of lexical choice

Source: The *Guardian* 23 January 1991

Alternative views of the world are not absent from press coverage. Divergent voices are to be found; the significant factor is how these voices are articulated; how they are framed; which parts of the newspaper they appear in and so on (see Fairclough 1995: 8). For example, the views of those who are considered outside the legitimate parameters of British politics are presented in the mainstream press. They are, however, presented in such a way that their voice is delegitimised. One example of this is in the *Sun*, a British right-wing tabloid newspaper (18 January 1991, on the editorial page), where the MP Tony Benn (an 'extreme leftist') is quoted, but he is characterised as 'Batty Benn'; he speaks 'sourly' against the allies in the Gulf conflict; he needs a 'whole hospital full of shrinks', thereby characterising both him and other opponents of the war as extreme and mad.

The language of the writing itself works to help build and maintain hegemony through the discursive construction of consent. An example comes from the *Guardian*, a British centre left broadsheet newspaper (6 May 1996, on page 2 of the News section). Subtitled the Monday Sketch (to indicate that this is a humorous piece, as regular readers would understand) under the heading 'It's my socialist party and I'll try if I want to' is a comprehensive ridiculing of the setting up of a new left-wing party under Arthur Scargill (the well-known miners' leader). The article wraps itself around a central photograph of the platform at the launch, with Scargill pointing his finger at the audience. The article opens with sarcasm:

> At long last, a new political party of the left! Strong men had awaited this day for generations – not the people who were going to join, you understand, but the Labour Party desperately keen to get rid of the ones who would

The article goes on to present the policy of the new party as unrealistic:

> Mr Scargill proposed the economic policy, which merely wanted to end capitalism.

The new party is represented as authoritarian:

> The platform won, as it did all day.

The article ends as it began with irony, claiming to be helpful by suggesting that there should be:

31

A little less socialism and a few more grins all round, maybe?

The writer of the article presupposes that most *Guardian* readers would find this amusing, on the grounds that they share the same underlying but unstated assumptions about and attitudes towards Scargill, the left outside the Labour Party, socialism and so on.

So far we have discussed the way in which writing, as it is produced by journalists, distributed and circulated in the press, works to maintain dominant ideologies through the discursive construction of consent. However, as Tony Bennett says:

> [t]o show that the media propose certain definitions of reality is one thing; but it cannot be inferred from this that such definitions are necessarily accepted in the sense that they are effectively taken for real and acted upon.
>
> (Bennett 1982: 297)

We develop this point further in Chapter 7, where we argue that it is important to look at actual reading practices in order to be able to determine how texts are actually consumed and interpreted.

Having set out some key issues regarding the discursive construction of consent through writing in the mainstream press, we now look more closely at the issue of the circulation of the printed word in the UK and its consequences for press 'freedom' and the availability of alternative representations.

A free press?

In liberal democratic societies there is much talk of the importance of the 'freedom of the press'. In reality, for example in the UK, this freedom is substantially curtailed. Firstly, government – purporting to represent the interests of the whole nation but in fact representing the interests of the privileged socio-economic groups – intervenes in a number of ways to limit the freedom of the press. Among these are: the Official Secrets Act; the Calcutt rules on privacy; libel laws; the 'd' notice system; the legal obligation (recently introduced) for journalists to disclose their sources; and the lobby system.[3] Secondly, there is an increasing concentration of ownership of the press, limiting the range of opinions in circulation in a 'market-driven' communications system. The meaning of 'market-driven' here is illustrated by a recent letter to the *Guardian* newspaper (20 April 1996), in which two readers lamented the decision of W.H. Smith, the largest newsagent in Britain, to withdraw over 100 publications from their shelves because of low circulation. John Pilger, a journalist working in Britain, says 'The narrowness of the British media, our primary source of information, is a national disgrace' (Pilger 1992: 58).

In Gramscian terms, the media in liberal democracies, as part of civil society, are relatively free of direct control and constraint by the state, yet they 'freely' articulate themselves around definitions that generally favour the hegemony of the dominant class. S. Hall and others in *Policing the Crisis* (1978) map out how the representatives of power elites tend to have special access to journalists, as sources of information and providers of the interpretative frameworks journalists then use in their stories. Hall *et al.* refer to these privileged sources as the 'primary definers' of news and to the journalists as 'secondary definers' (see McNair 1994: 48). The powerless are not seen as credible sources of knowledge and explanation and tend as a result to be marginalised. Scannell (1992) also shows that public persons are called on to give opinions whereas private people are generally called on for their experience (in Fairclough 1995: 40) This is largely because of the patterns of media ownership and the complex socio-economic relations that bind media owners to the dominant socio-economic political forces. For example, in the UK Rupert Murdoch owns 26 per cent of the press in the UK; 37 per cent of readership (McNair 1994: 10), as can be seen in Figure 2.2. If we add together the titles owned by Murdoch and the *Daily Mail*, the *Daily Express* and the *Daily Telegraph*, all of which support the same political party and share the same basic view of the world – and thus tell the same stories from the same point of view – we see just how limited are the ideas and meanings that circulate in the UK in such an important source of information as the press, and how negative that must be for democracy.

In global terms, the situation is equally shocking:

> 90% of international news published by the world's press comes from the 'big four' Western news agencies: two are American, one is British and one is French. . . . The largest news agency, UPI, gets 80% of its funding from US newspapers.
>
> (Pilger 1992: 66)

	Daily	Sunday
News International (*Sun, Today, Times, Sunday Times, News of the World*)	31.3	36
Mirror Group Newspapers (*Daily Mirror/Record, People, Sunday People*)	25.4	30
United Newspapers (*Daily Express, Star, Sunday Express*)	16.4	10.4
Associated Newspapers (*Daily Mail, Mail on Sunday*)	10.8	12
Hollinger (*Daily Telegraph, Sunday Telegraph*)	7.3	3.4
Newspaper Publishing (*Independent, Independent on Sunday*)	2.7	2.4
Guardian and Manchester Evening News (*Guardian*)	2.9	–
Financial Times Ltd (*Financial Times*)	2	–
Lonrho (*Observer*)**	–	3.3
Apollo (*Sport, Sunday Sport*)	–	1.9
Morning Star Co-operative Society (*Morning Star*)	–	–

Source: Audit Bureau of Circulation.
* Calculated on average figures for January–June 1992.
** In May 1993 ownership of the *Observer* passed to the Guardian and the Manchester Evening News.

Figure 2.2 Major proprietors and share of national newspaper circulation (per cent)
Source: McNair 1994: 10

This information imperialism prompted former Tanzanian President Nyerere to note sarcastically:

> the inhabitants of developing countries should be allowed to take part in the presidential elections of the US because they are bombarded with as much information about the candidates as North American citizens.
>
> (same page)

By contrast, the news on Africa reported in the West is famine, violence and political instability. As Jeremy Seabrook, another British journalist, wrote:

> Never is there a celebration of the survival, the resourcefulness and humanity of those who live in the city slums [of the developing world].
>
> (same book: 65)

When the editor of the *Washington Post*, Leonard Downie, was sent to England in 1982, he was shocked by the extent and nature of the limitations of press freedom, and said:

> In normal times, the British press accepts a far greater amount of government secrecy and news manipulation than American or foreign newsmen [his word] would put up with in Washington.
>
> (*The Washington Post*, 1982, quoted in Glasgow University Media Group 1985b: 3)

He goes on:

> More insidious, however, is a practice that most British journalists agree to voluntarily and even help to protect. . . . Newsmen (his word) participating in 'lobby' briefings and conversations are obliged to keep secret all their sources, all direct quotes, and even the times and locations of such contacts.
>
> They are sometimes forbidden by their sources to publish important information revealed in these contacts.
>
> This system enables the British government to manage much of what is reported by the national newspapers . . . and to escape responsibility for planting information – true or false.

It was, he said, as a result of this self-censorship that it had to be an American journalist to use sources from the war cabinet to report the controversial decision to sink the Belgrano[4] during the Falklands/Malvinas War, because as an American he did not feel bound to comply with the rules of the lobby system.

In this section we have mapped out the limits on the circulation of viewpoints and representations of reality, and indicated how difficult it is for citizens to have access to alternative representations in order to assess critically what they read in the press. These limits on the discursive construction of reality and the building of consent for a hegemonic world view are extremely serious. Ordinary people have little access to alternative views of the world and ways of representing it. It is hard for most people to unpack the ideological presuppositions and other significant discoursal features of written text. Texts do not usually contain alternative texts within them, as the text from the *Guardian* in

Figure 2.1 does, for readers to decide which makes more sense to them. We now consider the power of writing in terms of the status of writers, and of the political issues of who gets written about, and who gets the chance to have their writing published and read.

THE POWER OF WRITING

To talk about the 'power of writing' is ambiguous; it means both that writing is a very effective tool, as in a 'powerful piece of writing', in terms of ability to move and explain. But 'the power of writing' also means that writing gives access to power over others in terms of being able to influence the ideas and lives of others, and this is the meaning in which we are interested. People who write for public readerships, such as journalists, historians, lawyers, novelists and playwrights, can have an enormous amount of power, depending on their position in the wider hegemonic struggle.

Power and status interact in a way that makes it difficult to separate them out. Because writing in general, but certain kinds of public writing in particular, is highly valued in our society, it confers status on (certain) writers. Because these writers have status they also have the power to influence other people, to get things done, and the more successful they become, the greater their status and the greater their power. But, as we have hinted, some kinds of writing and writers are more statusful and powerful than others, and this is connected to the wider issues of economic and political power, ideological and cultural struggle and the relationship between writers and the building and maintenance of hegemony. Power, status, values and attitudes towards writing and writers are all closely interconnected with each other, and with the questions of who writes about what and for whom, why this matters and why it is like this. For reasons of analysis, however, we will try to separate out these issues.

The status of some writers, and the marginalisation of others

People think that if you are a good writer – powerful in the meaning of effective, good at expressing ideas – you will automatically be powerful in the other sense, namely of being recognised and rewarded and having influence. This is of course by no means always true. The patterns of ownership of the press in Britain that we described earlier and the effects of deregulation in television mean that dissenting journalistic voices, such as that of John Pilger, find it difficult to get the space to be heard and are marginalised. Pilger's voice may be a powerful one in terms of the effectiveness of his style and the persuasion of his arguments, but it is relatively powerless in terms of the ability to change dominant attitudes. Because his voice challenges the dominant consensus and its underlying presuppositions, constructed and maintained through the media, he is relegated to minority arenas where it will have less potential influence: late night slots on Channel 4, small-circulation journals and newspapers such as the *New Statesman and Society*, and the Sunday *Observer*.

This kind of marginalisation of writers happens in a range of domains. A similar process of conferral of power or silencing of oppositional voices also takes place around other kinds of writing, for example writing for television. In Britain in the 1980s and 1990s it has been very difficult for some writers whose work represents views of the world that challenge the capitalist order to get their work into the public arena. For example, Trevor Griffiths, the playwright whose work we discuss frequently in this book, managed against difficult odds to write plays for television in the relatively liberal 1970s, but has found it more difficult to get work accepted or repeated in the 1980s and 1990s. His play about Tom Mann, the trade unionist, written in the late 1970s for a BBC series on the Edwardians, was never produced – as Griffiths himself says in his preface to the published version:

> The ostensible grounds [for the rejection] were cost – they often are – but it's at least as likely that the play offered too brutal and too overtly political a contrast with the remainder of the series. . . . Tom Mann might have roughed up the series a bit, but it's arguable he might also have done something towards redressing its 'balance' too.
>
> (Griffiths 1988a: 182)

The BBC commissioned a play on the miners from Griffiths in the 1980s but then refused to go ahead with it; likewise they refused his play *God's Armchair*, written under commission for schools' television, because it was not 'suitable'. Mid-1990s programming policy in the UK prefers to give viewers a diet of soaps, hospital and veterinary dramas and thrillers.[5]

Another kind of marginalisation occurs when radical writing is 'emptied' of its radical content and praised for its 'revolutionary form', as is often the case, for example, with productions of Brecht in the West (see Bennett 1994: 33). Newspaper and journal critics play a powerful role in the maintaining of consent over what is 'appropriate' writing for the television and theatre. A recent example of this is Stuart Jeffries' piece in the *Guardian* (7 June 1995). In it he is ostensibly reviewing Tony Palmer's television film of Peter Sellars (American radical opera director). He criticises the film negatively and gives as part of his reason the following statement:

> Art has a negligible impact on changing politics and, what's more, when it presumes that it has a large role it falls into unconvincing didacticism.

Griffiths' 1991 play, *The Gulf Between Us*, was also criticised for being too overtly political, didactic, and therefore bad art (see reviews by Billington in the *Guardian*, 23 January 1992 and Coveney in the *Observer*, 26 January 1992 – both so-called liberal papers).

Although the political power of oppositional writers is limited, their work may be highly valued in certain sections of society that value their ideas and share their goals of challenging the status quo and offering different meanings and understandings. By contrast, a writer such as Jeffrey Archer, a pulp thriller writer whose writing sustains the existing social order, gets rewarded in terms of money and social status. He has been an active member of the (Conservative) political party that has run Britain since 1979 as an MP and Party chairperson; he clearly espouses and promotes conservative ideology and was knighted for his political services. As director on the board of several important companies, he combines political and financial power. It is at least likely that his financial success and recognition as a writer is connected to the fact that he belongs to the dominant social group and has had key positions in the dominant political party.

Dramatic confirmation of the power of writing and the effects it can have is given by the way in which governments and other institutions often react to oppositional writers. Historically, writers have been censored (directly and indirectly), banned, exiled, imprisoned, condemned to death and killed. They can even be incorporated into the political machinery of the state, as in the case of the Chilean poet Neruda who was nominated as Ambassador to Paris by the newly elected socialist government of Allende in Chile in the early 1970s. By contrast, the poet Victor Jara, who had campaigned for the election of Allende, was murdered by the Pinochet regime after its coup against Allende. When Antonio Gramsci, whose writing appeared in the influential left-wing journal *Ordine Nuovo* in Italy in the 1920s, was sentenced to internal confinement under the fascist regime of Mussolini, the judge said 'we must stop this brain from functioning'.

The value attached to writing

Many adults who were unable to learn to write at school often go through a lot of pain and effort in order to learn to write at a later stage in their lives (see Ivanič and Roach 1990; Ivanič and Simpson 1992; Ivanič forthcoming). It seems that there are three interrelated explanations for their desire to learn to write: firstly, writing has an intrinsic value for exploration of ideas and record-making; secondly, society demands that certain functions should be fulfilled by writing, though other means are in principle possible; and thirdly, being able to write is seen as a sign of being 'educated'. Why should writing be so highly valued?

The medium of writing itself allows socially prestigious forms of knowledge, information and codes of social behaviour to be recorded, stored and handed on in permanent form, unchanged by inaccurate or mischievous memory. Writing travels through space and time and so we can read from the past as well as from the present. This is particularly important in our society where the past is revered as cultural heritage, as if it somehow confers glory on the nation as a whole. The fact that Shakespeare's plays are available in written form makes it possible for them to play this role in British culture and particularly in British schools: a role strongly endorsed by Prince Charles, who accused schools of 'marginalising Shakespeare [which] seems symptomatic of a general flight from our great literary heritage' (reported in the *Guardian*, 23 April 1991; see also the *Times Educational Supplement*, 27 April 1991).

The fact that money and space are dedicated to storing what is written down gives it valuableness and worthiness. What has been and is considered at different times to be prestigious or useful writing (plays, novels, laws, parliamentary debate in Hansard, police records, letters between famous people) sits on our book-shelves and in our libraries and archives – unlike the unprestigious private writing of ordinary people which usually gets stored in attics, under the bed or at the back of drawers, or thrown away (there are some exceptions, such as letters recently found sealed in bottles and bricked into house walls, reported in the *Guardian*, 25 May 1993, and seen as useful historical evidence).

Who writes about what?

There are content conventions, such as what kind of person gets named and given central roles in most history books and who does not – kings and queens and prime ministers get named but ordinary people become generalisations such as 'the people' or 'women voters' or are unmentioned agents of passivisations or impersonal expressions. There are conventions covering what kind of people are suitable subjects for biographies and autobiog-raphies. These are generally the famous. This was brought home to one of us recently when an elderly working-class woman told us that she had been trying, unsuccessfully, to get an autobiographical story published. The title of her story is 'I was a butler's daughter'. We think the reasons for her lack of success in getting her story published are as follows. Firstly, she has not since become a famous person, so no one is interested in her origins (compared with, say, the interest in Mrs Thatcher's origins as a grocer's daughter). Secondly, these kinds of stories only seem acceptable as fodder for television situation comedies such as 'Upstairs Downstairs' and are based on stereotypes where the situation is more important for the laughs that it can raise than the real lived experience of class relations (whereas Trevor Griffiths' play *Country* focuses on these). Thirdly, the story would certainly not be salacious. Finally, she would almost certainly neither have nor want access to the sort of language of popular magazines or to the style of more prestigious literary magazines; and her 'telling it like it is', in her own rather timid and hesitant voice, would not be valued by most editors as worth publishing.

There are also conventions about who writes what about whom and for whom – the disadvantaged are mostly written *about*, sometimes written *for*, but hardly ever the writers. June Jordan, a black American writer, has written an essay about this called 'On listening: a good way to hear' (1967) (and not a lot has changed since then, despite the liberal rhetoric). In the essay she says that the best way to find out what somebody thinks and feels is to ask *them*, not somebody else. She argues that this self-evident truth is ignored when it comes to black people in the United States. She illustrates this in her criticism of a book by a white American writer, William Styrone, *The Confessions of Nat Turner*. The book is about the confession to murder by a black man and is written in the first person. She quotes a patronising review of the book:

> I think that only a white Southern writer could have pulled it off. . . . A Negro writer, *because of a very complex anxiety*, . . . would have probably stacked the cards, producing in a mood of unnerving rage and indignation, a melodrama of saints and sinners.
>
> (*New York Review of Books*, 26 October 1967;
> Jordan's emphasis)

Who does which kinds of writing?

The unequal distribution of the right to write for publication has been observed by Gunther Kress and Raymond Williams. Kress claims that:

> [T]he causes of the unequal distribution of active writing are of course social, deriving from the economic, political and ideological structures of any given society. It has economic, political and ideological effects: those able to produce meanings and messages are few by comparison with those who consume meanings and messages. Hence the control of messages and meanings is in the hands of a relatively small number of people.
>
> (Kress 1982: 3)

In his essay 'The idea of a common culture' (written in 1968, reprinted in Williams 1989), Williams says:

> If it is true that the creation of meanings is an activity which engages all men [his choice of generic], then one is bound to be shocked by the way any society which, in its most explicit culture, either suppresses the meanings or values of whole groups, or fails to extend to those groups the possibilities of articulating and communicating those meanings.
>
> (Williams 1989: 35)

41

One aspect of 'explicit culture' is the writing of texts of all kinds. In any talk of 'common culture' we must be demanding a 'free, contributive *process* of participation in the creation of meanings and values' (same book, his emphasis) through the act of writing and the circulation of writing.

Although we consider Britain to be a highly literate society, the actual distribution of the use of writing across the population is extremely uneven. It is uneven in both the amount of writing that most people do and in the types of writing they commonly engage in. Almost everyone uses writing to a greater or lesser degree as an integral part of their social life, as we discuss in Chapter 3. But very few people contribute through writing to the circulation of meanings by writing novels, history books or articles for the press, and even fewer get them published. There have been a number of grassroots movements that are trying to counteract this inequality of access. For example, in the north-west of England, the Labour History Workshop has published the accounts of 'ordinary people'. Commonword, a non-profit-making community publishing co-operative based in Manchester

> seeks to encourage the creative writing and publishing of the diverse groups in society who have lacked or been excluded from the means of expression through the written word. Black writers, women, lesbians and gay men all too often fall into this category.
>
> (Commonword 1988: 79)

We discuss the work of Commonword and other community publishers in more detail in Chapter 9, where we make recommendations for more democratic publication of writing.

Given the values reproduced by the school system and the distribution and circulation problems, community publications still have status in only certain relatively small sections of society; they do not get into the mainstream. So the vast majority of the writing that has high social value, prestige and power, governs our daily lives, and shapes our understanding of society is done by a very small minority of the population.

We now turn to examine the role of schooling in the building and maintenance of hegemony and the place of learning to write in this process. We look particularly at schooling as an institution where children not only learn to write but are also exposed to the values about writing that we have talked about and are effectively set on the path to becoming what Williams called 'transmitters' or 'receivers' of socially significant meanings (1989: 36).

A CRITICAL VIEW OF SCHOOLING AND LITERACY EDUCATION

Each time that in one way or another the question of language comes to the fore, that signifies that a series of other problems is about to emerge . . . the necessity to establish more 'intimate' and sure relations between the ruling groups and the national popular masses, that is, the reorganisation of cultural hegemony.

(Gramsci, quoted in Giroux 1989: 147)

For Gramsci, literacy was both a concept and a social practice that must be connected historically both to configurations of knowledge and power and the political and cultural struggle over language and experience. If democratic institutions and a democratic society are to be successful, that is genuinely representative and participatory in the sense that Williams argued for (1989), then the struggle over orders of knowledge, values and social practices is crucial. Both school as an institution and its linguistic and pedagogic practices are a site of the struggle for hegemony. In this section we first set out the way in which we see schooling as part of the struggle for hegemony, in order to provide a context for discussing literacy education.

Schooling and the hegemonic struggle

It is quite clear that there are inequalities in education, both in terms of access to and experience of it as well as in terms of its outcomes. These inequalities are primarily class based; there are also significant differences between the majority ethnic group and minority ones. Working-class pupils in Britain achieve less well than their middle-class counterparts on almost any measure of educational achievement: the lower the social class, the lower the attainment. This also chimes with what Herzberg says about education in the US:

The schools have generally failed to serve the interests of poor and working-class children. Rather they have perpetuated

43

class distinctions and reproduced the race, class and gender discriminations found in culture and society.

(Herzberg 1991: 104)

There is a huge body of research (for example, Westergaard and Resler 1976; Gibson 1986; Benn and Chitty 1996) that demonstrates that educational practices in state education (and private) consistently favour white middle-class children, and send the majority of working-class and ethnic minority children out of school earlier and ill-prepared for anything but the lowest paid and least skilled jobs or the dole queues. In this way the children of the low paid or the unemployed become the low paid and the unemployed of the future. The relationship between social class and educational achievement is represented diagrammatically in Figure 2.3.

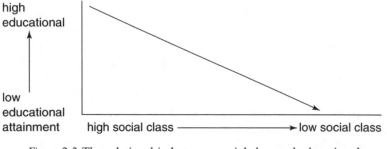

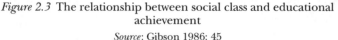

Figure 2.3 The relationship between social class and educational achievement

Source: Gibson 1986: 45

This inequality in education mirrors wider societal inequalities of wealth, income, power, prestige and opportunity. The evidence for this is remarkably consistent over time, and despite improvements in the material conditions of large sections of the working class the marked pattern of differences between the social classes remain. The questions we examine here are: what is the relationship between these two orders of inequality? How do we explain the fact that the liberal ideology, which for a century has argued that education for all would eradicate inequalities, has conspicuously failed to deliver?

It is tempting to see a mechanistic, deterministic relationship between the two orders of inequality and to argue that the school simply reproduces the dominant socio-economic structure of a society (as argued by Bowles and Gintis in relation to schooling in North America, referred to in Gibson 1986). It is obvious that as the state provides education for its children, no state is going to want schools that subvert the purposes, values and ideals of that state. So, schooling can in that sense be seen as crucial in terms of reproducing the values and purposes and the socio-economic order of the hegemonic forces whose interests are maintained by political society. At certain historical moments the economic forces of development require a widening of the school population (e.g. 1944 in Britain), or a shift in focus in general education or, more often, in vocational training. However, despite the direct national government intervention in education (through laws, finance, etc.) – and this has increased in Britain dramatically with the 1988 Education Reform Act – schooling remains part of 'civil society' and as such relates in a much richer and more complex manner to the state, or political society. Teachers themselves are not a homogeneous group and they bring to the school a range of beliefs and values, some of which may be at odds with the dominant ideologies about education within the Ministry of Education and within each local education site, leading to practices of resistance as well as of compliance. Pupils also bring with them different histories, different experiences and values. How is it that the experiences and values of some are more highly esteemed than others and how does this affect the educational experience and its outcomes?

The concept of 'cultural capital'

Various analyses have been made to explain the connection between education and cultural reproduction. We draw in particular on the work of Pierre Bourdieu, the French sociologist of education (Bourdieu 1977, 1984, 1991; Bourdieu and Passeron 1977). Bourdieu developed the notion of 'cultural capital' (in terms of language, meanings, thought and behaviour, values and attitudes) to describe and explain how cultural reproduction works. (Williams used the term 'cultural property' in much the same way [1989: 37]; see also Bernstein 1990.) According to Bourdieu, education favours a certain kind of cultural capital: that of the dominant culture. This process disadvantages those who do not accumulate the sort of cultural capital that is approved of and required for educational success in the present circumstances. Pupils who do not already have that cultural capital find their own culture denied or devalued. Their everyday knowledge, way of talking and writing, even their clothes and the way they hold themselves, become marginal and inferior to school knowledge and ways of behaving. Middle-class pupils, by contrast, come to school with the right kind of cultural capital to begin with, and through education they accumulate even more cultural wealth – just as money earns more money, so cultural capital earns more cultural capital.

The kind of cultural capital that is highly valued is represented in and by the curriculum and pedagogic practices. For Bourdieu, academic capital is

the guaranteed product of the combined effects of cultural transmission by the family and cultural transmission by the school, the efficiency of which depends on the amount of cultural capital inherited from the family.

(Bourdieu 1984: 23)

Writing represents a special kind of cultural capital. Firstly, children are expected to write in the standardised form of English, which is closest to spoken, south-eastern, white middle-class forms, and this makes it even more difficult for those children who do not bring these spoken forms to school with them. The equation of writing and standardised English sends clear messages about appropriacy and inappropriacy – as we discuss in Chapter 8 – and helps to undermine the sense of worth of children who speak non-standard forms of English. Secondly, few people continue to do much substantial writing once they leave school; those who do tend to fall into the professional/middle classes. Children from these social groups will see adults around them writing the sorts of things that are valued by school, will probably be encouraged and helped to write, and so will arrive at school with cultural capital to spend.

Connected to the notion of 'cultural capital' is Bourdieu's concept of 'habitus', or embodied culture (1977). It represents an 'internalised style of knowing and relating to the world that is grounded in the body itself'. Habitus is a set of dispositions that leads people to act and react in certain ways. These dispositions are learned through a slow process of inculcation, particularly through early childhood experiences. But the dispositions are also structured, in the sense that they are inevitably shaped by and reflect the social conditions, of class, ethnicity and gender, in which they are acquired (the same). In Britain, working-class children up until the late 1960s learned to expect to enter manual occupations; boys in particular expected to follow their fathers down the pit, into the factory, and so on. In the 1990s even this expectation is increasingly unrealistic in Britain, given the narrowing of the industrial base. Large numbers of working-class pupils can now expect years if not a lifetime of unemployment or low paid casual work. Working-class children have these expectations, according to Bourdieu, because they learn intellectually, emotionally, physically through their bodily experiences to think of themselves as subordinate: being told how to stand, sit, walk, write. We suggest that writing, as a physical act, has a special role in the formation of these dispositions: expectations and habitual reactions enter the mind through the muscles of the hand.

As we hinted earlier, the actual life in school is less mechanistically reproductive of class relations than the above somewhat schematic outline would perhaps seem to suggest – and Bourdieu would be the first to reject 'theories which explicitly or implicitly treat practice as a mechanical reaction to the . . . functioning of pre-established assemblies' (Bourdieu 1977: 73). Resistance may take three forms. Firstly, some working-class children do of course 'succeed' in educational terms, go to university and join traditional middle-class professions, such as teaching. They are strongly motivated to accommodate to the culture of the school and want to achieve the benefits they associate with enhanced cultural capital. So access to education and the acquisition of cultural capital may be seen as empowering for the minority of children who arrive at school with little but leave school with more. However, we are talking about a minority. According to a report in the *Guardian* on 20 April 1996, 80 per cent of children of unskilled fathers still leave school at 16, most with no qualifications; children from professional homes are twice as likely to stay on at school and three times as likely to obtain a professional occupation.

Secondly, the notion of struggle – and human agency – once again helps to explain why reproduction is never total but is opposed and resisted by some groups (of teachers and of pupils). The groups that do resist the dominant cultural ideologies at school bring positive images of their own culture which they draw on to counter the school culture. However, the act of resistance

47

by a particular pupil or group of pupils does not always succeed in achieving these positive outcomes. It may result in the 'failure' of this group and thereby contribute to the reproduction of inequality.

Finally, resistance practices contain the seeds for alternative, oppositional or emancipatory education: see, for example, the work of Paul Willis in Britain (Willis 1977), Paolo Freire in Brazil (Freire 1972) and Henry Giroux in the US (Giroux 1989).

The struggle is not between equals and does not take place in a vacuum. Schools are part of the society and as such are connected to the wider socio-economic struggles. At different moments of history, depending on the balance of power in society, those engaged in schooling will be more or less willing and able to resist and challenge the existing dominant values. As we argue in Chapter 9, the struggle for a properly democratic education cannot be separated from the wider struggle for emancipation in society.

In the next section we look more closely at how learning to write at school is connected to the wider socio-political issues in education that we have outlined so far. We argue that literacy education in schools, and especially the teaching of writing, is a site in which the reproductive tendency of schooling can be contested.

Learning to write at school

Kress, in his book *Learning to Write* (1982), makes the connection between the issue of who does which kinds of writing and how writing is learned. He argues:

> There are close connections between language, social structures and writing [which have] important consequences for the learning of writing. Access to writing is not equally available to all members of a society. Furthermore, the kinds of writing which children are taught and learn to produce at school may provide an insight into the value-system of our societies, particularly given the fact few children grow up to be writers in any significant sense of the word.
>
> (Kress 1982: 2)

Over fourteen years earlier, Williams spelled out the nature of the exclusion that this implies:

> It was perfectly clear that the majority of people were[6] both shut out by the nature of the educational system from

access to the full range of meanings . . . and excluded by the whole structure of communications – the character of its material ownership, its limiting social assumptions – from any adequate participation in the process of challenging and developing meanings.

(Williams 1989: 35 [written in 1968])

As Williams saw it, for a fully common culture to be realised, we need:

the creation of a condition in which the people as a whole participate in the articulation of meanings and values, and in the consequent decisions between this meaning and that, this value and that. This would involve, in any real world, the removal of the material obstacles to just this form of participation . . . it would [also] mean changing the education system from its dominant pattern of sorting people, from so early an age, into . . . transmitters and receivers, to a view of the interlocking processes of determining meanings and values as involving contribution and reception by everyone.

(same book: 36)

For this to be achieved, what is needed is an 'educated and participating democracy' in which 'education . . . provides its immediate means – developed speaking, writing and reading' (same book: 37). Despite the liberal ideology and its educational embodiments in the 1960s and 1970s in Britain, most pupils and the adults they become are still denied access to the active development of meanings. The arguments put forward by Bourdieu, as outlined above, help us to understand how difficult such a project would be because of the reproductive tendency of the schooling system. Schooling is not ideology-free, and language and language/literacy education is, in our view, the prime carrier of the dominant ideologies and cultural values in which school practices are consciously or unconsciously embedded.

But what kind of writing does school teach? To what extent *are* young writers able to become transmitters as well as receivers of a full range of meanings as Williams recommends? Kress, commenting on socio-political issues around learning to write, is pessimistic:

The kind of writing most widely taught and most highly prized in schools – such as essays, narratives, poetry – is

49

engaged in by very few members indeed of any society. It is quite clear, and reasonably obvious, that exclusion from the consumption of messages – being unable to read – carries with it heavy penalties in terms of exclusion from a wide range of knowledge, activities and hence power, in a society. Conversely, the ability to produce written messages is equally necessary for sharing and contributing to knowledge and ideological activity, and for gaining a measure of power.

(Kress 1982: 9–10)

He goes on to point out how the types of writing in school co-opt children into dominant values and contribute towards their socialisation into the dominant ideology:

the learning of the genres involves an increasing loss of creativity on the child's part, and a subordination of the child's creative abilities to the demands of the norms of the genre. The child learns to control the genre, but in the process the genre comes to control the child. Given the cognitive and social implications of these generic forms, the consequences for the child are immense.

(same book: 11)

Kress focuses in detail on genre because 'genres are . . . not neutral in their cognitive, social and ideological effects' (same page), as we argued in relation to both genres and discourses in Chapter 1. So the child learns what s/he is allowed to say (appropriate knowledge) and in what forms (appropriate ways of organising and telling that knowledge and the appropriate ways of representing the social relations between writer and reader) and what s/he is not allowed to say and what are 'wrong' forms. Kress argues that the learning of genre is 'intimately linked with the codification of knowledge in a society' (same book: 123). For example, the genre of scientific writing with its preoccupation with 'objectivity' and 'facts' – i.e. no 'I', no human agency, focus on process – grows out of the wider construction of science as being about truth and objective fact; the same is true of other genres. 'The child is being socialised into the structures and value systems of his/her society' through the texts that s/he is taught to value and to try and produce. What Kress says makes specific to writing what Bourdieu has said about 'cultural capital' in general.

Kress's views on genre intersect with what the critical discourse analyst Norman Fairclough has to say about notions of 'appropriacy' and the role of discourse in social change. In his article entitled 'The appropriacy of "appropriateness"', he argues that theories of appropriateness 'underpin controversial policies on the teaching of standard English [and] the development of a competence-based "communication skills" view of language education' (Fairclough 1992c: 33). He also argues that models of language variation based upon 'appropriateness'

> derive from a confusion between sociolinguistic realities and political aspirations. In no actual speech community do all members always behave in accordance with a shared sense of which language varieties are appropriate for which contexts and purposes. Yet such a perfectly ordered world is set up as an ideal by those who wish to impose their own social order upon society in the realm of language. So I argue that appropriateness is an 'ideological' category, which is linked to particular partisan positions within a politics of language – within a struggle between social groups in a speech community for control of (or 'hegemony' over) its sociolinguistic order.
>
> (same book: 3–4)

Although Fairclough is writing here about dialectal varieties, the same kind of argument holds for 'genre' and 'discourse'. 'Genres' themselves are ideological constructs, and the conventions associated with them are never monolithic (see Clark 1992) but the object of struggle. This is true of all genres, including literary ones, as exemplified by Griffiths' subversion of the adventure story in *Judgement over the Dead*, or of the hospital drama in *Through the Night*. Similarly, the discourses that are considered appropriate in school may be more or less contested.

In the same article, talking about appropriateness and skills, Fairclough says that competence-based views of language and language education dominate recent educational thinking in Britain. He chronicles a general shift 'towards seeing knowledge operationally, in terms of competence, what people can do; and seeing education as training in skills' (same book: 39). This is realised in the growth of vocational courses and qualifications in secondary schools (GNVQs) which, however pedagogically sound they may be in their own right, tend to create further divisions between vocational and non-vocational education along class lines. (We will take up this issue in greater detail in Chapter 9.) After a detailed discussion of the implications of this, Fairclough sums up as follows:

teaching the appropriate use of standard English . . . uses the educational system to transmit shared language values (if not practices) based around the hegemony of a particular dialect. . . . This use of the educational system corresponds to a traditional establishment (or 'old Right' as Barnes (1988) puts it) agenda. . . . teaching language competencies and skills is a priority of the modernising New Right (Barnes 1988, Hewitt 1989). It is based upon a planning perspective and the anticipation of new requirements for employers and citizens.

(same book: 43)

At school children are taught how to write and they spend many hours examining the writing of other, prestigious and professional writers. Concepts of good writing are handed out at school from one generation to the next; this is part of the process by which schooling contributes to the reproduction of established values. In England and Wales the recently introduced National Curriculum for English establishes guidelines for good writing and these are indirectly also embodied in the anthology of extracts from 'good' uncontroversial writers on which 16 year olds are tested nationally.

Notions of objectivity in academic writing are inculcated early on in the writing curriculum (in *The National Curriculum for English*, DES 1995.). Being able to write following the dominant conventions and in the prestige genres such as essays and narratives are considered to be a sign of a good education, intelligence, good social standing and are usually prerequisites for prestige professions that in turn confer high social status and good economic standing. With respect to the mechanics of writing, a new ruling in the 1990s demands that up to 5 per cent of marks in any school test (i.e. not just in English) must be deducted for 'bad' spelling (see the *Guardian*, 12 January 1991), and even a liberal newspaper like the *Guardian* argues that this is an issue of 'independence and power' for pupils (see our discussion of appropriacy earlier in this chapter and in Chapter 8). Non-standard grammar or spelling is often equated with low intelligence or sloppy thinking, and the complex reasons lying behind such attitudes are rarely confronted. These have to do with dominant and dominated cultures, control and conformising views of schooling, but are couched in terms of 'empowering' working-class and ethnic minority children. The emphasis is on standardisation and the system is self-perpetuating; middle-class practices, and hence values, are naturalised and presented as unquestionably right.

No distinction is made between aspects of particular genres that are intrinsic to their social purpose, and those that are socio-culturally established as 'appropriate'. For example, in academic writing we suggest that providing evidence to support a generalisation is intrinsic to the intellectual endeavour of showing knowledge and understanding, but that writing in long noun-phrases, using large numbers of abstract nouns, and using conventional spelling are not. These features may be useful, but they are not essential. For example, we use fairly long noun-phrases and a number of abstract nouns, but we try to do so only when they help to explain what we mean. Other academic writers use far longer noun-phrases, and far more abstract nouns. We use conventional spelling because we are used to it, but we do not consider it to be essential to expressing our ideas. This superficial veneer of formal conventions for academic writing is treated as if it is all that matters in learning to write, and is often what is taught, at the expense of the aspects of writing that really help to make and convey meaning. Learners are rewarded for their ability to ape the conventions, rather than for engaging in the underlying purpose for writing.

This system inevitably benefits those children who come from backgrounds that share these values but justifies itself because the occasional working-class or ethnic minority child manages to succeed within the system. The majority are failed by the system, as we argued above (see Figure 2.3).

Education, work and the issue of standards of literacy

The planning requirements for Britain's future are said to be to produce a more literate workforce, with the emphasis on 'good communication skills'. The Education Reform Act grew out of the New Right's response to the liberal education policies and agendas of the 1960s and 1970s which, they believe, have led to falling standards in education, increasing illiteracy and other ills. The panic over alleged falling standards and increasing illiteracy, the fears of politically motivated (or 'ideologically' motivated, in their terms) teachers and the alleged negative impact of 'immigrant intake' on standards have:

> turned the tide in the educational sphere towards themes and goals established by the forces of the right. The press have played . . . a quite pivotal role. They have publicised the 'examples' in a highly sensational form – and they have drawn the connections.
>
> (Hall, in Hall and Jacques 1983: 35)

The connections are, according to the above view of education, between 'trendy liberal' teaching and 'falling standards' in education, especially spelling and grammar; the emphasis is now on a 'return to basics'.

Even those newspapers that are not sensationalist, such as the *Guardian*, have helped to keep issues of alleged falling standards in the public domain, thus contributing to a climate of concern. In an editorial entitled 'The rights of writing', the *Guardian* argues that 'Employers have been increasingly exasperated by the state of literacy of some school-leavers' and championed the decision of the then Education Secretary, Kenneth Clarke, that spelling should be penalised if there are frequent mistakes. On April 23, 1991, the front page of the same paper carried two articles, one of which was the lead story, on school 'illiteracy'. The main story reported the concerns of the Prince of Wales at what he called the 'functionally illiterate' and in the words of the journalist 'had harsh words for both the standards of education children attain in England and Wales, and for the child-centred methods used to teach them'. He went on to attack literacy education, reiterating the 'increasingly common impression that standards of handwriting, spelling and punctuation are not at all what they should be'. The second front-page story carried the headline 'Inspectors attack English teaching for primary pupils', and in the opening paragraph stated 'Up to ⅓ of the pupils now sitting the first national tests for 7 year-olds had unsatisfactory teaching in the basics of English . . . '.

The following Education Secretary, John Patten, in a speech at an Adult Literacy and Basic Skills Unit (ALBSU) conference in 1993, referring to an ALBSU survey which indicated that one in seven of those surveyed had low literacy levels, said that 'The problem has been swept under the carpet for decades.' He added that the new National Curriculum would take a number of years to improve standards of literacy.

In the essay quoted earlier, Hall (in Hall and Jacques 1983) points out that the main witnesses to the alleged alarming trends of falling standards are employers who complain about the quality of job applicants – especially spelling and grammar in writing – and the detrimental effect this has on efficiency and productivity. For working-class or black parents, on the other hand, he says that given the failure of liberal education to redress disadvantage in any significant way, the answer seems to lie in the past more conventional, traditional approach. This, in our view, matches the aspirations of employers and illustrates another aspect of the reproduction of class relations in education. Let the working-class children train for work; hence the emphasis on skills for the work-place and GNVQs at school, and 'transferable skills' in Higher Education.

CONCLUSION

The consequences of the unequal distribution of access to socially prestigious and socially shaping types of writing are in our view extremely important. Vast numbers of people as individuals but, more importantly, powerless social groups are excluded from contributing to the collective store of knowledge, cultural and ideological activity; from the production and projection of ideas that fundamentally shape society. Whole social and ethnic groups are largely voiceless, their experiences unrecorded and their right to contribute to the shaping of society virtually denied. In Williams' words they remain 'receivers' and are not encouraged to be 'trans-mitters'. In Britain in the 1990s there are still disproportionately few black novelists, women playwrights and working-class poets. This is clearly not because they/we have nothing to say or would be incapable of writing. They/we are not less 'intelligent'. The reason for this inequality in distribution of prestigious writing lies in the dominant class, gender and ethnic relations in our society which are largely reproduced, we have argued, by the education system.

However, what we have described is not inevitable and fixed for all time. The issue of what are the mainstream dominant practices and prestigious genres and who has access to them is an arena of social struggle. Writers of the working class like Trevor Griffiths have struggled in the past and are still struggling to write for popular audiences on television with work that challenges the dominant conventions of form and content of popular drama.

Black dub poet Benjamin Zephania's poem about Liverpool was used as an introduction to *The Gifford Report* (Gifford and others 1989) on racial discrimination in Liverpool. This was a deliberate attempt to bring a marginalised genre (dub poetry) and marginalised experiences (black working class) into a prestigious document. The document itself is 'oppositional' and challenges the complacent assumptions about (the lack of) institutional racism in the UK; Lord Gifford is a 'class rebel'. So the situation is fluid; hegemony is unstable and there are opportunities for change – sometimes more, sometimes fewer, depending on conditions in the wider socio-economic context. This is why it is so important to fight for an educational and cultural climate that encourages challenge and change, real empowerment and emancipation and not just a woolly tolerance of plurality of voices, where the critical voices remain enclosed within the confines of cultural ghettos.

3

WRITING AND SOCIAL CONTEXT

INTRODUCTION

In Chapter 2 we set out what we see as key aspects of the broader socio-political context in which any act of writing takes place. Drawing mainly on insights from social theory, we showed how writing, and the right to write, is tightly woven into the fabric of socio-political action and the shaping of ideologies and social structures. In this chapter we focus more closely on the immediate social context for specific acts of writing. Drawing on linguistics theory, literacy studies and composition studies, we examine different ways of conceptualising 'context', and how these relate to claims about the 'autonomy' of writing. We show how both the act of writing and the linguistic realisations of texts themselves are shaped by the context in which they are embedded.

There is a body of literature that claims writing is 'autonomous' (for example Ong 1982; Olson 1977) – i.e. that it is independent of social context, that it is language free, pure, 'solid like . . . a diamond formed under pressure' (Halliday and Hasan 1985: 87) and able to be carried or transmitted across time and space. The view that writing is independent of social context has been challenged by the social anthropologist Brian Street, who argues (1984, 1995) that there is no such thing as 'autonomous literacy' – all literacy practices and written texts are ideological, that is shaped by the wider socio-cultural environment in which they happen. There is an analogy in approaches to literature (in itself an aspect of literacy) here. On the one hand, there is the timelessness of great writing: it speaks down the ages; on the other hand, it is important to recognise that twentieth-century readers will under-stand different things from, say, sixteenth-century readers, because of the change in socio-historical conditions. We suggest that these opposing views are associated with different ways of thinking about *context*, and in this chapter we challenge the view that writing is 'autonomous' and context-free.

In our discussion we distinguish between the physical context and the wider socio-cultural context and argue that writing is an activity embedded in and dependent on not only the immediate social circumstances and people participating in it but also on the social and cultural values, beliefs and patterns of privileging surrounding it. This is what makes writing a *political* act, in its broadest sense. We first explain why social context is essential to the study of writing. We then outline three views of context, explaining how they throw light on what is involved in writing and on the similarities and differences between writing and speaking, drawing on several other attempts to define 'context'. We use as a starting point Halliday's definition (as summarised in Halliday and Hasan 1985, Chapter 1) which draws a broad distinction between 'context of situation' and 'context of culture'. We distinguish two aspects of context of situation. We then attempt to spell out more thoroughly what 'context of culture' is, and how it is connected to context of situation. We then point out the importance of viewing social context as heterogeneous, as a way of understanding how writing can be socially constructed yet not socially determined in a mechanistic way. This is what makes it possible for writing to play an important part in challenging the patterns of privileging among values, beliefs and power relations in socio-political contexts. We then provide two case studies to illustrate the distinctions we are making and their implications. We conclude the chapter by arguing that these often neglected aspects of the social context must be incorporated into any theoretical account of the writing process and of written language.

WHAT HAS 'SOCIAL CONTEXT' GOT TO DO WITH WRITING?

Firstly, context is relevant to the study of almost anything. Volcanoes have to be studied in relation to the geology that creates them; trees have to be studied in relation to the soil and weather conditions that nurture them; Ford Escorts have to be studied in relation to the market forces that affect their design. Physical objects all exist in a context that gives rise to them and/or affects them in some way. This information about what causes things to be as they are is essential to understanding them. Written texts are objects too, and in the same way they need to be studied in relation to the context that gave rise to and affects them. However, writing is not only an object, it is also an act. This idea has been captured in the study of literacy by referring to 'literacy events': occasions that involve reading and/or writing in some way. In order to emphasise the role of the writer in writing, we refer to 'acts of writing'. 'Acts of writing' often involve reading and/or speaking too – but in this book we will always look on such literacy events from the point of view of the writing. In short, each written text has a context that gave rise to it. Since a written text is produced by a human act of writing, this is not just a physical, but also a social context. In order to study writing, we need to understand how it is related to its social context, and in what ways it is dependent on it. Before discussing context in more detail we want to make a further important point concerning the so-called 'autonomy' of writing compared with speech.

Most spoken language is face-to-face communication, and does make use of the physical presence of participants in the communicative event, whereas most written language has to compensate for the fact that the interlocutors are separated in time and space and do not share a physical setting. It is important to recognise that this difference in context-dependency hinges on whether the interlocutors are communicating face-to-face or not, and is not in principle related to the spoken or written medium. Passing notes to someone sitting next to you during a lecture is an instance of face-to-face communication that uses the written medium; listening to a taped lecture or 'letter' is an instance of communication without access to shared physical context that uses the spoken medium. But even the line between face-to-face and non face-to-face is not clear-cut. For example, telephone conversations (spoken medium) and electronic mail (written medium) share time-reference, even though the interlocutors are separated in space and physical surroundings. A note left in the kitchen by one member of a household for another shares physical surroundings but not time or eye contact. There is no clear dividing line – the degree of 'autonomy' differs from one act of writing to another, and from one act of speaking to another.

In what follows we will distinguish three aspects of 'social context', discuss how they affect writing, and how far writing differs from speech in relation to each.

59

CONTEXT OF SITUATION

Context of situation is what Halliday and Hasan call 'the immediate environment in which a text is actually functioning' (1985: 46). It includes the place, the time and the people involved: what they know, their unique configurations of interests and beliefs, their sense of self-worth and control over their lives, the social relationships between them. When applied to written language, it concerns the immediate environment of both the act of writing and the act of reading. In what follows, we distinguish between the physical and the social aspects of the immediate environment, in order to show the limits of the 'autonomous' view of writing.

Context of situation as a physical scaffolding for meaning

A part of context of situation is the physical setting in which language is embedded, and what is actually going on at the time – that is, the local circumstances. Here we discuss how language is related to this aspect of context, how the local setting interacts with language, and ways in which speech and writing differ along a continuum in this respect.

Many meanings can be conveyed without language: pictures, gestures, actions, facial expressions 'say' a lot. For example, if a woman holds a door open for another in a corridor without speaking, it 'says' 'I am noticing you walking behind me, and acknowledge you' – mainly an interpersonal kind of meaning. Language is used only when other forms of communication are insufficient, and only as much will be said or written as the circumstances require (a point made by Grice [1975] in his 'maxim of quantity').

In some types of writing there are other means of conveying meaning physically present alongside the written language. For example, the words of a song will be accompanied by its music. Writing for magazine advertisements is likely to be accompanied by various other visual means of communication: layout, graphics, typeface and pictures. In writing a set of instructions or directions the writer is likely to use diagrams to complement the written message. Young children often write in the physical context of other visual forms of communication, particularly drawings (for some examples see Hall 1989; Moline 1996; Johnson 1996). In all these cases, the other means of visual communication provide a

60

physical context for the writing as well as conveying meaning in their own right.

When people talk, they do not need to use language to put into words those ideational and interpersonal meanings that are conveyed by other means in the physical context of situation. In this respect a lot of writing, particularly continuous writing, is different from speech. As we write, we cannot point to things around us, we cannot see how the reader is reacting at the same time that we are writing. In this sense, when we are writing, the language often has to make more meaning explicit than when we are talking. In the following section we indicate how written language differs from spoken language in this respect.

The effect of the lack of shared physical context on many types of written language

Figure 3.1 summarises some of the ways in which language differs according to whether its users share the same physical context or not. (See Ivanič 1994b for further discussion of the differences between spoken and written language in this respect.)

ASPECTS OF LANGUAGE	Physical context shared (usually spoken)	Physical context not shared (usually written)
Reference to people, things, time and place	Can use indexicals (e.g. her, this, now, here)	Must make who, what where and when explicit in the language
Interpersonal meanings	Can be indicated by stance, voice quality, prosody, gesture and facial expression	Must be conveyed by lexico-grammatical choices
Taking account of interpreters' knowledge, values, feelings, attitudes, beliefs and understandings	These can be monitored on-line	These must be guessed in advance

Figure 3.1 The effect of physical context on spoken and written language
Source: Adapted from Ivanič 1994b: 184

Reference to people, things, time and place

When people are using language in a shared physical context, they often use pronouns and other indexicals such as 'this', 'those, 'now' and 'there', without saying exactly what they are referring to. Because the speaker and hearer share the same physical context, they can assume that these are understood. This is common when they are talking face-to-face, as they can point to what they are talking about, but not so common in a telephone conversation. Many acts of writing – for example letters, articles for newspapers, schoolwork – have to put into words those things that the physical context contributes to many acts of speaking. Writers cannot write 'he' without having made clear in words beforehand who 'he' is.

Interpersonal meaning

When they are using language in a shared physical context, people often use means other than language to convey interpersonal meanings. To indicate respect for the person they are talking about, they may choose a particular position to stand or sit in, they may adopt a particular voice quality or prosody, they may wear particular clothes. They may also choose particular words, but are not *forced* to use language to convey this meaning: it is one of many options available in face-to-face communication. When writers and readers do not share physical context, writers have to put into words the relationship they want to set up between themselves and their readers. They do this by their use of modality markers such as 'may', or 'possibly', and politeness strategies ranging from direct impositions on the reader in the form of imperatives and categorical statements to indirect requests and statements that leave room for readers to have their own opinion.

Taking account of interlocutors' knowledge, values, feelings, attitudes, beliefs and understandings

Communication involves establishing 'common ground' between the interlocutors. We are using the term 'common ground' here, rather than 'background knowledge' or 'shared knowledge', because we think this is more than a question of 'knowledge'. We are talking about not only information but also ideology: values, feelings, attitudes and beliefs – types of meaning that straddle the 'ideational/interpersonal' distinction. In face-to-face communication, interlocutors can monitor moment-by-moment whether their meanings are coming across. They can see by a shadow on the listener's face that s/he has not understood something, and fill in some detail. They can pick up from their interlocutor's questions, gestures or tone of voice when s/he does not agree and needs more explanation, or more persuasion. In many situations where people are using written language, however, they do not share physical context. They have to make guesses about the common ground and points of contention between themselves and their readers and, if in doubt, state them in their text (as we discuss further in Chapter 7). If they are not sure that their readers will share their ideological presuppositions, they may want to make sure that they spell out potential sources of disagreement more carefully than if they are writing for someone they know shares their point of view. Alternatively, they may intentionally choose *not* to spell out their ideological presuppositions (as defined in Chapter 1), intentionally assuming shared ground and thereby conveying messages ideologically rather than explicitly.

In these ways, a lot of written language is more 'autonomous' than a lot of spoken language, meaning that it has to make sense independently of its physical context. But this is where the value of the term 'autonomous' stops. In all other respects writing is embedded in context just as much as spoken language is. In the next section we will continue to write about the context of situation, but focus on the way in which the social elements of this context shape writing just as much as they shape speaking.

Context of situation as a social environment for meaning

In this section, we are still focusing on the particular context in which people write, but extending our attention to the wider social environment which includes, but is not limited to, what is audibly and/or visibly present at the time. Firstly, writing is dependent on its social context in the sense that purposes for writing, and hence writing practices and characteristics of texts, differ from one context to another. Writing is a part of people's lives in all domains in which they are active: at home, in the community, at work, in leisure activities, as students, as citizens of their countries and of the world. Each of these broad domains is an umbrella for infinite variations in social context: for example, in the work domain, writing as an employee of a hospital differs enormously from writing as a teacher or writing as a waitress. Ethnographic studies of literacy in different workplaces have uncovered the detail of this diversity (see, for example, Odell and Goswami 1985). Studies have also pointed to the richness and specificity of literacy at home (see, for example, Taylor 1983; Barton and Padmore 1991), and the extreme differences among literacy practices from one social setting to another (see, for example, studies in Hamilton *et al.* 1994; Barton and Ivanič 1991). Such studies show conclusively that there is little in common between the writing done in all social contexts, other than spelling words in the same way – and even that is not an absolute constant. For example, 'writing a note' may sound like a type of writing that can be learned once and for all, and then used in a wide variety of situations. But a note to a friend at school is very different from a note to the milk-deliverer or a note from a shoe-shop assistant to a customer. These will be written for different purposes, on different types of paper, in different physical conditions of time and place, using different kinds of language. Individuals move from one domain to another from hour to hour in the course of their everyday lives, and they are likely to encounter new social contexts frequently across their whole lifespan, as their social roles and conditions change. They have to be aware of and cope with all the different constraints and demands of these contexts, and this includes encountering new writing practices and new genres.

Secondly, the context of situation for an act of writing includes the social action in which the writing is embedded. By 'social action' we mean the on-going web of interests, pleasures, ideas, relationships, positionings, needs, tasks, demands, desires, feelings, attitudes, beliefs, values, plans, activities, intents and conversations that people engage in as they go about their daily lives. Within the welter of social action that makes up our day-to-day existence, some juxtapositions generate a need to write something, and the conditions for writing it, and cause a person to write it in a particular way. In this respect writing is just as 'context-dependent' as speaking. (See Barton 1994 for 'an ecological approach to written language' and Barton and Hamilton forthcoming for a detailed ethnography of the way in which literacy is embedded in social life.)

An important part of the context of situation is the relation of power between its participants. For example, a student writing for a university lecturer is likely to be in an unequal relationship in which the lecturer has more power and status than the student: the lecturer is the one who assesses the piece of work and can therefore affect the very future life of the student; the lecturer is usually perceived as more knowledgeable and experienced than the student; the lecturer is usually older than the student. But this may not be absolutely straightforward. In a particular context of situation, a particular, physically strong male student from a socially statusful family background may feel relatively powerful in relation to a particular more tentative female lecturer, in spite of the other factors that tip the balance of power in her favour. Here, personal and political aspects of context are interacting.

A functional view of language, as represented in the work of Halliday, is that the texts we say or write are determined by the exact configuration of characteristics in the actual social context. This view of the language–context relationship suggests that the words will flow almost automatically, driven by the context. Taken to extreme, this functional view would mean that, if it is possible to specify all the features of the context of situation precisely, it is possible for a writer to know exactly what to write and how, and it is possible for a socio-linguist to predict the characteristics of a text, down to the minute detail of syntactic and lexical choice. This explains why it has had such appeal to educators, especially those concerned with vocational programmes: all they have to do is specify everything precisely, and their students will have no problems with writing. In principle we see this as a powerful view of the relationship between language and context, provided that it takes account not only of more superficial aspects of context, but also of the ideological positions of the participants: their interests (in both senses), values, beliefs, commitments, allegiances, and their sense of self-worth. Once these are treated seriously as part of the immediate social context, then the idea of context determining text is compatible with heterogeneity, and recognises the possibility of socio-cultural struggle over meanings. In practice, however, we have found that participants' commitments and positions are rarely treated as significant features of the immediate context. As a result, functional views of the context–text relationship are often unitary and mechanistic. This may be adequate to account for certain more ritualised acts of writing, such as jotting down recipes for our own use, or giving journey directions. But we suggest that the vast majority of acts of writing are embedded in social action that consists of complex constellations of factors, some of which may be in conflict with one another, and that most acts of writing are contested or contestable in some way. The concept of 'context of situation' needs to take account of this political complexity.

We suggest that the complexity of the context of situation is often responsible for people having difficulty with writing. In situations with which we are very familiar, where we are on safe and comfortable ground – for example, when we write a shopping list or the labels on storage jars – we do not usually have problems with the context. The writing of Christmas cards is also a fairly automatic task for most British people, but even this can get complicated if we are sending the card to someone we do not know very well and do not know how it will be received. In any situation that is more complex and slightly unfamiliar, everyone has the experience that words do not flow automatically; particularly in extended writing, words often dry up altogether. It seems to us that one of the hindrances to fluency is that there are so many aspects of context of situation, and writers have to weigh up all these aspects simultaneously. Writing is not simply the translation of a set of ideas into words, dependent only on ideational meaning. It is also a social interaction, and has to convey the identity of the writer, the writer's assessment of the reader(s) and the relationship between them. These interpersonal aspects of meaning are in turn affected by the writer's sense of the power relationships involved, and of her or his own status; for example, writing a letter to the bank manager for a loan if you have a big account is very different from writing for one if you are young, poor and unemployed, as we discuss further in Chapter 7.

This is where the idea that writing is 'autonomous' is very misleading. Because the act of writing *is* often 'autonomous' in the sense of being separated physically from the act of reading, the writer may approach writing as if it were 'autonomous' in relation to the social context too. The physical 'autonomy' of writing deludes writers into discounting the crucial social-contextual factors, making them think that the reason that writing is difficult is because they are bad at it, rather than realising that the complexity of the context is the cause of the difficulty. Even when writers recognise that writing is not autonomous of its social context, the physical separation makes it difficult for them to assess aspects of the social context associated with the reader, and to decide which words to use.

In this section we have been arguing that writing, like all language, is embedded in its immediate social context, and that it is particularly important to recognise that this is true of writing as much as speaking, because superficially writing appears to be 'decontextualised' in terms of its physical context. (The two case studies at the end of this chapter provide detailed illustrations of how particular contexts of situation shape particular acts of writing.) We have also been arguing that a narrow view of what constitutes the immediate social context leads to an overly deterministic view of the relationship between language and context. Context of situation must include not only the observable characteristics of participants, but also their interests (in both senses), their values, beliefs, commitments, allegiances, and their sense of self-worth. In the next section we look at the wider cultural and socio-political context as the source of these actual individual characteristics, and of the norms that people draw on in their context of situation.

CONTEXT OF CULTURE AS THE SHAPER OF CONTEXTS OF SITUATION

In any particular context of *situation*, the context of *culture* provides the range of possibilities that are in struggle, competing for dominance. It is the whole historical and socio-political context in which language is used; the 'cultural knowledge', the competing systems of values and beliefs of which writers need to be aware and which condition the choices they make in any act of writing. The context of culture consists of all the values, beliefs, constructions of reality, possible social roles and relationships, and associated norms and conventions for practices, genres and discourses which are in principle available to members of that culture. Different members draw on different configurations of these, as we discuss in Chapter 6. This may sound like a free-for-all, but it is not. Firstly, any context of culture may accommodate several, but not infinite, sets of values and beliefs. These can in principle be specified, and they are systematic. Secondly, there are patterns of privileging among them whereby particular values and beliefs are more dominant in a context of culture at a particular time in history, and there is powerful social pressure to adopt them, and to conform to the conventions that follow from them. (See Wertsch 1991 for the concept of 'patterns of privileging'.)

The context of culture consists of several levels that interact with each other (see Fairclough 1992a for a discussion of different levels of context). There is the 'national context': the context of a country such as the UK, which we described in Chapter 2. This level of context of culture provides the values, beliefs and associated conventions that are applicable in a wide range of contexts of situation. Within the national context there are more specific, local, cultural contexts of particular institutions. An 'institutional context' supports particular values, beliefs, associated practices and conventions, and patterns of privileging among them that are specific to the remit of that institution. So, for example, the British Medical Association allows for a particular array of beliefs about the ethics of heart surgery, among which one will be dominant at a particular moment in history. Narrowing the focus even further, one particular hospital will have its own culture, which is likely to be influenced by the British Medical Association but have its own particular characteristics. And narrowing further still, a particular department or a particular ward of a hospital may have its own culture: some aspects of the context of culture can be extremely local. At the other end of the continuum, the 'national context' is often hard to distinguish from larger-scale contexts that overlap with it, such as 'the Muslim world', and even 'the global context' of values, beliefs and patterns of privileging among them that are currently dominant. For example, the ideological struggle over what sort of action must be taken in order to preserve the environment is part of the global cultural context, not just the national context. While it is useful to distinguish these levels for purposes of discussion, it is also important not to see them as separate from each other, nor even to think of them in a hierarchical relationship. A particular array of beliefs in a particular institution may be partly influenced by a national institutional body, but partly independent of it. It may be possible to find similarities in the context of culture of two individual hospitals in different countries, while there are other aspects of the national cultures of those countries that may differ. There are likely to be aspects of the culture of 'the Muslim world' as part of the plurality of most national contexts, though how highly this culture is valued will differ greatly from nation to nation.

The concept of 'discourse community' is sometimes used to refer to institutional contexts of culture in order to focus attention on the role of language, particularly written language in that institution. (See Ivanič forthcoming, Chapter 4, for further discussion of the concept of 'academic discourse community'.) The term has the advantage that it focuses on people: there are members of communities, but not members of contexts. However, 'discourse community' is just as difficult to delimit as a 'context of culture': for example, an 'academic discourse community' may be a particular institution, such as 'Lancaster University', which has its own particular set of values, practices and patterns of privileging, or it may be a national 'community' of those who work in academic institutions in the UK, or it may be the global 'community' of academics world-wide. The term has the disadvantage that it suggests homogeneity – a community is associated with a single set of norms – whereas a 'context of culture' is easier to envisage supporting a wide array of competing ideologies and practices.

The context of culture cannot be materially described, yet its characteristics are usually quite specific, and can be inferred from their instantiations in actual contexts of situation. People know exactly what is or is not expected and acceptable within a particular context of culture, and this cultural knowledge covers all the aspects of context of situation that we outlined in the previous section. A description of the context of culture for the context of situation for a particular act of writing would consist of abstract statements about possible ideological positions, possible social relations among participants, possible ways of doing things and the patterns of privileging that make some of these more sociopolitically legitimate than others.

In Chapter 2 we wrote in more detail about one aspect of the context of culture: writers' power and status – who we expect to have the right to do certain kinds of writing, our expectations for norms of behaviour according to class, gender and ethnicity. Another aspect of context of culture that specifically affects writing is the cultural expectations as to whether we achieve a particular purpose through writing or other means. For example, writing a letter of condolence is the British way of showing solidarity with the bereaved. Writing an academic essay is the British way of proving to your tutor how good you are at your work. In both these cases, it is specific to British culture that the action should be achieved by writing. Many cultures would consider a written condolence insincere compared with a personal visit; some cultures prove intellectual capability by oral tests, some by reading and ticking boxes. We discuss the issue of culturally shaped purposes for writing in more detail in the next chapter.

Moving from the large scale to smaller-scale considerations, the context of culture also includes the discoursal, generic and syntactic conventions that are associated with its values, beliefs and practices: conventions of what to write and how to write it, of how to represent different people in writing, and of how to represent oneself in particular acts of writing. For example, in the UK we learn that if we are writing a letter of condolence to a neighbour we do not say in the letter that we are pleased that the deceased person has died, even if this is true because we know how much s/he had been suffering. The social convention is that we say we are sorry, and it would be very difficult to flout this convention because of the social consequences on our relations with our neighbour. A more contested convention of syntax is the so-called generic 'he'. More and more writers (and speakers) are finding this offensive to women and are choosing to write, as we do, s/he. Other, more radical writers use 'she' as a generic, in order to redress the balance.

In terms of the context of culture there is no difference between writing and speech. They are both embedded in and dependent on context of culture in the same way. When, why and how people write is determined by socio-cultural attitudes to writing, including accepted conventions of handwriting, spelling, public and private behaviour (what to 'put in writing' and what not). Writers use language the way they do because of the socio-cultural norms that operate in the context in which they are writing: following some and flouting others, conforming to or challenging the patterns of privileging among them.

HETEROGENEITY IN THE CONTEXT OF CULTURE

We think it is essential to recognise that culture is not monolithic. The context of culture is socially produced and reproduced, but most societies are open enough to contain alternatives. Through-out the previous section we have been emphasising the fact that a context of culture may accommodate a variety of possibilities, but at the same time privilege one of these possibilities over others. We see this as a dynamic way of representing multiplicity without overlooking dominance. Both the array of possibilities and the pattern of privileging are socially constructed, and both, but particularly the pattern of privileging, are open to contestation and change over time.

British society is made up of different social classes, different ethnic groups, men and women, young and old; these groups have differing, often conflicting, needs and interests and very different positions of power. As a consequence, each act of writing is a potential site of struggle because there are competing systems of values and beliefs at work. For example, a parent trying to write a letter to her child's teacher may feel pressure to be formal and respectful towards the teacher, but at the same time want to show that she has a valid point to make: the writer is influenced by the traditional view of teacher as authority, and another, 'Parent–Teacher Association' view of parents and teachers as equal. For this reason we do not think it is possible to identify a one-to-one relationship between types of context and types of writing, nor to draw up a typology of writing 'registers' or 'genres'. Rather, we take the view that each act of writing and its resulting written text is unique, and can play an important part in the struggle among the various ideological positions and associated practices and discourses in its context of culture.

THE RELATIONSHIP BETWEEN CONTEXT OF SITUATION AND CONTEXT OF CULTURE

For strictly analytical purposes we have distinguished between context of situation, or local writing environment, and the wider socio-cultural context. However, it is in practice difficult to separate them out because the local circumstances themselves are in part determined by the socio-cultural context. The actual writing task, what it is that the writer has to carry out, is part of the local environment and will affect what the writer has to do in order to carry it out. However, what the writer brings to the task in terms of attitudes towards it, beliefs about what is expected from the task, the purposes that lie behind the setting of that particular task, all connect into the wider context of culture and affect the process and the outcomes.

The participants in the context of situation – the people, the readers and writers – are what link it to the context of culture. They bring with them their experience and knowledge of the socio-political context they live in, and their own alignments, positions, values and beliefs. All the elements of cultural knowledge that we identified above are brought into the local situation through the mind-sets of the individual readers and writers. This link is represented graphically by Figure 3.2. The inner box represents the 'context of situation' in which an actual person, John, is engaged in an act of writing an assignment for a university course and anticipating the response to his writing of the tutor who will read it. The outer box represents the 'context of culture' in which this context of situation is embedded, consisting of values and beliefs about Aids, the topic he is writing about, about the nature of academic assignments, and about other, less directly relevant, things. The link between the two types of context is 'through the heads' of the participants.

Both John and his tutor are represented with their minds opening into the outer box, for they act as filters through which elements of the context of culture enter into the context of situation. In addition, the books and other texts are represented as open to the outer box, since they have been produced by

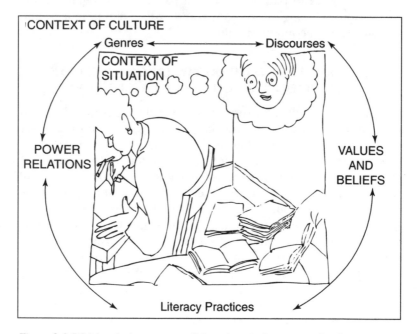

Figure 3.2 Writing in its context of situation and context of culture

72

people who have, in turn, been shaped by the context of culture. An individual will have access to some of the possibilities that are in principle available within a context of culture only through their life experiences and their past and present encounters with its texts. Many will be constrained by the patterns of privileging within the context of culture: that is, they will bow to the pressure to adopt only the dominant values and beliefs, and conform to the conventions that follow from them. The participants in an act of writing are likely to have both knowledge of and commitment to some aspects of the context of culture, but are likely to differ in other respects. Thus the whole of the context of culture does not necessarily enter into a context of situation, only those elements of it that have been available to, and in turn adopted by, the individual participants. Not represented in the figure are the processes by which individual participants in a context of situation come to align themselves with some aspects of the context of culture and not others. This depends on the social groups and values and beliefs they identify with and other texts with which they are familiar, as we discuss further in Chapter 6.

To end this section, we illustrate how the context of culture affects writing practices, and how, in turn, writers may either conform to or resist the patterns of privileging within the context of culture by the way in which they act in a context of situation. We know many women who do extremely important writing on the corner of their kitchen table late at night after the children have gone to bed, while their male partners write on their personal computers in their studies. These two different physical situations are an expression of the different values accorded to men's work and women's work, of the embedded patriarchal view that men's work is more important and that women's writing – stories, course-work or perhaps writing associated with their employment for a 'second income' – have to come after her 'natural' duties of looking after the family and the house. Some of the women we know accept this state of affairs as 'the norm'; others dispute it and are fighting for more 'space', both physical and mental; fighting to establish different norms of greater equality; others again choose to write in the kitchen because of its association with nourishment and creative confusion. In this way the flow can be seen not only inwards on Figure 3.2 from the context of culture to the context of situation and the act of writing itself, but also in the opposite direction, with individual acts of writing themselves, through not only the words writers choose but also the practices they engage in, challenging and contributing towards changing cultural norms. This is represented by the outward arrows on the diagram.

So far in this chapter we have examined the concept of 'social context' and made a distinction between context of situation and context of culture and how these shape both the writer and the act of writing. We now give two case studies to illustrate these arguments more concretely.

WRITERS IN THEIR SOCIAL, POLITICAL AND HISTORICAL CONTEXTS: TWO CASE STUDIES

Rachel: a struggle for identity

Rachel is 28. She is at university. She is doing the professional year of a four-year degree in social work. The writing she does consists of academic essays for the course, case notes on her placement, and some editing notes for papers she has written collaboratively with a friend and with her tutor. We will focus on the time when she wrote an assignment about one of her placements.

Part of the context of situation is the way in which the assignment was set. There was a very strict deadline. There was no choice. The students were told that they must show the relationship between their fieldwork placement and relevant theory. So what could be written about, and how, was very restricted. Another part of the context for this writing was Rachel's personal history. She left school at 16 with no qualifications. At that time she read and wrote very little; she found reading hard, and viewed herself as someone who 'couldn't write'. She worked for nine years, doing mainly catering and seasonal work. During that time she learned a lot from the people she met. She decided to study more. She enrolled for two 'O' level subjects at a college of Further Education. She then took a part-time 'Fresh Horizons' course which gave her the confidence to apply to university, and on the strength of her performance in an interview she was offered a place. However, these courses had not given her the experience of writing she needed in order to write academic assignments. In her first three years at university, she struggled with every assignment, using a vast network of support systems to get the written work done. She also worked in a café, and was embarrassed because she had to write down orders on the spot, and was not sure how to spell 'salad'.

Another aspect of the context of situation is the physical circumstances in which she worked on this present piece of writing. Rachel wrote this on her own. Her network of friends from the previous three years had split up; she no longer had access to a word-processor. She worked in her own bedroom, with a small desk. She had only one person left from her network of friends whom she asked for some advice on her final draft.

The participants in the context of situation include Rachel herself, who was struggling to achieve satisfactory grades for her course: she did not have confidence in herself as a writer, although she was a self-assured person in other respects. Rachel got on well with her tutor, who in turn thought highly of her and was interested in her ideas, so one of her readers was someone Rachel expected to be sympathetic to her. Her tutor's view was that if she could be examined verbally she would get first class marks. Rachel knew that her work was also likely to be seen by an external examiner, but knew little about him. The power relations among these three participants in the actual context of writing are that the external examiner is the most powerful and Rachel is the least.

The richer characterisation of context of situation that we are working with includes people's ideological commitments: their values and beliefs. Rachel expressed her own commitments in the piece of writing that we are focusing on. The following is an extract from the final version of it:

> Personally I think that Ms A's 'problems' and sense of powerlessness was part of a wider social problem: that of 'compulsory heterosexual relationships' (Rich, A. 1981), the institution of marriage, the family, motherhood and unequal social relations, all of which I think social work/ers take for granted as being so 'natural'.

Rachel expected her tutor to share her commitment, but she suspected that her external examiner would consider these views irrelevant to the essay. Because of her own commitment and her assessment that the tutor would share her belief, Rachel did include this sentence, and distanced herself from the word 'natural' with quotation marks. Because of her worry about the external examiner, however, she confined these views to this single sentence near the end of her essay, hedged them with the modality markers 'personally' and 'I think', and appealed to the authority of a published author to validate the views with '(Rich, A. 1981)'.

These details give a sketch of the local context in which this particular writer did this particular piece of writing, and of some of the textual decisions she made about it. These aspects of the context of situation are further embedded in the 'context of culture' in which she was writing, that is, the socio-politically and historically shaped values and conventions that were current in the UK in 1990. This includes values and beliefs about writing in general, norms and conventions of practice and product for the particular type of writing she was doing, and conflicting beliefs about heterosexuality and how its dominance affects women's lives. In that context of culture not being able to write fluently is stigmatised as a sign of low intellect, poor education and/or low social class. Another important part of this context of culture were certain practices that are seen as 'male' and elitist among feminist academics. These include many of the dominant writing practices within the academic discourse community, such as the 'fragmentation into specialisms' and the fact that academic knowledge is 'so divorced from real everyday life experiences' (Karach and Roach 1994). Finally, in the context of culture of the department in which Rachel was studying, heterosexuality was seen as a norm, and not a cause of women's problems: to identify it as a cause of problems was a minority view, and deemed 'radical'.

The processes of identification of people involved in the context of situation connect it to the context of culture. Rachel knows, consciously or subconsciously, a certain amount about the competing systems of values, beliefs and norms in her culture, societal and institutional. She also has made an assessment about which systems her tutor adheres to, and which the external examiner adheres to. Both her own allegiances among those aspects of the context of culture, and her prediction of the allegiances of the readers, influence the specific act of writing in which she is engaged, and the discoursal choices she makes as she writes. So, for example, it was the privileging of heterosexuality in the context of culture, along with the unequal power relations between her and her external examiner, that caused her to leave her radical views to the end. In some small way, her individual action as a writer will contribute to the shaping of cultural resources in the future, as the outward arrows in Figures 1.1 and 3.2 represent: the privileging of heterosexuality has been challenged, but only hesitantly. In Chapter 6 we discuss further the way in which writer identity is at the heart of this connection between the context of culture and the context of situation.

Trevor Griffiths: a struggle for space

Trevor Griffiths was born in Manchester in 1935 in a working-class family. His early years were marked by the poverty caused by the Great Depression. He won a scholarship to a Catholic grammar school and then studied English at Manchester University on a state scholarship. In the 1960s he became involved in CND and also became the chairperson of the Manchester Left Club, a reader group associated with the *New Left Review* (then edited by Stuart Hall; see Poole and Wyver 1984). He taught for a while, became a Further Education officer for the BBC, and finally turned to full-time writing in 1972.

This very brief sketch of Griffiths' background is part of the general context of situation that indirectly or directly affects each piece that he writes (for further detail see Poole and Wyver 1984). We now explore the issue of social context with reference to one specific piece of writing: the play *Who Shall Be Happy?* (retitled *Hope in the Year 2000* by the BBC when it was broadcast in 1994), set on the eve of Danton's execution in 1794. The wider social, historical context of the play is directly significant to the writing of the play. Firstly, it was

> conceived, set up, researched and written . . . over the year that followed the last election [i.e. 1992] . . . [It] constitutes a raid on the past, an address to the present and a rejection of the future currently on offer. . . .
>
> (Preface to the published version of
> *Hope in the Year 2000*, 1994a)

1994 was the 200th anniversary of the death of Danton, and the play was written to be broadcast in 1994, and was finally produced on stage in 1996. Theatre and television-wise, the play was conceived and written at a time when it was and still is very hard for radical, political plays to get the space they need to reach wider audiences. *Who Shall Be Happy?* was eventually staged by a small company, with very few resources; in London it was put on at The Bush Theatre, so back to the fringe for Griffiths, after 30 years of writing, including plays staged by the National Theatre with Laurence Olivier and other major actors (*Independent*, 5 June 1996).

77

The immediate or local context of situation in which Griffiths wrote the play, originally for television, consists of a wide range of conditions. Firstly, the play had to 'fit' into the allotted time slot of 80 minutes – time on television is rigorously apportioned. The deadline was in part self-imposed, in that Griffiths wanted the play to be broadcast in the summer of 1994, to coincide with the 200th anniversary of Danton's death. But he also had deadlines imposed by the working practices of television: pre-production, production and post-production needs. Because writing plays for production inevitably involves later collaborative work with directors, actors, set designers and so on, the actual writing of the play is also affected by the anticipated needs and roles of and struggles with these collaborators. So, for example, the shot (or stage) directions are a crucial part of the writing. Some particularly important stage directions (pp. 15–16 of the play), describe a scene in the Palais de Luxembourg, and refer to a broken-down chair. Of these, Griffiths says:

> what you see there in this broken down chair, what you get in that signifier is an ancient order destroyed and it's the only place in the play where the old ruling class is represented. But the significance of the present is that it can't stand up on its own. It's a chair which is skewed. Now, when Danton goes and sits on it, it's saying the revolution is also skewed. There's a complexity of meaning there which needs to be understood.
>
> (Griffiths 1993)

Griffiths struggled to make the proposed director understand these directions and commented:

> [the director] is actually saying: 'why don't you leave the shots to me? I'll do the shots, you do the dialogue. That's what film directors do.'
>
> (the same)

Because the play was to be shown on the BBC, their producers also affected the writing, albeit at a later, in-production stage:

> The BBC didn't like my title. It was thought to be archaic. I don't think I've had a single title accepted by the BBC in 26 years of writing for them. . . . It's like they think somehow you lose your ability to write at the point of the title. They

have a greater understanding of the audience than you do. And it's so demeaning.

(*Independent* 5 June 1996)

Precisely with the audience in mind, Griffiths had woven the original title, *Who Shall Be Happy?*, into the play, as a kind of conundrum: this acts as an important thread in the weaving of the web of the play and the 'hooking' of the audience and keeping them engaged. With the BBC's title, much of this is lost.

Griffiths was writing a play that he knew would be produced with a limited budget. Hence, for example, there could be only two main actors and limited on-location shooting. This meant that a lot of meaning had to be concentrated in The Prisoner's monologues, and the historical references, such as the 'Noyades' of Nantes,[1] had to be understood mainly through the words of the text: there could be no dramatic reconstructions as in big-budget historical movies. In turn, however, these contextual constraints led to a taut, almost Greek, dramatic unity and purity, achieved by the very tight focus throughout the play.

The content of the play is also affected by the times in which it was written. Some of the concerns of post-modernity are apparent, particularly the notion of identity – who *is* The Prisoner? Is he really just an actor pretending to be Danton? Or is it Danton himself? And who is the real Danton, anyway? – a complex web of competing and conflicting identities, desires and allegiances.

Finally, part of the context of writing the play was also Griffiths' inevitable contemplation of his own life and death, and his political beliefs. Of writing this play he said:

the Danton play was a (much more) imprisoned play; I mean, I felt awfully trapped inside a world that I was creating and I knew that world reflected subjectively a lot of my own desperation, fear, pain, unhappiness. . . . I remember saying to people that while writing it I'd been in a place where I didn't really want to go and I'd always felt this place to be inside me and that I'd visited old terrain, and I didn't want to get back there in a hurry. . . . It's not jolly. You are enter-taining your own death or the prospect of your own death all the time.

(Griffiths 1993)

CONCLUSION

We have described the two case studies in order to show how, far from being 'decontextualised', writing is embedded in social aspects of its context. The chapter as a whole has presented an overview of what we mean by 'the social context of writing'. A central claim of this book is that the social context of any specific act of writing constructs both the way in which the writing is carried out and the written language of the text itself. In Chapters 4–7 we elaborate on this claim, examining first the nature of the processes and practices involved in the act of writing, and then three specific aspects of its social context: the purposes for writing, the role of the writer and the role of the reader.

4

WRITING PROCESSES AND PRACTICES

INTRODUCTION

In this chapter we first discuss writing as a physical and social activity, arguing against the assumptions implied by the term 'procedures' and the widely used term 'skills', in favour of our preferred term: 'practices'. We then focus on mental processes involved in writing, briefly comparing writing with speaking as processes of language production, highlighting some key differences that make the writing process more difficult than talking for most people, and identifying the linguistic characteristics of written language that result from particular mental processes of production. We look at different attempts to describe what is involved in writing and the respective 'models' proposed. We describe an alternative representation of the writing process, building on the very important contribution that Hayes and Flower have made in emphasising the dynamic, non-linear nature of writing as a thinking process. Our view of writing treats it not merely as a set of physical procedures, and not merely as a cognitive process, but as a social practice consisting of a complex set of physical, socio-political, cognitive and affective elements. We argue that there is no right 'route' through the physical procedures and mental processes involved in writing and no right set of practices, but that the routes and practices selected are affected by the context in which the writer is operating, including the teaching of writing approaches that s/he has been exposed to and the nature of the writing task itself, as well as the individual writer's ideologies and preferences. To illustrate the generalisable application of our representation of the writing process, we draw on interviews with the playwright Trevor Griffiths about his writing practices as a playwright and his responses to some of the elements we believe are central to writing.

THE TERM 'PRACTICES' VERSUS 'PROCEDURES' OR 'SKILLS'

As we indicated in Chapter 1, we view writing practices as social practices and include in these physical, interactive and discursive practices. We use the term 'practices' and not 'procedures' or the even more widely used 'skills' to emphasise the social nature of what we do as writers. Practices are not just what people do, but what they make of what they do, and how it constructs them as social subjects. The physical act of organising your work in a certain way before starting to write, browsing for ideas in books on library shelves rather than reading set books from cover to cover are, for example, socially and ideologically shaped ways of behaving. In the British academic community, independence is valued; in others less so. Students from some other countries and cultures are more 'obedient' in the way they approach reading lists and texts. There are competing views of what constitutes good writing 'behaviour' and what not; the activity of writing is an arena of struggle as well as of conformity. We feel that the term procedures does not capture all of this. It decontextualises writing, does not capture the three dimensions of the act of writing in Fairclough's diagram (Figure 1.1) and has prescriptive connotations, as in 'the correct procedures'.

Writing practices are culturally conditioned. Even the apparently technical aspects of writing, such as the choice of implement, are deeply embedded in socio-economic relations and have ideological implications. These are the visible aspects of prestige practices which are more open to scrutiny than the social aspects we discuss below. For example, using a word-processor in order to put thoughts into words is very different from writing by hand, with all the crossings out and inhibitions to redrafting this involves; there is also the option to resist the social pressures to adopt certain practices, such as to use a word-processor and to get ever more powerful (and expensive) ones. The drive to ever more powerful and complex – and expensive – technology for writing is at least in part driven by commercial and economic needs and leads to technocratic elitism. In Britain families are under pressure to buy the latest technology for their children. While so much is claimed about the benefits to the child in educational terms and the advantage later in the job market, another wedge is lodged between the well-off and the poor. Indeed, as we know from our experience in Tanzania, some African universities which do not even have basic electricity supplies guaranteed are under pressure to buy computers. The pressure to conform is very difficult to resist. (Romy still works on an Amstrad PCW 8256 because she does not want to be sucked even further into the technologising of her work and all that that implies, including the financial cost. She is consequently regarded as a 'dinosaur', and constantly reminded of the advantages of buying something more powerful and faster!)

Practices vary not only from culture to culture, but also from person to person and from one context to another. For example, writing in the classroom is different from writing at home: the way the learner writer writes in the classroom will be affected by the length of the class period, by the kind of supervision, by the encouragement or otherwise of collaborating with peers, etc. Some professional non-academic writers like to write early in the morning, others, like Griffiths, prefer to write at night; some set themselves a target of so many words a day, others do not.

With respect to the interactive/interpersonal aspect of writing, writing collaboratively is a very different activity from writing alone. Particularly, the reader's response is built into the writing process itself in collaborative writing, as we have experienced in writing this book. Again, attitudes towards collaborative writing are highly ideological: in British society, emphasis is primarily placed on the individual and individualism is encouraged, at school and beyond. We have notions of the 'artist' as the creative individual, and in the educational world we have notions of individual effort and reward. Most student academic writing is supposed to be done individually and suggestions of collaboration are actively resisted by many lecturers.

As we argued in Chapter 1, the term 'practices' does not refer only to such obviously physical acts as going to the library, and interactive practices such as collaborative writing, but also to the linguistic and discoursal choices that the writer makes. The plural 'practices' implies that there is no one right or appropriate way of behaving or communicating, but multiple competing ways of being. These competing ways of being are not equally valued or accepted, hence the struggle for hegemony. For example, when a student writer chooses to use the pronoun 'I' when s/he is referring to her/his own ideas in an academic essay for, say, the Department of Accounting and Finance, s/he is making a social statement about the right of students to have opinions of their own; s/he is also breaking a dominant convention in many disciplines that says that academic writing should be 'objective', and is therefore inscribing him/herself in a particular ideological view of knowledge, and in a particular view of social relations. S/he is also taking risks because of this challenge to the dominant convention.

These differences in *practices* seem to us to be of enormous significance and often interact with the cognitive *processes* involved in writing. For example, the choice of writing technology will have an effect on the cognitive work that the writer does: using a word-processor is likely to lead to a greater willingness to revise and redraft. The widespread practice among university students of writing their essays with textbooks open in front of them must have an effect on the process of formulating their ideas into written language.

Physical and social behaviour surrounding writing is often lumped together with mental processes under the broad heading 'skills'. We challenge both this unanalysed lumping together, and the connotations of the term 'skills'. The term skills, like pro-cedures, suggests a set of neutral technologies or techniques that are somehow separate and separable from the social context that favours them. The term is associated with competence-based models of language and language learning (see Fairclough 1992c: 39–43) and has its origins in Chomsky (1965). It has led to the viewing of language activities as consisting of discrete, apparently manageable and 'teachable' components, and so appears to facili-tate teaching and learning. It implies a normative, prescriptive view of communication, namely that these competencies/skills constitute 'writing' and writers need to acquire them in order to achieve effective communication. Because of this, we do not think it is possible or desirable to describe the writing process as a set of skills, or to reduce language education in general and writing in particular to skills training. The teaching of writing as a set of 'skills' rests on an unproblematised view of sociolinguistic appro-priacy and an acceptance of the existing sociolinguistic order. The (liberal) aim is to help individual learners, who at present do not have certain desirable 'skills', to acquire those skills in order to fit into the existing order, not challenge or change it. This is in line with the reproductive tendency of education we mentioned in Chapter 2. Conceptualising writing in terms of 'skills' focuses on writing as a technology and disregards writing as meaning-making, negotiation of identity, and social participation. 'Skills' are deemed to be independent of content and transferable to any context: a view we would hotly contest.

In pedagogic terms, the term 'skills' is prescriptive and seems to reproduce a deficit view of the learner writer, that is as some-one who does not have this desirable package of technologies and needs to acquire it. A further pedagogic implication is that these technologies can be acquired in an unproblematic fashion – learning 'effective communication skills' is like learning to ride a bike (see Johnson 1996) – whereas our experience tells us that learning to write is in fact an extremely painful and sometimes traumatic experience. We try to capture the socio-cultural com-plexity of writing practices, where we present our alternative view of 'the writing process', later in the chapter. But first we consider a particular aspect of writing as a mental process: the ways in which it compares and contrasts with speaking as a mental process.

THE WRITING PROCESS COMPARED WITH THE SPEAKING PROCESS

One important difference between speaking and writing is that most people acquire the ability to speak in their first language without making any conscious effort, whereas writing has to be learned. This has the effect for most people of making writing a more self-conscious activity, and carries with it the association of 'school' which for many people is not always a happy or successful experience (see Chapter 2). It is impossible to compare writing and speaking processes without saying what types of writing and speaking we are referring to. Some communicative events have clear differences between them; for example, writing an essay is very different from chatting to a friend. On the other hand, some types of writing and speaking are quite similar; for example, a phone conversation and passing notes to a friend. And some forms of communication are hard to classify categorically as 'speech' or 'writing' at all; for example sign language and e-mail. Most differences between types of writing and types of speaking are a matter of degree and are related to the actual social context of the writing (see Chapter 3). Stubbs (1980, 1987) was one of the first people to address the issue of the different dimensions that distinguish speaking from writing, talking in terms of overlap or continua between the two modes. Biber (1988) has explored the same issue through corpus-based studies, and Barton has integrated it into a social view of literacy, arguing also that there are 'many complex configurations of language involving both writing and speech' (1994: 83).

In spite of these difficulties with clearly distinguishing the writing process from the speaking process, we suggest that it is still useful to recognise two aspects of the cognitive process of language production that make prototypical writing different from prototypical speaking. Firstly, all language use involves some form of mental planning, and there is a continuum between slow, carefully planned production of language and fast, relatively spontaneous production of language. Most types of writing tend to be at the carefully planned end of this continuum, and many types of speech tend to be at the relatively spontaneous end. However, factors other than the medium of communication affect the degree of planning too, particularly the context, the content and the relationship between the producers of the message. Figure 4.1 illustrates this point.

This continuum can also be explained in terms of flexible processing versus fixed processing. Most types of writing allow the

---

CAREFULLY PLANNED   SPONTANEOUS
...1........2......3.................4..........5..........6........7.............8..

1 Writing a letter of condolence to a friend
2 Writing a lecture
3 Making a complaint to a company over the phone
4 Writing an essay in an exam
5 Writing a shopping list
6 Writing notes to a friend
7 A telephone conversation with a friend
8 Chatting to a friend face-to-face

Figure 4.1 The nature of planning in different types of speech and writing

producer to draft and redraft flexibly in order to get the wording just right, whereas most types of speaking require the speaker to produce their message on-line, with no chance to repair it until after it has been heard. Having more time to think about what to write and how to write it often makes people more self-conscious, and this can make the process of writing slow and painful compared with speaking. When people are talking they usually have to think and speak simultaneously, and therefore no one expects a polished version of their thoughts, however articulate they are.

A second difference between the cognitive processes of writing and speaking is that many types of writing are done at a distance from the reader, whereas many types of speaking and listening are interactive, simultaneous and/or face-to-face. In Chapter 3 we discussed the way in which the context of writing is often separated from the context of reading; here we consider how this separation between the writer and the reader affects the *process* of writing. When people are writing they have the disadvantage of not having immediate feedback from their addressee which would help them to develop their message. Widdowson (1983: 34) says that in his experience 'writing is usually an irksome activity and an ordeal to be avoided whenever possible. It seems to require an expense of effort disproportionate to the actual result.' He suggests (p. 39) that the main reason why writing is such an 'ordeal' is that the interactive process of negotiation in written discourse is covert and non-reciprocal. The writer has to enact both roles in the interaction, and because of the lack of immediate feedback can only anticipate what is the likely reaction of the reader. The writer therefore has, in Widdowson's term, a 'conveyancing problem'. The lack of immediate feedback from reader(s) means that writers have to manage the dialogic aspect of writing by trying to anticipate their reader's reactions to and disagreements with what they write. This is very difficult to do, especially when writers are not sure who their readers will be. Similarly, Ong (1982: 102), in discussing the problem of the missing 'extratextual context' that, in his words, makes writing 'so much more agonising an activity than oral presentation to a real audience', refers to the writer's audience as 'a fiction' (quoting himself from 1977: 53).

The lack of instant feedback in combination with the permanency of writing (unless we tear it up, of course!) often has inhibitory effects on the writer. Once something is written down it seems definite, unchangeable and open to criticism, whereas spoken language is fluid and negotiable. People usually have the chance to qualify or elaborate what they are saying according to other people's reactions, especially in conversation where participants take turns at speaking and listening. Once something is committed to paper and seen by someone else, we cannot deny it in the same way as we can pretend spoken words were never said.

The effects of writing processes on written language

As we argued in the previous section, there is no neat dividing line between writing and speaking, and consequently there is no neat dividing line between spoken and written language. However, the mental processes we identified above do shape the language they produce. Particularly, the fact that writing usually allows for slower, more carefully planned language production has some specific linguistic consequences. Firstly, slow production allows for hesitation, reformulation, repetition and redundancy to be ironed out, so that the resulting text appears seamless and smooth-flowing. Secondly, the more carefully planned writing is, the more opportunity there is to pack meanings in relatively long, complex noun phrases which are in turn combined into long, lexically dense clauses (see Halliday 1985/89 for a detailed analysis of this characteristic). This characteristic of written language is seen by many as a defining feature of academic writing, although it is in fact simply a function of time available for planning, and not intrinsic to the knowledge-making purposes of the academic community. Long noun phrases are also common in bureaucratic and legal writing, and in some forms of literary writing where the writer wants to create tightly packed description. Finally, the separation of producer from receiver means that a great deal of written language is in the form of relatively 'long turns', whereas spoken language often consists of short, interacting turns.

These differences between written language and spoken language have been characterised by Halliday (1985; 1994) as the difference between a product and a process; as the difference between the static and the dynamic; as the difference between a diamond formed under pressure and a rapidly running river. We are claiming that these differences are caused not by the characteristics of the linguistic medium, but by the nature of the cognitive processes of production. In principle these are independent of the medium, but in practice most writing involves one configuration of processes of production, and most speaking involves the other.

Models of writing try to capture in an economic and graphic way what is involved in writing. We now look at three different attempts to provide such a description.

MODELS OF WRITING

A linear 'model'

The term 'linear model' is used extensively in theoretical discussions concerning approaches to writing, particularly in comparison with the 'process approach' but, in reality no one (as far as we know) has ever actually produced a linear model as such. It is an implicit model. Much of the early research on composition, as described, for example, in Beach and Bridwell (1984), focused on the effects of teaching methodologies that rested on a set of prescriptive assumptions about 'good' writing. One of these assumptions was that writing progresses logically and sequentially through a set of discrete steps or stages, hence the word 'linear'. These stages, as can be deduced from the teaching materials and methods proposed, could be presented as follows:

1 Choose a topic.
2 Write an outline.
3 Develop the outline.
4 Edit and proofread.

So from the above stages we can deduce a linear model, and from the accompanying advice to teachers on how to use published materials in their classrooms it is also clear that the accompanying pedagogy is product-based. There are usually recommendations to learner writers to 'plan carefully before you begin writing', and it is still common practice in many academic departments in our university to expect students to write their introduction to, for example, their dissertations before they write anything further, and then to write sequentially according to the outline that has been approved. As we argue later in this chapter, this undermines the concept of writing as a thinking process and a space where the writer is negotiating his/her identity, and encourages students to think that writing is simply a translation into words on the page of the thinking they have done beforehand. In one department in another university the students are given a mark for their outline and plan, reinforcing by this the linearity of the process of writing and creating problems for their students who feel ashamed that they cannot do what they are asked to do. Considering what the finished academic product of writing looks like – with an intro-duction, a development and a conclusion, or, in the case of simple narratives, a clear beginning, middle and end – it is clear why this kind of linear approach to the actual order in the writing process appealed (and still does) to teachers and went unchallenged for such a long time. It is neat and unmessy and mirrors the order of the product. It appears seductively easy to teach because it divides the task into manageable chunks, both in terms of class time and in terms of description, and is still widely advocated by teachers of writing to all ages all over the world. As a result of the implicit assumptions about writing mentioned above, learner writers are expected to produce 'perfect' writing in a single sitting in the classroom, and are thus indirectly encouraged to think of them-selves as 'poor' writers because most of them find this very difficult to do and usually get back their texts covered in red ink! Slightly less rigid versions of this approach have been developed but remain essentially tied to the separation of the writing process into the discrete stages embodied in pre-writing (thinking about and planning what you want to say), writing (actually composing in sequential fashion) and post-writing (checking spelling, grammar, etc.).

In the late 1970s and early 1980s some researchers, such as Hayes and Flower (1980), Matsuhashi (1982), Murray (1978) and Rose (1984), began to challenge the assumptions behind this approach and published studies that showed what it was that writers actually do, compared with the idealised picture reflected in the linear approach we have just outlined. In the late 1970s and 1980s further research has found that a more recursive or cyclical view of the writing process is needed to capture what it is that writers do in their heads while composing.

A recursive process model

We are now going to examine in some detail a model of writing as a cognitive process that was first proposed by Hayes and Flower in 1980, and discussed in detail in Hayes and Flower 1983.

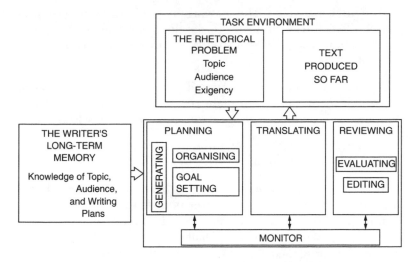

Figure 4.2 The Hayes and Flower model of the writing process
Source: Hayes and Flower 1983: 208

First of all some explanation of the terms used by Hayes and Flower in this model will be necessary before we comment on the model itself.

1 The task environment:
   This includes everything outside the writer, including the assignment and the need to write, the audience and eventually the written text-product itself (Hayes and Flower 1983: 208); this does not refer to the wider socio-cultural context as portrayed in Fairclough's diagram (Figure 1.1).
2 The writer's long-term memory (LTM):
   According to Hayes and Flower this includes knowledge of the topic s/he is writing about and knowledge of writing plans.
3 The writing processes (contained in the largest box in the model):
   These are, according to Hayes and Flower, the mental processes involved in the actual act of composing.

   Planning: this involves generating content, organising it and setting up goals and procedures for writing. That is 'the whole range of *thinking* activities . . . before we can put words on paper' (same book: 209; our emphasis).

   Translating: this is the act of expressing the content of planning

91

in written language. This moving from plan to composing in full 'often forces the writer to develop, clarify and often revise . . . ' (same page). This means that the writer often has to return to planning.

Reviewing: this is the act of evaluating (their term) what has been written or what has been planned, mid-text or at the end of a draft. (This evaluation may be conscious or unconscious.)

The monitor: this is the mechanism that determines for the writer when to switch from one process to another.

In their description of the model we have just outlined, Hayes and Flower make the following three important comments. Firstly, writing processes do not typically occur in a fixed sequence, such as plan, translate, review (we shall return to this point later). Secondly, writing is goal-oriented; a lot of time is spent developing what they call 'global goals' for affecting an audience and developing ideas, and more 'local goals' and plans that guide the writing process, that is the way we translate the former into actual words, phrases, sentences, etc., each with their own specific aims. Thirdly, 'writing stimulates the discovery, of new goals' (same book: 210). That is, the act of writing itself is a process of discovery, and new goals may be discovered through 'insights triggered by the act of writing'. This, Hayes and Flower say, is an important aspect of the writer's creativity. This is why there can be no fixed sequence in the writing process.

We share this view of writing as a non-linear, recursive thinking process in which the writer moves backwards and forwards from one element to another as s/he explores what s/he wants to say. However, we have a number of serious reservations about this model. Our first reservation is that it concentrates only on the psychological processes of the individual mind, without relating the writer to the social context in which s/he is writing (see Chapter 3). And because they decontextualise, the implication is that the cognitive processes that they describe are universal. While Hayes and Flower recognise the importance of the writer engaging with content, they ignore the equally important interpersonal aspects of writing and the pressure of convention (cf. Widdowson 1983). The process of writing therefore is not located, as it should be in our view, in the context of writing practices (see Flynn 1991 and Newkirk 1991 for similar criticisms). Even if it is argued that

92

these additional elements are covered either by the 'long-term memory' box (context of culture elements in our representation) or by the 'task environment' box (context of situation) of the model, we still feel this is inadequate. By not spelling them out clearly and by banishing them to what could be described as the 'ragbag' box,[1] diminishes their importance and foregrounds even more the psychological aspects of the process.

Secondly, this model implies that there are discrete constellations of elements such as, for example, planning elements. We believe that the interrelationships of elements are more complex, and therefore less 'tidy' than this model makes them seem.

Our third reservation concerns the fact that Hayes and Flower focus on writing as a cognitive process, rather than thinking of writing in terms of culturally shaped practices. This, in our view, adds to the prescriptive air of their model, and ignores the relationship between cognitive processes and practical procedures (as Stotsky calls them) on the one hand, and what we are calling 'practices' in a broader sense on the other. Hayes and Flower, coming from a psychology background, see processes as something inscribed in our brain cells, a neurological process; as Stotsky says (1990), they are hazy about what it is that writers actually do in physical procedural terms. We need, for instance, both to distinguish between and to recognise the relationships between the psycholinguistic process of planning (mental plans) and the practice of producing some sort of written plan: making an outline or drawing a spider diagram. Teacher-rewarded practices like writing an outline or a linear plan before starting an essay are also easy to see and therefore to copy, and these also affect the cognitive activity of the writer by forcing him/her to do a lot of generating of ideas early on and perhaps not doing enough later on. The writing process is therefore treated not as a thinking process but more as the translation into connected sentences of the outline.

Similarly, the notion of 'translating' is problematic. The mental process of translating in Hayes and Flower's model needs to be placed within the different practices that actualise the mental process (we develop this issue in the next section). For example, writing an assignment and being able to refer to other people's ideas in books is very different from dragging up all your ideas from memory and/or experience in an exam and leads to different kinds of writing and approaches to the writing. Hayes and Flower's notion of 'translation' also seems problematic when trying to explain discursive practices such as flouting generic conventions. This is not just an issue of 'translating' a mental plan but the result of a complex ideological struggle and is bound up with issues of writer identity.

We have consequently suggested additional components in our description and representation of the writing process. Our representation is an attempt to show the interplay between cognitive processes and writing practices.

Towards an alternative view of writing processes and practices

We deliberately avoid using the term 'model' for this view of what is involved in writing, because it suggests a fixed, predetermined and hence prescriptive route through the process and does not allow for differences in practices. (This was borne out by the reaction of a group of students with whom we used our representation early on, who expected to find or to be shown the 'right route'. In discussion afterwards they said that it was the term 'model' that had misled them.) Our representation attempts to capture the dynamic interplay both between all of the elements of the writing process and between the psycholinguistic and social features, and also to convey the message that there are no prescribed routes through the process.

The list is composed of those elements that we think are crucial to writing, including some things that do not generally get included in discussions of writing.[2] Our list is in no significant order other than a division into (a) long-term components (that is, those that develop over time) and (b) components of each individual act of writing. For example, the 'accumulation of knowledge, opinions and feelings' appears in both sections. It is an ongoing, lifelong developmental experience that is always there as something to draw on in our writing. But we also accumulate new knowledge, opinions and feelings specifically as part of each act of writing.

Long-term components

1 Accumulating general knowledge, opinions and feelings.
2 Developing the ability to use language.
3 Developing familiarity with types of writing (genres).
4 Developing socio-political identity as a writer.

Components of each act of writing

5   Accumulating knowledge, opinions and feelings for this particular task.
6   Establishing goals and purposes (global and local).
7   Analysing the assignment.
8   Planning.
9   Drawing on familiarity with types of writing (genres) (i.e. making use of what you know about the conventions of different types of writing and deciding whether to follow them or not).
10 Considering constraints of time and space.
11 Making the neat copy.
12 Drafting.
13 Formulating your own ideas.
14 Revising.
15 Experiencing pain, panic and anguish.
16 Clarifying your commitment to your ideas (i.e. deciding what you wish to say, how strongly you believe it and whether you are prepared to risk saying it.
17 Establishing your socio-political identity as a writer (i.e. deciding how and how much to show the reader who and what you are through the way you write and what you write about and how you treat your reader).
18 Considering the reader (i.e. both being considerate towards your reader and also bearing him/her constantly in mind while writing).
19 Experiencing pleasure and satisfaction
20 Deciding how to take responsibility: whether to mask or declare your own position (e.g. whether to use the pronoun 'I' or to passivise).
21 Putting your knowledge of the language to use and developing this knowledge.

Before we proceed to a diagrammatic representation of the actual process of writing, we need to make a number of explanatory comments about the components of writing that we have listed. Firstly, because we have presented them in list form, the dynamic and interdependent nature of the relationship between them does not come across. We will come back to this later in this section. Secondly, some of the components we include involve a degree of conflict and opposition that will vary from writer to writer. For example, 'drawing on familiarity with types of writing' as it stands suggests an unproblematic dipping into a well of accepted norms and conventions. But of course some writers will use their knowledge of these conventions in order deliberately to resist or flout them (cf. Chase 1988). And as Kress (1982: 124) points out:

> Other conventions can be imagined; . . . children constantly invent their own modes of organising and knowing, which do not, however, become recognised as such but rather are categorised as errors.

Thirdly, we think it is crucial to include and emphasise the socio-political dimensions to the writing process (cf. our view of language in Chapter 1), as expressed in particular in the components 'clarifying your commitment to your ideas', 'establishing your socio-political identity' and 'deciding how to take responsibility'. The socio-political context is also central to the components 'establishing goals and purposes', 'drawing on familiarity with writing', 'formulating your own ideas' and 'considering the reader'. We deal with these aspects of the process in detail in the next three chapters. Also important are the long-term aspects that cover the way in which a writer develops over time, because different elements will come more or less into focus as the writer learns more about him/herself and what is involved in writing and the different genres they have to deal with. We also think it is wrong to neglect the affective factors involved in writing, and these are represented in particular by the components 'accumulating knowledge, opinions and feelings', 'experiencing pain, panic and anguish' and 'experiencing pleasure and satisfaction' (for a more detailed discussion of these components see Clark and Ivanič 1991). We have also tried to represent more truthfully the seemingly 'chaotic' nature of the writing process.

The representation of the process of writing that follows is the result of discussions with thirty students in Lancaster University's department of Politics and International Relations in 1990. Each of the components of the individual act of writing was written on a piece of card, and the students worked in small groups, each with a 'pack' of cards. The students were asked to discuss the meaning of the cards and any difficulties they thought the components might cause them and to share their experiences of writing as they reflected on each component. Finally, they were asked to arrange the cards in such a way as to represent what they thought the process of writing 'looked like'. Figure 4.3 is what one of the groups came up with and, not surprisingly, for them 'pain, panic and anguish' was central to the process and 'pleasure and satisfaction' was near the end.

Several points emerged from attempting to incorporate physical, affective and social elements alongside cognitive ones in a representation of the process of writing. Firstly, as Hayes and Flower, we and the students found it impossible to suggest any type of linear progression through the writing process. The use of a word-processor even makes it difficult to see the 'neat copy' as the final stage in the process. Secondly, 'revising' is fundamental to and ongoing throughout the whole process. Writers revise their plans in the light of new thinking or new information; they revise the identity they wish to project to the reader by, for example, changing sexist language to non-sexist; they revise their understanding of the reader's needs in the light of rethinking or after discussing with an intermediate reader. Writers revise mentally and they revise as a physical 'procedure'. So, although it appears on our original list of components it perhaps should not appear separately but be subsumed in the other components. Thirdly, all the components are in some way interrelated; e.g. 'analysing the assignment' draws on 'familiarity with types of writing', 'knowledge' and 'considering the reader', and all these in turn belong in other 'constellations'. In other words, some arrows are missing. Fourthly, different types of writing need a different amount of each component, but probably even the simplest labelling task involves a small amount of each.

Fifthly, neither the list nor the representation shows the often interrupted nature of the writing process: writers often write ourselves into a corner and do not know how to go on; one solution is often to stop and go and do something else! But it is at moments like this, when we are 'stuck' or when we feel we are 'on to' something new, that we most consciously move from one element of the process to another. We may consciously decide that we have to change our overall plan, for example, in order to incorporate new thinking. This in turn can create problems for other parts of our writing and so we stop and maybe go back to goals, etc. This is nicely captured in the following extract from a letter from one of the student writers who had, earlier on in the term, devised Figure 4.3.

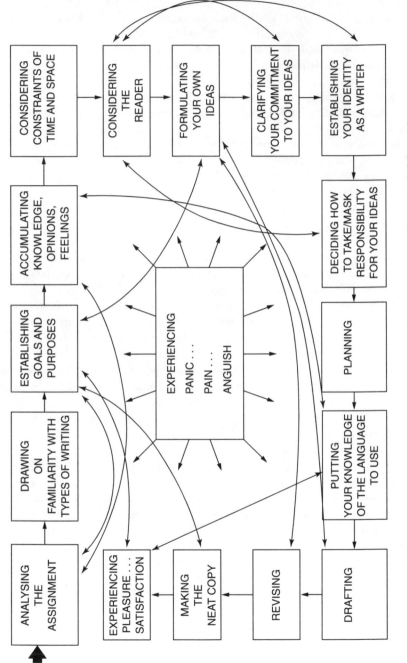

Figure 4.3 An alternative representation of the process of writing as a social practice
Source: Clark and Ivanič 1991

Do you remember our first session that we have drawn the 'elements of an assignment writing'? We had designed a continuous loop/circle of essay/dissertation writing. . . . And, this happened to me! At the end of my essay, after reading an article, I completely changed my mind about the construction of my essay! I found out that I missed some very important and interesting arguments!.[3]

Finally, even with the directional arrows drawn in and the proviso made under point three above, the printed version of the representation still inevitably looks static.

We have turned the activity we have just described into a pedagogic tool for raising consciousness among learner writers of what is involved in the writing process. We briefly describe the classroom procedures we have used with our classes in Chapter 9 (for full details see Clark and Ivanič 1991). In the last part of this chapter we present what the playwright Trevor Griffiths said about how some of these components of the writing process apply to writing a play.

THE WRITING PROCESSES AND PRACTICES OF A PLAYWRIGHT

This section puts some flesh on the bones of the explanation we have given of what is involved in the process of writing. We suggest that the components of the writing process that we outlined above and the sort of fluid representation of the writing process captured in Figure 4.3 apply to all types of writing and not just to academic writing. The differences between types of writing is not that the elements are different but that different kinds of writing involve different issues in relation to the same elements and different degrees of emphasis on each of the elements. To illustrate this we show how some of the elements we have listed apply to the writing of plays (we have written about how these components apply to student academic writing elsewhere: Clark and Ivanič 1991; Clark 1992).

As part of her work on the writing of Trevor Griffiths, Romy asked him about his own writing processes and practices. In one conversation she used the elements we outlined above as cues for the discussion. We believe that the playwright's responses support our view of the writing process as well as enriching our understanding of it in important ways. The rest of this section consists of some extracts from Romy's conversations with Trevor (Griffiths 1992/3) in which he elaborates on what some of the elements of the writing process mean when applied to playwriting. They are just a selection from a longer paper containing quotations which illuminate all the elements in the list (Clark 1997). We are presenting these comments as far as possible in Trevor's own words, with minimal intervention from us.[4] The final editing of these extracts was approved by Trevor himself. The other 'I' in what follows refers to Romy.

Planning

At the beginning of the conversation, I recalled something that Trevor had said about his planning processes at a public talk in Leeds (about *Comedians*, which was playing at The West Yorkshire Playhouse at the same time), suggesting that his approach to planning was now less linear. When writing *Comedians* in 1975 he said he had started with a step outline, whereas in writing *Who Shall Be Happy?* he worked using what he called a mosaic on A3 drawing paper. He also talked about a different mind set that was less linear. I asked him if he could elaborate:

> it's a very rough and ready account of strong but subtle changes over a number of years. All I did in the talk in Leeds was take two moments as it were, 1975 and 1993, and try in a broad way to describe what I think are the important differences in process. It may be that the plays I am writing now are different and I sort of organically discovered that they needed different processes from the earlier ones . . . or that I believe that something has changed about the way in which the social world, social reality, constitutes itself for my reading of it that makes it very difficult to examine it linearly or using the earlier rational structure.

I asked him if this had something to do with the greater fragmentation of reality and the less obvious connections between things:

> I think it probably has. If you take grand notions like causation, it's much more difficult to explain the causes of social reality than previously, or than we previously imagined.

Or maybe we were wrong and the world was always just as complex. Or it may be that the world has become hugely more jumbled and complex and you have to have a different way of looking, but I'm not sure. I mean, we can say some clear things about the change in process, the change in method to attack a project but as to what causes those, why they are necessary is more difficult to pin down. In a sense what you put in you get out and if you put a mosaic in as the structure to a play, you get a kind of mosaic play.

And this, in a sense, is what *Who Shall Be Happy?* is, in its finished form: a mosaic.

Trevor's comments reveal two approaches to planning when writing a play and the relationship between the planning process and the shape of the play that emerges from it.

Drafting, revising and making the final draft

In talking about drafting, we discussed how much of writing is consciously planned. Trevor talked about the way in which writing is not just the translation of pre-found ideas, but is itself part of the creative process:

[I]t's true of all writing that you're kind of aware of what you are doing, but there is a contradiction at the heart of it; you're aware of what you are doing at one level, even when you are doing stuff that surprises you. That's the contradiction. It's not a distraction, but you're watching certain key things when you are writing and you're aware of rhythms and counter-rhythms, resonances and colorations and correspondences. But there are other things happening on the page that you are less aware of, and when you come back to reading, particularly as I come back to a reading of it usually in typewritten form – whereas it leaves me in manuscript form – you then find these other things that happened and many of them are, for want of a better word, poetic or imagistic.They are about subconscious or uncon- scious things that begin to accumulate meanings almost on their own, without your intervention. I mean such intervention as you've made is not highly conscious, not consciously fashioned. *Thatcher's Children* [1993] was like that, and so was *Who Shall Be Happy?*.

101

On the question of revising, Trevor said:

> a lot of revising goes on in the writing. When I write the piece, I can't go on if something needs rewriting; if something needs revising then I have to get it right. Every piece has to connect with every other piece in a way that feels right; for example I can't write out of sequence. I can't say to myself, look I know this area very thoroughly, I can write that, and still need to know more about that; I can't do that. I suspect it's something to do with my character that makes me very empirical, so I have to feel concrete, not be abstract. It makes writing quite difficult but once I'm in it, once I'm weaving the web, then it has to be little by little by little by little, so finally that draft is like *it*. But it never is, because when you look again, when you come at it in a different way rather than as the weaver of the web, you begin to see that there are parts of it that don't actually work on the page; or there's a better thing to be done, there's something that strengthens it, makes it tauter in a practical way.

I asked him if this is why he writes the first draft by hand, because of the need to be so deliberate. He thought it probably was.

Talking about the final draft, he said:

> when you've finished something, when you've completed the final draft and that's it in a sense, there is a sense of fear that you've said that, you've cut the ambition. When you've done that, you feel awful because you've killed, you've slaughtered a thousand other possibilities. In order to make that one you have to kill off a lot of things and now you'll never work around that notion or around that subject or character again. For the moment, anyway, you feel awful. The act of writing is a resolution of [the range of possibilities].

Considering the reader

As a playwright, Trevor is ultimately writing for an audience, but part of the process of getting his work made into a stage or television play or a film involves showing the written text to a number of readers, such as directors, producers and actors.

> It's like producing your first audience and so on the page you need to surprise, to stimulate, to intrigue, to weave the

reader's attention into the piece that you've written to get the reader on the journey. . . .

We include further comments by Trevor on ways in which he considers the reader in Chapter 7.

Considering constraints of time and space

I recalled an interview with Misha Glenny (1986) in which Trevor talked about writing for television where producers impose time slots (the 60 minute slot or the 90 minute slot), and he said that he didn't write for 60 or 90 minutes, but wrote what was necessary, but then someone else comes in and does the cutting (pp. xx–xxi):

> It's the best way of proceeding. It's interesting to see them [the constraints] set out quite starkly as constraints, though I suppose in an obvious way they are. They may also be great aids in writing. You can get so enmeshed that you never come out; maybe having just one or two little markers like: if it's longer than 100 pages then I'm not saying it properly or whatever helps.

Trevor went on to talk about other constraints on a playwright:

> the budget is hugely important because that will confine what you can do. You don't yell about it; you're always saying I have to accept that I have a producer. I have to accept this little world of production. The Arts Council is slashing its grants and theatres are losing their funding and I write plays for somewhere where you don't know where its next budget is coming from, so you accept this.

The question of budgets has a direct influence over the writing. For example, in 1979 Trevor felt that:

> we needed something on the Tories and I said [to the BBC] I would do six linked plays, taking a nexus of interconnected families and following them through watershed moments in Conservative history, from 1945 into the late 80s. But then when I was writing [in 1980] it became obvious I was not going to get the conditions of production: the films, the money, the budget. So, bizarrely, *Country* turns out to be all six of the plays put together; that's the problem with *Country*,

103

it's a hugely compressed text because I knew I just had this one shot. It's carrying more meaning than it needed to have done. . . .

Putting your knowledge of the language to work

Trevor commented particularly on the way he used language in stage directions:

> I know that frequently when I'm writing stage directions, using language which is somehow different from the language of dialogue, in order to address a particular reader or ultimately the audience – a gesture of one sort or another on the screen or on the stage – using the language which is affective and sensory, sensuous even, in the sense that I'm trying to suggest what it's like to be there, what it feels like, what it smells like, what it tastes like, quite frequently I'll do this in a sort of encoded language so that only an actor/actress would get some of that; would get a sense of what I'm after. I know that when these directions are read by other people they are felt to be very strange, not part of the register of that text.

Some directors have problems with this, as Trevor illustrated by explaining the problems a potential director for *Who Shall Be Happy?* had with a particular set of directions:

> frankly, he didn't understand [the directions]. But I mean, if you take a word like 'jags', it seems to roar and jags around the space, [it's] saw-edged and there's an image there. There's a meaning to that and there's a lot of language there in the work which is resonant language. Like poetry, it's impressionistic language that needs a director who sees the intention but not drawn up in detail. It's inviting the reader to savour something and by savouring it in touch, and taste, and smell, and seeing, to understand it, and then to be able to apply it in the way that that creative person then approaches the play. The problem with writing like that is that most of the people involved in the creative decision making of that sort really aren't equipped to handle language of that kind.

Clarifying your commitment to your own ideas

Trevor recalled what he had said earlier about writing to find out what he thinks, and developed the point:

> I think that is not quite true because a lot of the understandings that you've got you've developed over a long time, and they're unlikely to change simply because you've gone into the writing mode. But you put them under intense scrutiny when you're writing, and then are forced to clarify what you mean to yourself.

IMPLICATIONS OF TREVOR GRIFFITHS' COMMENTS

These extracts from Romy's discussions with Trevor Griffiths clothe in detail and add complexity to some of our set of components of the writing process. While his comments highlight the specific nature of playwrighting, they also show that the framework we originally designed to account for what is involved in academic writing applies to this very different type of writing, too. Some of his comments bring out contrasts between literary and non-literary writing and bring to life in exceptionally vivid ways just what is involved in the writing of a literary work. For example, what he said about 'watching for rhythms and counter-rhythms' is less likely to apply to non-literary writing. Some of his comments reflect less apparent interpretations of our suggested components. For example, what he said about the fear that 'you've slaughtered a thousand other possibilities' when you finish a piece of writing may apply less to, say, writing a lab report for a chemistry course. Some of his comments show how the particular discursive practices of production and interpretation of a play differ significantly from the discursive practices associated with, for example, a business letter: for instance, what he said about the financial constraints of production budgets is specific to playwrighting. Overall, we have found that Trevor Griffiths' responses to our set of components of the writing process shed a great deal of light on what is involved in writing, and validate the use of the list of components as a framework for drawing comparisons and contrasts between different types of writing.

CONCLUSION

In this chapter we introduced the view of writing as a set of social practices, rather than a set of 'procedures' or 'skills'. We briefly compared the writing process with the speaking process and looked at why writing for most people is more difficult. We then examined different approaches to writing and their respective implicit or explicit models and assumptions. We offered an alternative understanding of the writing process which takes account of both literacy practices associated with writing and the cognitive, affective and socio-political processes involved in it. We ended the chapter with extended extracts from discussions with the playwright Trevor Griffiths about the writing process as it applies to playwrighting. We concluded that the framework we have developed is a useful one for talking about and understanding similarities and differences between different types of writing. In the next three chapters we take up three aspects of the social context of writing that have a crucial bearing on the processes and practices we have been discussing here.

5

WHY WRITE? PURPOSES FOR WRITING

INTRODUCTION

In an interview with a magazine (*Good Housekeeping*, June 1993), the novelist Jilly Cooper[1] said:

> I don't do much housework . . . because I have other people to do it for me – that is one of the main reasons for wanting to write books.

Her purpose for writing as expressed here was to make enough money so that she did not have to do something that she disliked – housework. This is an extrinsic purpose for writing, dependent not on the writing itself but on its power to make money for the writer.

Just a few days earlier, in an interview with a journalist from the *Guardian* newspaper (17 May 1993), the playwright Trevor Griffiths said that in his then latest play, *Thatcher's Children*, his purpose as a writer was to 'recover a language for the Left', and to ' . . . make the audience laugh'. These two purposes are intrinsic and communicative: purposes dependent on the writing being not just bought, but read and responded to by others.

Anne Paley, a poet published by Commonword (1988), says:

> I find poetry an ideal way to express feelings which are either too intense to talk about, or so nebulous that the only way they seem to hold together is in a poem.

For her the communicative purpose (to 'express feelings' and to 'hold [them] together') leads inevitably to the genre poem. This is an intrinsic purpose, and, in comparison with the previous set of examples, to some extent independent of the writing being read by others: there is the suggestion that expressing feelings in a way that helps her to understand them for herself might be a sufficient end in itself.

In this chapter we examine the meaning of the word 'purpose' in relation to writing, and the sorts of intrinsic purposes – as exemplified above – people have for writing. We take the view that 'purposes' are the fundamental driving forces behind all social activity. Writing is part of a range of resources at people's disposal for achieving those purposes and one of our recurring questions in this chapter is: why writers choose or are told to write rather than use other communicative means of doing something. The purpose for writing is – or should be – integrally bound up with what the writing is about. Indeed, in order to specify the purpose of any act of writing it is usually necessary to say, among other things, what message the writer is intending to convey. We begin the chapter by discussing the relationship between purpose and content in writing, both globally and locally.

We then distinguish between what we are calling the 'functions of writing' – those things which writing, as a semiotic medium, is particularly well designed to achieve – and 'purposes for writing' – those social goals for which people use writing. We use the term 'function of writing' to mean 'something writing can achieve because of its fundamental characteristics', focusing on the properties of writing as a technology, rather than the people who use writing. This is distinct from 'purposes', 'intentions' and 'goals', which exist consciously or subconsciously in the minds of writers. We identify the functions to which writing is particularly well suited by virtue of its special characteristics as a semiotic medium: record-keeping, helping to sort out ideas, communicating with others across time and space, providing evidence of understanding, and the dissemination of ideas.

We then consider 'purposes for writing' from two perspectives, distinguishing between the macro-purposes that writing serves in society at large, and the more specific, micro-purposes of achieving different kinds of social action that drive people to write in specific situations. Writers' purposes are socially constructed in two ways that correspond roughly to the outer layer and the middle layer of Fairclough's diagram (our Figure 1.1 in Chapter 1). Firstly, the motivations that drive people to write are deeply embedded in the socio-cultural context in which they live, part of which is their own personal or group life story and cultural patrimony. Secondly, the daily social demands of people's lives construct purposes for writing: writing can often fulfil the desire to get something done, to express a feeling, to make something available for consultation. To show what we mean by the first of these, we discuss the macro-purposes of regulation and reproduction that are embodied in the law, education and cultural institutions, and the role of writing within them in literate cultures, but also other, oppositional, macro-purposes of maintaining non-dominant values and beliefs, and challenging patterns of dominance. We then ask whose purposes are served by particular acts of writing. We consider both imposed purposes and the sorts of purposes for writing that social groups and individuals generate for themselves, discussing the difference between being told to write by someone else and writing for your own purposes. In the context of these broader aspects of 'the purpose of writing', we discuss the wide range of more immediate, situation-specific purposes people have for writing: micro-purposes such as writing to amuse, writing to educate, writing to complain, writing to challenge and change the socio-political order; writing to represent others, and/or writing to represent yourself. We give three examples to show how these 'micro-purposes' interact both with each other and with what we have been calling 'macro-purposes'. We end the chapter by discussing briefly the way in which purpose shapes written language both globally and locally.

THE MEANING-MAKING PURPOSE OF WRITING

We are using the term 'meaning-making' to refer to the topic/ content of writing: the ideas that are written about. The term 'meaning-making' contrasts with other ways of talking about the relationship between writing and content that suggest that writing is simply a technology for making visible pre-formed content. Terms such as 'writing out', 'writing up', 'presenting' and even 'communicating' misrepresent writing as something that happens after thinking. We strongly oppose this view, and argue that meaning-making is fundamental to the very definition of writing, since written language is a semiotic system: a system of signs for conveying meaning. 'Meaning-making' is more than simply a function of writing of the sort we discuss in the next section; it is more than just a purpose for writing: it is a type of purpose that is built into the very nature of language as social action.

In some types of writing the meaning is so ritualised that it needs little thought, as for example in making a shopping list or writing a receipt. But for many types of writing shaping the meaning is a central part of achieving the purpose. This applies to both the ideational and interpersonal meaning, and in our earlier example of writing a letter of condolence, the writer is likely to pay careful attention to both. But there are some types of writing where the ideational meaning, the 'content' as it is commonly called, is particularly salient: all types of literary, media and academic writing involve the extensive shaping of information and ideas. People who do this sort of writing usually choose their own content, and are driven to write and rewrite in order to get their story or their message exactly right. We ourselves are a good example of this. Our main purpose in writing this book is to clarify, distil and shape up our ideas about 'the politics of writing' in such a way that you, the reader, will understand and engage with them. It is the topic that is motivating us, as much as any other aspect of the social context in which we are writing.

Writing serves a unique function in relation to meaning-making by holding thinking still for inspection, and allowing writers to take their time over shaping their ideas. In our role as advisers on academic writing at university, we make a great deal of this, impressing upon students that they must start writing even though they do not know exactly what they want to say, because writing will in itself help them to clarify their ideas. In other words, writing is a process of meaning-*making*, not just a process of transcribing ready-made meanings.

By emphasising the essential meaning-making purpose of writing, we are in danger of presenting an overly romantic view of writing as a creative process of producing original meanings. On the one hand, it is 'creative' in that each individual act of writing produces a unique text containing unique meanings to serve a unique configuration of purposes in a unique situation. But on the other hand, these meanings are created within the constraints of a cultural and socio-political context. They there-fore serve macro-purposes in the way we outline later in this chapter, and in that respect are far from 'creative' in the sense of 'original' and free. The creativity of meaning-making is in this respect little more than the opportunity to reproduce existing meanings: existing constructions of reality, values, beliefs and power relations. However, as we have argued elsewhere, cultural and socio-political contexts are never unitary or monolithic. Meaning-making can be 'creative' in a more politically robust sense, by reproducing non-dominant constructions of reality, values, beliefs and power relations, and thereby contributing towards challenging and changing patterns of privileging among them.

Of all the definitions of purpose we explore in this chapter, purpose as meaning-making is the most 'micro', the closest to the linguistic choices. Writers choose their words to match the subtle turns of interpersonal and ideational meanings they need to convey at particular points in their texts. These subtle turns of meaning become the driving forces that determine writers' lexico-syntactic choices. We take up this issue at the end of the chapter.

We suggest that an understanding of the fundamental meaning-making purpose of writing has important pedagogical implications. It helps to explain why children often become disenchanted with writing at school, as we argued in Chapter 2. If they are not committed to meaning-making on topics of their own choice, they are likely to see writing as an exercise in correctness, rather than an opportunity to say something worth saying. The grammar and punctuation of writing are not elements that can be learnt in isolation, but only in the process of writing meanings which matter. People are unlikely to learn the mechanical aspects of writing unless they are engaged in the content of what they are writing and have a personal commitment to communicating it, as we argue further in Chapter 9.

THE SOCIAL FUNCTIONS OF WRITING AS A SEMIOTIC MEDIUM

Writing is only one of a range of available means for achieving life purposes, so what makes people select writing rather than one of the other tools for a task? Written language is visible and relatively permanent compared to spoken language, and writing as a mental process is usually slower, more carefully planned and less interactive than speaking, as we discussed in Chapter 4. Because of these characteristics of writing there are some social functions, such as record-keeping, that can be fulfilled more satisfactorily or in greater detail by writing than by speaking or other, non-linguistic, forms of social action. According to Halliday (1985: 39), writing developed to serve social functions that arose as communities changed 'from a predominantly hunting and gathering economy to a predominantly agricultural one' – a change that happens at different times in different cultures. These functions grow, diversify and become more institutionalised as literacy becomes more widely available in a particular cultural setting. There are many social functions that writing may serve, but they may also be served by other semiotic means such as talking, touching, sending flowers, physical aggression. These may be fulfilled by writing in some cultures and periods of history but not in others, or some individuals may prefer writing and others may prefer to use other means. In this section we identify some of the functions for which writing, because of its characteristics, is particularly well suited, and discuss them in terms of socio-cultural and individual preferences for using writing to fulfil them.

Writing for record-keeping

One of the fundamental uses of writing is to record something for future reference. This is probably the original and most common use for writing. There is historical evidence of written records dating back nearly 5,000 years (Barton and Hamilton 1996). Records notched on sticks or scratched on stone helped humans to store information that they did not want to waste mental energy committing to memory. Today millions of people use writing for such things as shopping lists, inventories, family trees, recipes and instructions, even if they use it for no other purposes.

Writing for record-keeping serves to remind the writer by producing a permanent record that is easy to consult in the future. An example in everyday life is writing a recipe someone showed you or told you. An example in school is writing notes from a lesson. Writing also helps the writer to remember things even if the piece of paper is lost or destroyed. The act of writing in itself helps the writer to digest the information.

Writing also often serves the function of providing a record of events for people other than the writer, often for people who live in future times. This is the purpose behind such public documents as the register of births, marriages and deaths in Great Britain. Written records of events such as coronations, declarations of war and the acquisition of territory are history in the making. These are public records, but the desire to record something for future reference inspires private writing too. Recently, personal letters dating back to 1864 have been found in bottles bricked into a wall in a house. Someone must have written them, put them in the bottles and bricked them up with the intention that they should be read by later generations as testimony of earlier experiences. Many women and men in the twentieth century in Britain responded enthusiastically to opportunities to record their 'ordinary' lives and struggles, to fill the gaps and silences in official publications – opportunities provided by community publishing initiatives (see Morley and Warpole 1982), and invitations offered by the Mass-Observation Archive.[2]

It is the permanent quality of writing that makes it so ideal for record-keeping. This characteristic of writing also makes it an ideal tool for another fundamental use: helping the writer to think.

Writing for thinking

Thinking in your head is difficult because ideas leak away. Writing is a way of pinning thoughts down and holding them still in order to examine them, as Anne Paley suggests in the words we quoted at the beginning of this chapter. We can go back to these thoughts, refine them, build on them, discard or develop them in a way that is difficult to do when talking. We can order and reorder ideas in writing until we have found the best relationship between them. Writing allows us to shape our thoughts 'at the point of utterance', as it was called by Britton (1983: 13), with more opportunity for contemplation and control than is afforded by speaking. Trevor Griffiths says:

> I don't like to go into the writing process with everything
> decided because then I don't know why I'm writing plays
> . . . I usually write . . . to find out what I think.
>
> (Griffiths 1993)

People often use writing just for the sake of sorting the ideas out for themselves, without any intention of this writing ultimately being read by others. For example, a lecturer often uses writing for thinking what s/he is going to say. A personal diary works like this too. Diary-keepers say that writing in their diaries helps them to sort out what they think about what has happened and to understand their lives better. Teaching methods pioneered by

Britton (1970) and recently developed by the National Writing Project (1989/90) in Britain recommend that children write in 'think books' in all their subjects across the curriculum as a way of understanding and learning all their subjects.

Writing for thinking is also an integral part of the process of writing something that will go beyond the writer: for communication with others, for study purposes, or for publication. When writing for thinking is a part of something that will eventually be read or heard by someone else, it includes thinking about the reader or audience and about discoursal and generic choices, as well as the ideas.

Writing to communicate with others

An enormous amount of personal and official communication is carried out by word of mouth. Spoken interaction has many advantages in fulfilling this function, the main one being that the communication is explicitly interactive, giving interlocutors the opportunity to gauge each other's interpretations and reactions, and to adjust their message accordingly. Characteristics of spoken language itself also favour its use for communicating with others: its many prosodic resources can convey infinite subtleties of meaning. Face-to-face spoken interaction has the added advantage of integrating verbal and gestural modes of communication. Finally, spoken interaction is for most people easy and economic: it does not require any materials or aptitude other than opening your mouth. So why write? We suggest that there are at least five factors that cause people to prefer writing as a means of communication with others: distance between communicators; the need to *avoid* interaction; the opportunity to take time and care over wording; the opportunity to integrate verbal and visual means of communication; the need to keep evidence of the communication; and finally, in some cultures, to add weight to the message. Of course, these reasons are interconnected, and several are likely to apply at the same time.

When people need to communicate at a distance, written language is likely to serve their purposes, since it is 'language that can be carried'. Changes in technology are constantly changing people's preferences for spoken or written means of communicating at a distance. In times and places without modern communications and broadcasting technology, writing became the main way in which people kept in touch at a distance, did business, and disseminated information. With telephones, radios and televisions becoming more and more widespread globally, many of these forms of communication at a distance that may previously have been achieved by writing can also be done orally. Business with people at a distance that would have taken several days to conclude by letter can be conducted instantly on the telephone. Even more recent developments in technology now mean that it is possible to pass written messages to and fro at a distance with no delay. Those who have access to fax machines and e-mail often prefer to use this written means of doing quick business – official or personal – with someone working elsewhere. This may be because people are not always easy to contact by telephone, but we suggest that other characteristics of writing make it preferable to speaking for communicating with others in many circumstances. Even without access to these latest means of communication, people may prefer to write rather than telephone for one or more of the following reasons.

Writing avoids face-to-face interaction. Communicating face-to-face or even by telephone is sometimes intrusive. For example, when someone has suffered bereavement, the norm in some cultures is not to intrude on their grief. Face-to-face interaction can be face-threatening for one or both parties, for example when needing to apologise for or complain about something. Writing is often less intrusive, avoids embarrassment, and can save face.

Writing is often better than speaking for something that has to be worded very carefully, such as a complaint. Writing allows the writer time to work out the precise wording. This reason often interacts with the previous one: situations that are highly emotionally charged are often the ones in which people 'can't find the words to express. . . . ', and face-threatening acts often need to be very carefully worded to maintain as much face as possible of all concerned. Writing gives the opportunity to choose careful wording in such circumstances.

A less emotionally charged reason for choosing writing rather than speaking to communicate with others is the way in which it gives the opportunity to integrate verbal and graphic means of communication. Television allows spoken language to be integrated with the graphic, but video-making is not usually an option for individuals or even institutions for communication on a daily basis. Sometimes communication is best achieved by bringing

115

together a diagram and some writing, a cartoon and some writing, or a sketch and some writing. Further, writing allows characteristics of layout to add to the salience of the message. Although layout features of written language can never compete with the full resources of prosody available in spoken language for modulating meaning, they can achieve slightly different communicative effects, which may be preferable in some circumstances.

People also usually choose writing as the mode for messages that have to last longer than the moment of utterance. Messages often need to be relatively permanent so that they can be referred to by different readers over time (for example a set of laws, or road signs), or frequently by the same reader (for example an important letter). In cultures where people travel away from home without personal guides to accompany them, they need written language to provide directions and place names to help them find their way, and someone has to take the responsibility for writing these. The need to provide a permanent record in writing rather than in speech is sometimes imposed by others. For example, applying for employment almost always involves completing a form and/or supplying a curriculum vitae, or CV, as evidence of what the applicant has to offer, rather than being able to use the resources of spoken interaction to communicate her/his suitability for the job (see Davies 1994 for discussion of this). Having the written document helps the employers to speed up their task of selection, but providing it may be a burden on the applicant.

Finally, people often choose to communicate in writing to add weight to the message. In official communication, the written form gives words authority. This includes making the message legal (for example a contract) and making the message official (for example a notice on a railway station). Often legal and official documents or notices require very precise wording so that no one can be in any doubt as to what has been stated. This would be impossible in speech, which leaves no mark for future consultation. For personal communication, the written message is thought to represent more effort, forethought and care in some cultures. For example, in British white middle-class culture a birthday card is more highly valued than a birthday phone-call, and a written thank you is considered to have come more from the heart than a spoken one. The function of adding weight to a message interacts with the function of providing a lasting record. If an official message is written, it both has authority and can be kept or displayed as a permanent record. If a personal message is written on a card or in a letter, it can be displayed in a special place, and kept as a memento.

Writing as evidence of understanding

A good deal of writing for academic purposes is either writing to keep a record ('notes') to remind yourself of something in the future, or writing for thinking. However, there is an additional purpose for writing in school and college: to show the teacher or examiner what you know and what you think. This is not really 'communication' in the sense of the above. It is a specialised type of writing that exists only in the educational institutions of some countries; other countries do their assessment of students' knowledge and understanding entirely orally. It is questionable which method is most efficient and best for the learner: writing is by no means intrinsically superior for fulfilling this function. Certainly in a country that uses written assessment it is essential to understand 'the rules of the game'. On the whole, courses in writing for academic purposes concentrate on this particular aspect of writing for study, but it is important to remember it is not the only one. Writing for thinking is just as important.

Writing for the dissemination of ideas

It is the permanence of writing that makes it so well suited to the dissemination of ideas. Without writing, ideas can be spread slowly by word-of-mouth, but they are restricted to those who meet the speaker. Such dissemination can be very unreliable, as anyone who plays the whispering game knows. Since the development of printing in the fifteenth century in Europe there has been a massive increase in the dissemination of ideas in literate cultures. Once written, something can be reproduced in quantities and distributed far beyond the original producer of the ideas. Until the technological boom of the middle of the twentieth century, printing was virtually the only means of disseminating ideas. Now, in the industrialised countries of the world, there are many means for the dissemination of ideas. Writing competes with other mass media: radio and television broadcasts of the spoken word, films, video and audio cassettes.

Published writing includes poems, plays, stories, all types of books, articles for newspapers, magazines, journals, letters to the editor. Publication requires a lot of time and energy and above all confidence to believe that your ideas or creations are worth disseminating. Not many people write with the conscious purpose of publication and dissemination: publication is considered the prerogative of a privileged few, and the institutions of publication in many industrialised countries serve to perpetuate this discrimination, as we argued in Chapter 2. This is a function of writing that we believe can and should be as widely diversified as possible, and we return to this issue in Chapter 9.

In this section we have outlined what we see as five main social functions that writing can fulfil by virtue of its characteristics of visibility, permanence, transportability, slow, considered production and isolation from the reader. We have argued that some of these functions are to a large extent dependent on a high degree of literacy, but that most can also be fulfilled by other forms of social semiotic action. Whether writing is actually chosen to fulfil these functions depends on socio-economic factors such as what sorts of communication technology are available, on cultural factors such as what form of communication is considered most weighty, or most heart-felt, or on factors to do with the nature of the message to be communicated, as our examples later in the chapter show. We now turn from considering the social functions to which writing is well suited to considering purposes in terms of what people might be wanting to achieve through writing. Some of these are, we argue, ideologically motivated, and therefore often operate subconsciously. Others are more locally motivated by the conscious or subconscious desire to achieve immediate social goals.

MACRO-PURPOSES FOR WRITING: ITS ROLE IN MAINTAINING AND CHALLENGING IDEOLOGIES

Writing is, ultimately, always maintaining or promoting certain interests. By choosing to write rather than use another form of social action, by engaging in particular writing practices, by putting certain messages or ideas into writing, by participating in certain discourses and genres through writing, people are reproducing particular sets of values, beliefs and power relations. A great deal of writing reproduces dominant values, beliefs and power relations in the social context, thereby reinforcing the existing hegemony.

However, writing can also serve non-dominant interests, reproducing alternative values, beliefs and power relations, thereby
challenging the existing hegemony. Some people's socio-cultural
context is aligned to the dominant values and practices of their
society, and the macro-purpose behind their writing is likely to be
hegemonic. For others, the socio-cultural context that motivates
them is at odds with the dominant culture. For the majority there
is an uncomfortable tension between these two extremes: engaging
in the writing tasks of the dominant culture is in their interests, in
order to succeed in that culture, but at the same time it may be
denying other cultural allegiances they espouse. It is these underlying, usually subconscious, ideological motivations for writing that
we are calling 'macro-purposes'.

In this section we discuss how writing serves the two functions
of the modern state identified by Gramsci (see Forgaçs 1988: 235):
the *regulatory function*, which concerns maintaining orderly behaviour, and the *reproductive function* of ensuring that dominant values
are maintained. The reproductive function concerns firstly the
'production' – the systematic raising of the mass of the population
to a particular level of technical, cultural and moral development
(same book: 234) which corresponds to the needs of production
as defined by the dominant social groups; this is carried out prin-
cipally by educational institutions and by government employment
training schemes. Secondly it concerns 'reproduction' – the maintenance of hegemony and the status quo which is in the interests
of dominant and powerful social groups (the ruling classes, as
Gramsci calls them); this is achieved by cultural institutions
'protected by the armour of coercion' (Gramsci in the same book:
235). In this way the reproductive function and the regulatory
function are interdependent.

Because the state has to make sure that society is orderly and
that certain dominant values are maintained, it needs laws. In
order for these laws to be applied by the courts and magistrates
and judges and adhered to by the public they need to be conven-
tionalised and written down. Once they are written down they
are recorded and can be changed only by repeal or reform. Any
reforms are written down, and new versions are recorded in
writing. Very few people have access to either the writing or the
reading of these laws; in fact most ordinary people would have
great difficulty in reading them because they are written in very
obscure Latinate English. Some people, usually from the legal

119

profession, argue that this is necessary because no ambiguity in wording can be allowed, and so the complicated phraseology and syntax serve the function of legal clarity. Others argue, as we do, that the obscurity of the language has the social function of excluding the non-professional from legal discourse and so justifying the role of solicitors and lawyers in writing legal documents and interpreting the law for the lay person.

Apart from criminal and civil law of precedence, the state also legislates through Acts of Parliament, first presented as Bills for debate. Most Bills are presented by the government (and prepared by civil servants) and occasionally by private members of parliament. Once a Bill has been passed in both Houses of Parliament it becomes the law of the land. The overarching purpose of the writing of the Bill, particularly in its final form, is to regulate the sections of society to which it refers. Acts of Parliament and laws are written, made permanent, so that they can constitute a reference point for future action. In this way writing contributes to the regulation of human action. For example, The Education Act of 1988 introduced for the first time into British education a national curriculum that has the reproductive function of transmitting national values and notions of what is legitimate knowledge by controlling the content of teaching and testing and, increasingly, the pedagogic methodology too. Many of the provisions of this Act are controversial but most people who are actually affected by them, including teachers, knew what they were only after they had come into operation, and did not have the chance to contribute to shaping them.

Another aspect of the regulatory function of the state is gate-keeping: the regulation of status, educational opportunity, employment and financial benefit. In Britain, writing is used as the main form of evidence in all these processes – for completing forms that give people access to benefits, for job applications, as the means of educational assessment. Davies (1994) discusses the way in which writing is the dominant medium for showing that a person is suited to a job, and for obtaining unemployment benefit, rather than face-to-face communication which many people might find more congenial for representing their qualities and abilities. Davies and others (1994) discuss the way in which the dominant practice of using writing for gate-keeping purposes in Britain robs people of strength and identity that they would be able to demonstrate through other means.

Writing also serves the reproductive function of the state. The sorts of things that get published and, more crucially, circulated, make the dominant values of any culture more stable. So, for example, it is possible to identify the currently dominant cultural values of a nation by looking at the books in its mainstream bookshops, the notices in its public places, the newspapers and magazines it has on sale, the sales figures for different publications (as we showed in Chapter 2), and at the National Curriculum. In some socio-political contexts the values and beliefs promulgated in writing will be relatively varied, showing a tolerance for diversity; in other contexts patterns of domination will be apparent; yet in others the values represented in writing will be singular, suggesting repression of alternatives. Even in a nation that exhibits cultural pluralism in its available publications, the relative sales figures of these publications will indicate the implicit dominant values of the society.

The sorts of things that learners are encouraged to write, the discourse conventions they are taught to follow and the practices in which they are expected to engage within the education system tend to reproduce the dominant values of the society supporting that education system, and to reproduce existing class relations. As is always the case with the reproduction of ideology, this process works insidiously. Children who succeed in school gain pleasure from writing the sorts of things they are taught to write, usually because their home values, meanings and practices overlap with 'school' values, meanings and practices. They start school with what Bourdieu calls 'cultural capital' (see Chapter 2), and they capitalise on it and contribute to reinforcing its dominance through their successful school careers. In this way, white middle-class children are favoured and the majority of working-class and ethnic minority children excluded. One of the reasons why many students do not learn to enjoy writing at school is that they cannot identify with the kinds of reading they are offered, and they cannot engage with the writing tasks they are given. The narrow canon of what constitutes 'literature' embodied in the 1992–3 National Curriculum for English assessments in the UK favoured white middle-class children and left little for other children to identify with or feel motivated by. Few would be likely to feel 'Oh, I could write something like that.' Nearly all small children love to 'write' as soon as they can hold a pencil, but so many of them hate it at secondary school and do so little of it in later life. Part of the reason for this may be that the tasks are other-imposed (see below), but another major reason, we think, is that they are being asked to write types of texts with which they do not identify. For many children also, whose life out of school is filled with conversations in a different variety of English or in another language altogether, the combination of the type of writing task with the requirement to use standardised English may prove doubly alienating.

In spite of the reproductive power of writing, publication and circulation, these processes are, fortunately, open to contestation. The current values of a state have been established by socio-historical processes, and can also be changed for the future by active resistance. For example, in some societies or institutions with relative freedom of speech, people with alternative views can circulate their own publications, put up their own posters and notices. A British university campus is an interesting example of this. A large number of posters and graffiti representing various alternative views are tolerated. However, when the administration feels under threat, or when a particular student group with un-acceptable views becomes active, the posters are torn down and the graffiti removed. Recent research has drawn attention to the way in which social resistance is one of the purposes for which people use writing, particularly in the form of graffiti, and in written messages that oppose rules and regulations that have been imposed by people in authority. This use of writing for social participation is not just restricted to university students or active campaigners in organised groups, but is widespread in vernacular uses of literacy among people in general (Barton and others 1993, Barton and Hamilton forthcoming).

It is perhaps misleading to use the term 'macro-*purpose*' to refer to the uses of writing described here. The word 'purpose' suggests conscious intentions, and a conspiracy among those who use writing to serve the regulatory and reproductive functions of the state. It may be that those in powerful political positions, such as the Minister for Education in Britain, are consciously manipu-lating the ideological apparatus of nations through the Bills they propose. However, for the majority of people who contribute to this reproduction there is probably nothing conscious about the operation of writing in this way, as we mentioned above, and it is therefore all the more insidious in its effects. Those who are a product of an ideology see themselves as promoting what is unquestionably right, of high quality, and to everyone's advantage, and not as reproducing an ideology and maintaining their own interests. They cannot see that it is a question of cultural capital, not of neutral 'knowledge' and 'skill'. Neither the successful children nor their teachers are necessarily aware of the way in which they are participating in the reproduction of dominant values, practices, conventions and genres by requiring or engaging in such writing at school. The children who do find the writing tasks at school compatible with their own values, practices and beliefs and engage enthusiastically in them cannot be seen as having the conscious purpose of reproducing an ideology. However, we have stuck with the word 'purpose' in order to highlight the way in which an act of writing can be serving macro- and micro-purposes at the same time, at different levels of consciousness.

On the more conscious level, writing is also serving a constellation of immediate social purposes. Before discussing the nature of these 'micro-purposes', we introduce the issue of whose purposes are being served by an act of writing which spans the distinction between the 'macro' and the 'micro', between the unconscious and the conscious.

WHOSE PURPOSES?

Sometimes people write as the result of some driving force within them – whether it is an impulse to be creative or the need to respond to a social situation, or both. At other times people write because they have been told to. Whether the purpose for writing is self-generated or imposed has a crucial effect on the writing process (see Ivanič and Moss 1991 for further discussion of the distinction). The difference between self-generated and imposed writing connects the macro-purposes we discussed in the previous section to the micro-purposes we discuss in the next section. The sort of writing that people do in response to the demands of state institutions is imposed – demanded by the system. Filling in an application form for unemployment benefit is writing for a purpose imposed by bureaucracy. Writing an essay for a GCSE examination is a purpose imposed by the British practice of discriminating children on the basis of written products. In the British university context, assessment is mostly done by writing and most students see the writing as an imposition and a chore to be got through. Very few write with enjoyment or with the sense of writing for their own purposes, to explore their own ideas or to contribute to thinking in the discipline. It is possible for writers to make these tasks their own, to take control over them and turn them around to serve their own, self-generated purposes. However, it is far easier and more likely for people who share the dominant values and practices of the state to do this. And when they do make such writing tasks their own they are, as we mentioned before, wittingly or unwittingly contributing to the reproduction of those dominant values and practices.

Purposes for writing can also be 'imposed' in a more local way by people who have some sort of power over the writer: parents often impose the task of writing thank you letters on their children, and line managers impose innumerable writing tasks on clerical workers. Again, writers can make these tasks their own by investing them with their own interests, values and beliefs. If a child is genuinely grateful for a gift, and/or believes in showing appreciation in order to show respect, and finds writing their most congenial medium for expression, then the imposed task will become a self-generated one. If clerical workers identify strongly with the company for whom they are working, share its goals, and agree with the means of achieving them suggested by their line managers, then they will generate their own purposes for writing whatever has been set them. But the number of 'ifs' shows that it is rare for a writer to make tasks their own when they have been imposed by someone with authority over them.

Gramsci, talking about illiteracy in Italy in 1917, said that 'if literacy is not a need it becomes a torment, something imposed by the wielders of power' (in Forgaçs, 1988: 67). This captures very tellingly the alienation that many children still feel if schools demand that they write the sorts of things that reproduce the values of cultural groups with whom they do not identify. Gramsci went on to argue that culture and literacy needed a purpose, a social purpose through which the individual is no longer locked in their private family world but becomes a 'citizen of the wider world, with whose other citizens one needs to exchange ideas, hopes and sufferings' (same book: 68).

Self-generated purposes for writing include writing personal letters and notes to people we choose to write to: to family members and best friends, or to prisoners. Many people write diaries, stories, or family histories of their own accord, either in order to keep records, or to make sense of what happened for themselves, or to share with others. This type of writing is much more widespread than is commonly believed, as has been shown in ethnographic studies such as Barton and Hamilton (forthcoming), articles in Barton and Ivanič (1991) and in Street (1993). We give some examples of the sorts of purposes possible for writing, if not repressed by state institutions, in the next section. On the whole, writing for your own purposes – your own macro-purposes and your own micro-purposes – is easier and more enjoyable, and the end result is more satisfying and worthwhile. Even when the task itself is hard, the struggle is rewarding if the writer(s) see it as worth engaging in. For example, writing this chapter is a self-generated writing task for us: it has been difficult, but at the same time we relished the opportunity to thrash out our ideas and our differences in opinion!

MICRO-PURPOSES: WRITERS' IMMEDIATE MOTIVATIONS TO WRITE

Writing is used to respond to particular life demands, not practised for its own sake. What we are calling 'micro-purposes' differ from macro-purposes in that they are generated by the immediate 'context of situation' in Halliday's terms, rather than fulfilling larger, political ends. They are the individual writer's motivations, goals and intentions underlying a specific act of writing in a specific social situation: purposes such as letting someone know where you have gone, showing a tutor what you know and think about political changes in Eastern Europe, giving a friend the fun of hearing about what happened to you, and simultaneously cementing your friendship. The last of these examples brings out the way in which any act of writing may have multiple, interrelated goals. To use the Hallidayan terminology we intro-duced in Chapter 1, every act of writing has both an 'ideational micro-purpose' of conveying a message, and an 'interpersonal micro-purpose' of defining the social relations between its writer(s) and its reader(s). Taking the issue of multiplicity of purposes further, people may write a particular piece to achieve a number of micro-purposes at the same time, as the quotation from Trevor Griffiths at the beginning of this chapter shows.

'Micro-purposes' are almost certainly more accessible to consciousness than the 'macro-purposes' we discussed above.

Writers are often able to talk about the social action they hope to achieve by writing, and this has been researched through think-aloud protocols (as in the research of Linda Flower [1990]) and in retrospective interviews (as in the research of Simon Pardoe [1994a] and Romy's research with Trevor Griffiths). 'Micro' social purposes of this sort are the driving forces that determine writers' choices of genre for their writing: for example, the need to plan a family celebration with a sister who lives in another country generates the decision to write a personal letter rather than a research article.

While those people whose interests are served by the dominant culture have no problem with engaging in the purposes for writing imposed upon them and making them their own, we suggest that factors we have discussed so far militate against the majority of people finding any use for writing. The majority of people are excluded from engaging in the types of writing they see all around them, written by privileged writers, as we discussed in Chapter 2. The majority of people hold different values and beliefs from those encoded in the discourses and genres that they encounter and are encouraged to reproduce in school. The majority of people experience writing as something imposed by bureaucracy, the education system and/or by other more powerful individuals, as we discussed in the previous section. In spite of these powerful social factors, people do turn to writing to fulfil immediate purposes, and they do choose writing rather than other forms of social action such as speaking, giving gifts, and physical means such as kicking or caressing. We suggest that this is not only because they are enculturated into the dominant values represented by many forms of writing, but also because, as we argued at the beginning of this chapter, writing is intrinsically well suited to getting certain things done. But beyond that, we suggest that writing can also serve more socio-politically salient micro-purposes of self-representation, and of explicitly challenging, subverting and even overturning dominant values, as is true of the writing of Trevor Griffiths. In such instances, micro- and macro-purposes become hard to distinguish.

Another way in which the micro- and the macro- interact is that micro-purposes for writing are in themselves culturally and insti- tutionally marked. For example, the social purpose of indicating respect for elders is associated with some cultures more than others. The social purpose of taunting people for their physical characteristics is common in some sub-cultures rather than others. Some institutions have particular purposes associated with them: for example, in the UK giving explanations for our actions is associated with the law, giving explanations for physical and social phenomena is associated with academic institutions, and not vice versa. These purposes may be fulfilled by writing in some cultures, by other means in others. The sorts of micro-purposes people engage in thus serve macro-purposes of identifying them with and reproducing a particular culture, while disassociating them from, and contesting, others. Ethnographic studies of literacy practices in various settings (such as those mentioned in the previous section) provide many examples of the culture-specific micro-purposes for writing of different social groups in many parts of the world.

There could be no such thing as an exhaustive list of micro-social purposes for writing: writing can be turned to an infinite number of social purposes in an infinite number of combinations. This is to a large extent what distinguishes the 'macro-' from the 'micro-': micro-purposes are situation-specific and unique, just as the texts they shape are unique. Micro-purposes could perhaps be generalised and categorised into a finite set of categories, similar to a list of 'speech acts' such as to inform, to apologise, to report, to instruct, to request. Halliday (1985: 40–1) suggests that the roles written language plays in our everyday lives can be broadly categorised as primarily for action, including social contact, primarily for information, and primarily for entertainment. However, such categorisations take attention away from the coexistence of many purposes for a single act of writing, and erases the subtle differences between particular purposes for writing in particular settings. It also suggests a neutral sameness among purposes for writing, failing to recognise the ways in which micro-purposes might interact with macro-purposes, as we have outlined above. We find the situation-specific particularity of people's real purposes in real situations more interesting than such broad generalisations. Writing involves communication between individuals who have particular social identities, values and beliefs, a particular (probably complex) interpersonal power relationship, with particular (though not necessarily shared) social purposes. Rather than attempting to be comprehensive in this section we therefore give three examples of acts of writing by very different writers. In each example there is an overarching social purpose, but there are others intertwined. In these examples we attempt to make connections between the more immediate micro-purposes of the writers, the macro-purposes we discussed above, and the issues of writing and power we raised in the previous section and in Chapter 2.

Suzanna writing a birthday story for Romy

Suzanna, a 7-year-old middle-class British girl, decided of her own accord to write a story for Romy's birthday, called *The Alley Cats and The Robber Swag and Grannie Swag*. This story was part of a birthday card, with 'Happy Birthday' written at the end on doors that opened to disclose the words 'The End'. This is a good example of 'self-generated writing' as we described it in the previous section. Suzanna put a lot of time and effort into writing this and was enormously pleased with it. The constellation of micro-purposes included making Romy happy on her birthday, entertaining her, and showing warm feelings for her. She wanted to explore particular themes she associates with Romy: cats, old age (!), living in terraced houses. She was also creating her own story in a genre she enjoyed, the genre of *Funday Times* comic strip, to make that genre her own. In doing so she was appropriating and being appropriated by a dominant genre, reproducing dominant ideologies about 'old people' and life in terraced houses, exactly in the way Kress theorised.

A university course co-ordinator writing a 'feedback sheet'

The university tutor we are describing is responsible for running a large first-year course in a department of linguistics with over 100 students. The course had already been fully programmed for the year with a timetable of lectures and seminars. The students had done their first assignment for the course and several weaknesses had recurred in many of the assignments. The course co-ordinator therefore wrote a feedback sheet: a single side of A4 with seven points on it, each pointing out what some students had done wrong, and giving some suggestions as to ways of avoiding this shortcoming. His main purpose for writing this was, presumably, to give the students advice that would ensure that they had both an understanding of the assignment topic on which they could draw for the exam, and guidelines that they could use for future assignments. There were probably other purposes intertwined: he wanted to save tutors in future from having to deal with the same weaknesses over and over again and he wanted to fulfil his role as course co-ordinator impeccably (not least because there was a teaching audit in the university). He chose to write it rather than speak it because there was no time allotted on the lecture timetable for it, but also because it made the advice permanent and easy to refer back to. This contrasts with a tutor in another department who had given the same sort of advice orally.

This sheet served regulatory and reproductive functions for the institution, helping to ensure the students fell in with its expectations. However, it also broke with convention in an interesting way. In the past students had been expected to sink or swim on assignments: if they did not know how to do them, that was their failure and not the responsibility of the course co-ordinator. This tutor did not conform to this belief, believing rather that it was his responsibility to demystify these expectations and conventions as far as possible, and so he established a new practice, writing a new type of document which had not been part of the course procedures in the past.

Trevor Griffiths writing plays

Trevor Griffiths' plays are deeply embedded in both his own personal experience and in the socio-cultural and political context that envelops his experience: he writes as a member of a class, the working class (despite his own eventual class translation as a result of becoming a relatively successful professional writer), who wants among other things to give voice to working-class experiences, and to challenge the dominant interpretations of history. Much of his work is an attempt to recover parts of the past or to examine issues that have been rendered invisible or denied and distorted. For example, the play *Such Impossibilities*, part of a series on prominent Edwardians, is a working-class success story about Tom Mann's leadership of a successful dock strike in Liverpool at the beginning of the twentieth century – 'restoring however tinily an important but suppressed area of our collective history . . . and to celebrate a victory' (preface to the play, 1977).[3] He writes in order to contribute to the examination of important socio-political issues (in, for example, *The Party*; *Occupations*; *All Good Men*), and to contribute to wider socio-political change by challenging dominant versions of reality (*The Gulf Between Us*) or dominant cultural practices (*Comedians*). His immediate purposes are to examine and explore these alternative perspectives with his audiences, and to provide them with the opportunity to contemplate new ways of understanding.

Trevor Griffiths' purposes for writing illustrate the effect of socio-cultural context on purposes. His other-imposed purposes are difficult to separate from self-generated motivations for writing: he writes plays because he 'chooses' what to write and how, but he is constantly responding to the wider socio-political and cultural context that informs his writing, in both content and form. His plays not only criticise dominant views of reality but also challenge dominant television and theatre genres (*Country* exploits and criticises the Country House family drama; *Through The Night*[4] criticises the hospital drama genre). (This contrasts strikingly with the observations we made about Suzanna, who was enthusiastically trying to reproduce the genre of *Funday Times* comic strip in her story for Romy.) Because of the topics that he writes about and because of how he writes about them, his writing is differently valued depending upon the socio-political, ideological positions of his audience, professional and other (see Clark 1993a; Clark, forthcoming).

THE OVERARCHING ROLE OF PURPOSE IN SHAPING WRITTEN LANGUAGE[5]

In this section we develop the idea implicit in Halliday's 'functional view of language' (see Chapter 1) that purpose determines both the local and global linguistic characteristics of texts. However, we argue that there is no mechanical, one-to-one, deterministic relationship between social purposes and characteristics of language, but that the issues we have raised earlier in this chapter construct tensions around this relationship. What we say here applies in principle to all language, but it is particularly important to state in relation to written language, since written language is the focus of so much teaching and learning. We agree with Pardoe (1994a, 1997) that teachers and learners of writing benefit greatly from recognising the importance and nature of 'purpose' in shaping the linguistic characteristics of texts as a way of getting beyond the usual focus on form.

Swales, in a book that makes a detailed study of written genres in academic settings, emphasised 'the primacy of purpose' (Swales 1990: 46) in defining genres. In a famous passage, he writes:

A genre comprises a class of communicative events, the members of which share some set of communicative purposes. These purposes are recognised by the expert members of the parent discourse community, and thereby constitute the rationale for the genre. This rationale shapes the schematic structure of the discourse and influences and constrains choice of content and style. Communicative purpose is . . . a privileged criterion [in defining a genre].

(same book: 58)

This means that the main factor that causes differences between the linguistic characteristics of, say, an academic essay and a thank you letter is that they are serving different communicative purposes. By 'communicative purposes' we understand Swales to mean what we have called 'micro-purposes' earlier in the chapter: the purposes that belong in the middle layer of Fairclough's diagram, as part of the social interaction between the participants in the immediate social context.

Swales is claiming that purpose shapes the linguistic features of

1 *structure* – the length, the component parts, and the organisation of the text,
2 *content* – what is written about, and
3 *'style'* – lexical and syntactic features.

For example, writing an academic assignment for a course in anthropology appears to have the communicative purpose of 'informing' the reader. It therefore cannot be short, it must contain reference to anthropological theory and research, and lexico-syntactic characteristics associated with this field. Another purpose shaping this genre is, we suggest, for the student writer to present a position in relation to the body of knowledge, although this purpose is often not explicitly stated or recognised by either tutors or students. The structural elements of an argument therefore need to shape either part or all of the text. A third, usually unstated purpose is, we suggest, to negotiate identities for and relationships between the actual participants in the communication, in which the student writer constructs an identity as a member of the academic discourse community, but a suitably modest one, and the status of the tutor–assessor–reader is not threatened. The modality of the writing needs to be fine-tuned to achieve this purpose.

This is a powerful claim, and one that is certainly more useful both to researchers and teachers than one that suggests that the linguistic features just have to be the way they are for no apparent reason. However, there are two interrelated difficulties with this relatively simplistic view of the relationship between purpose and linguistic features, focusing on 'micro-purposes'. Firstly, the very attempt to define 'genres' by identifying their recognised purposes suggests a typological approach to social life in which there is a finite set of types of social situation and associated purposes, rather than an approach that treats each social situation as unique, and a possible site for struggle over what sorts of purposes might be served by it. This can support an overly prescriptive view of the relationship between purpose and linguistic characteristics. It suggests that, in any situation such as the writing of the academic assignment for an anthropology course, there can be only one 'correct' set of communicative purposes which are shaping an 'appropriate' configuration of linguistic characteristics. This smacks of 'imposed purposes', not allowing room for contestation or even negotiation of the purposes a student writer might choose to fulfil through undertaking the assignment. (For further discussion of this issue, see Pardoe 1991, 1994a, and for pedagogical implications, see Chapter 9.)

Secondly, this view does not take account of what we called macro-purposes for writing earlier in this chapter. Following Fairclough (see Chapter 1) we are claiming that language is shaped not only by the micro-social purposes associated with social interaction, but also by the macro-social purposes associated with the maintenance of dominant power relations, values and beliefs. To follow through our example of writing an academic assignment for an anthropology course, we suggest that it is also serving the regulatory function of requiring students to demonstrate their grasp of a body of knowledge. Its linguistic characteristics may be subject to such macro-purposes in the cultural context of the academic discourse community as maintaining an objective view of knowledge (see Pardoe 1997), maintaining an academic elite based on the use of exclusive lexis and syntactic conventions, and maintaining the status hierarchy among members of the community.

These reservations with Swales' theory do not diminish the

power of the central (Hallidayan) insight that language is shaped by purpose. Rather, we are suggesting that the meaning of this insight needs to be extended by incorporating a richer and more theoretically powerful view of purpose. We would want to emphasise that, firstly, what sorts of purposes might be served by a particular act of writing is a site of struggle which is, ultimately, realised in the language of the resulting text; and, secondly, the generic resources of written language are shaped not only by micro-social purposes, but also by macro-social purposes.

CONCLUSION

In this chapter we have explored the question 'Why write?' from a number of perspectives. We considered why writing might be chosen in preference to other semiotic media, and the functions to which it is particularly well suited on the grounds of its physical characteristics and the nature of the mental processing associated with it. In terms of the outer layer of Fairclough's diagram, we discussed the way in which writing serves the macro-functions of regulation and reproduction, thereby playing a role in the maintenance of hegemony. At the intersection of the macro- and the micro-, we considered the difference between writing for other-imposed purposes and self-generated purposes. We then discussed 'purpose' as it relates to the second layer of Fairclough's diagram: the way in which a particular instance of interaction involving writing might be serving a number of interrelated micro-purposes. We emphasised that writing can be serving micro- and macro-purposes simultaneously, and provided three examples to illustrate this. We ended by presenting the view that purpose plays an overarching role in shaping the linguistic characteristics of texts, and discussing how the aspects of 'purposes for writing' that we had presented earlier could be incorporated in this view. In the next two chapters we discuss what we see as the other two key elements in the social context of writing: the writer and the reader.

6

WRITER IDENTITY[1]

INTRODUCTION

It is common to pay attention to the identity of the writer of fiction, autobiography and 'creative' writing (see, for example, Mace 1992, Chapter 5; Mace 1995), but many books about academic writing say little about the writer. They take it for granted that the writer produces the written product, but they do not say much about the presence of the writer in that product. We think it is important to focus on the writer as well as the writing: how authoritative s/he feels, what s/he wants to say, how s/he wants to represent herself in the writing, and the conflicts s/he faces between what s/he might ideally want and the constraints imposed by conventions. Writing cannot be separated from the writer's identity.

The importance of identity in writing has been brought home to us by our work with students who find academic writing difficult. They often say things such as 'this doesn't sound like me' which seem to be associated with the conflicts of identity they experience in higher education between their former selves and their becoming-selves. For many students, other adult commitments and experiences – other social worlds – are juxtaposed with the academic world. They are caught up in conflicting social pressures that cannot be ignored while writing. Their experience throws the issue of multiple and conflicting identities into particularly sharp focus. (See also Gardener 1992 for illuminating discussion of these issues.) While our discussion in this chapter is illustrated with examples from the writing of such students, we think that the broader issues we are raising apply to all writers and all types of writing.

The question of writer identity was also highlighted in the work of the Teaching of Writing Research Group at Lancaster University when we were attempting to identify key elements in the writing process. We felt that the widely recognised model proposed by Hayes and Flower (1980, 1983) of the writing process did not sufficiently represent the social aspects of writing, and tried to invent our own alternative (see Chapter 4 for further details of this). Three elements which we felt to be important that were not specifically mentioned by Hayes and Flower were:

- clarifying your commitment to your ideas
- deciding how to take responsibility: whether to mask or declare your own position
- establishing your socio-political identity as a writer

These particular elements usually provoke great interest among students and teachers who work with our alternative model because they are not used to thinking about them as part of the writing process. As a group we became interested in what these elements really mean, whether there are other aspects of writer identity that are important, and how they relate to other, more widely recognised aspects of the writing process such as 'formulating your ideas' (which we discussed in the previous chapter) and 'considering the reader' (which we discuss in the following chapter).

Bartholomae wrote about the way in which student writers take on an identity in academic essays:

> The student has to appropriate (or be appropriated by) a specialized discourse, and he [Bartholomae's generic] has to do this as though he were easily and comfortably at one with his audience, as though he were a member of the academy or an historian or an anthropologist or an economist; he has to invent the university by mimicking its language while finding some compromise between idiosyncrasy, a personal history, on the one hand, and the requirements of convention, the history of a discipline, on the other. He must speak our language. Or he must dare to speak it to carry off the bluff, since speaking and writing will most certainly be required long before the skill is 'learned'.
>
> (Bartholomae 1985: 134)

In this chapter we explore what this 'compromise between idiosyncrasy, a personal history, on the one hand, and the requirements of

135

convention, the history of a discipline, on the other' means, and what sorts of consequences this 'compromise' might have for people's sense of self.

In the following sections we argue first that writers' identities are socially constructed through the possibilities for self-hood, the 'subject-positions' that are available to them, and that this availability is socially constrained in the ways we discussed in Chapters 2 and 3. We then discuss three aspects of the identity of actual writers. Firstly, writers bring to any act of writing an 'autobiographical self': their personal autobiography up to that moment. Secondly, writers create through the act of writing a 'discoursal self': a particular representation of self through the practices and discourses they enter into as they write. This representation is shaped partly by their personal history, partly by the subject-positions available in the prototypical literacy practices and discourse types available, and partly by other factors in the immediate social context. Thirdly, writers differ in how far they have a sense of 'self as author', and in how, and how far they establish their authority and authorial presence within a piece of writing. We illustrate each of these aspects of writer identity with examples from Roz's recent study of mature students entering higher education, in which she worked collaboratively with the students to investigate the way in which they were positioned by their discoursal choices in specific academic assignments.

We suggest that these three aspects of the identity of a writer can be thought of as a sort of 'clover-leaf' in which the three parts are inseparable, and are all affected by the socio-culturally available subject-positions and patterns of privileging among them that exist in the socio-cultural context. We illustrate this in Figure 6.1.

SUBJECT POSITIONS: SOCIALLY AVAILABLE POSSIBILITIES FOR SELF-HOOD

This is the most 'abstract' aspect of writer identity, in that subject positions are not characteristics of any specific individual. 'Subject positions' are possibilities for self-hood that exist in the socio-cultural context of writing, both the broader context of society at large, and the more specific institutional context of a particular act of writing. For example, two contrasting 'subject positions' that are available in the British socio-cultural context are the possibility of being the sort of person who treats men as more intelligent

136

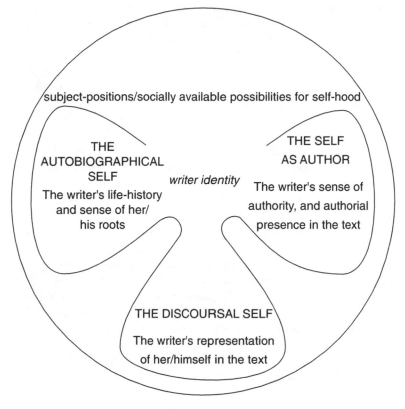

Figure 6.1 Aspects of writer identity

than women, and the possibility of being the sort of person who treats women and men as equally intelligent. Subject positions are identities that are set up for people by the conventions for all types of action, of which writing is one. By 'conventions' we mean abstract 'rules of behaviour', or prototypical ways of doing things: practices that are ratified by the social, cultural and institutional context, as we explained in Chapter 1. (In what follows we use the terms 'conventions' and 'practices' more or less interchangeably.) Interests, values, beliefs and relations of status and power are all encoded into conventions, and by drawing on particular conventions a person takes on what is encoded in them. Individuals can only have identities that the conventions they are drawing on allow them to have. In other words, the practices people enter into position them in particular ways, and to some extent everyone is at the mercy of these possibilities. However, as we have been arguing throughout, contexts are normally heterogeneous: there is almost always a range of possibilities for self-hood within any context of culture, although there are also patterns of privileging among them. People have the chance either to accept those patterns of privileging, taking on the identity set up by the dominant conventions, or to contest it by drawing on alternative conventions.

As we argued in Chapter 1, writing includes both the physical, mental and interpersonal 'literacy practices' that constitute and surround the act of writing, and 'discourse conventions': ways of using language in the writing. Both literacy practices and discourse conventions have subject positions inscribed in them, and writers are positioned by both of these simultaneously. While taking account of both of these, in the rest of this chapter we focus particularly on the way in which subject positions are set up for writers by discourse conventions. Discourse conventions differ from one 'discourse type' to another (we introduced this term in Chapter 1). We use the term 'discourse types' to mean sets of discourse conventions associated with a particular purpose for writing or with a particular topic being written about: resources 'in the air' on which people draw as they write.[2] The word 'type' in itself means something abstract, something that consists of a set of norms and conventions that are generally known about by many people, rather than an actual instance of discourse in a specific social situation. When someone uses the discourse conventions of a particular discourse type, they identify themselves with the interests, values, beliefs and power relations that are associated with it.

As we mentioned above, all conventions are not equal: some conventions are more 'conventional' in the everyday sense than others. In every cultural context some conventions have a privileged position at a particular historical moment, so that there is particularly strong pressure for people to conform to them, and to adopt the interests, values, beliefs and status encoded in them. The prestigious conventions are used by the people with status and power, and so they are more highly valued by the majority of members of the same culture. For example, the prestigious literacy practices for students writing most types of academic essays include undertaking the assignment alone, working at a desk in a study bedroom, treating existing theory and research with reverence, and presenting the essay on A4 paper in one of a small range of plain types of folder. The prestigious discourse conventions for this discourse type include using Graeco-Latin vocabulary, using a lot of abstract nouns, avoiding the use of 'I', and writing long clauses. The majority of students will attempt to conform to these conventions, as they seem to be associated with success, and they will thereby take on the subject position that is inscribed in these conventions: someone for whom learning is set apart from other aspects of daily life, someone with a competitive rather than collaborative approach to knowledge-making, a member of an exclusive group – and a conformist.

It can seem as if these abstract conventions have power over us, forcing us to conform to them, but this power is socially constructed, and can be socially challenged. The patterns of privileging among conventions are in a constant state of flux: they are not so fixed and constraining as is sometimes suggested. Social contexts nearly always support a variety of alternative sets of practices. For example, there are many subtle variations in the conventional practices for writing academic essays, some of them having less status in the academic community than others. Each actual social situation is unique, not least because the people involved in it are unique individuals, so there is no one-to-one relationship between conventions and actual use. Different people draw on different conventions, depending firstly on their opportunities for access and secondly on their preferences – shaped as these are by their life-histories. People are to some extent free to opt into particular ideologies, willingly adopting the practices in which they are embedded. However, this identification process is almost always subconscious, as are most processes to do with ideologies. With more critical awareness, people might want to question and resist being appropriated by the dominant and statusful conventions, and thereby disassociate themselves from the interests, values, beliefs and power relations they represent. (For a discussion of the idea of accommodation and resistance in writing, see Chase 1988.)

We have established the idea that the subject positions embedded in conventions for different types of writing are something abstract, but used by real people, and affected by the way in which real people use them. Because subject positions, conventions and discourse types are abstract entities, it is not possible to present concrete examples of them. We will nevertheless be using these concepts in the rest of the chapter, as we talk about more 'down to earth' aspects of writer identity. Discourse conventions carry with them prototypical identities: possible selves for real writers, 'subject positions' that they inhabit when they participate in this discourse. In the following sections we discuss three aspects of real writers' identities that are shaped by these socially constructed resources. Our examples are all of mature students writing academic essays, but we believe that the aspects of writer identity we are talking about apply to all writers and all types of writing.

THE AUTOBIOGRAPHICAL SELF: THE WRITER'S LIFE-HISTORY AND SENSE OF HER ROOTS

We call this the writer's 'autobiographical self' because it is to do with the way in which writing is affected by the writer's life-history up to the moment of writing. This is perhaps the most intuitively obvious meaning of writer identity. Everyone is different, because everyone has a unique life experience, and this life experience affects how people write. Teachers know this all too well: if 1,000 students all answer the same exam question at the same time in the same place, they will all do it differently. This is not just because some know the information better than others; it is because each will have made their own sense of it, and each will have their own ways of writing about it, depending on what they are bringing to the task.

There is an important connection between this aspect of writer identity and the 'abstract' socially available subject positions discussed above. People's life-histories and sense of their roots are not inevitable and natural. They are themselves constructed not only by socio-economic factors but also by possibilities for self-hood that have been made available to them by discourse conventions and literacy practices that they have encountered. Individuals are introduced or exposed to only a restricted range of conventions, and are to a large extent positioned by the social opportunities that have been available to them. A person's life-history includes his/her opportunities and experiences, and the people s/he has encountered, which are shaped – enabled and constrained – by socio-economic factors and differences in status. These different experiences and encounters lead to differential access to discourse types: people are immersed in and imbued with the voices and practices of their social circumstances. As a result of these experiences, a writer identifies with particular people and social groups rather than others. S/he takes on their interests, values, beliefs, practices and voices, and thereby inhabits the same subject positions as they do. People's life-histories also shape the sense of self-esteem and status with which they approach all aspects of social life, including writing.

To illustrate this, we will very briefly tell the life-history of Sarah, gradually focusing in on a particular essay she wrote at university. Sarah had done well at school in all subjects except English language. She was the first person from her family to go to university, getting a place to study chemistry. But she did not finish her science degree, and went to work as a research assistant for the UK Atomic Energy Authority (UKAEA), where she met and married her husband, who was the official photographer for the institution. She has two children and left her job for (UKAEA) to concentrate on them and on things that she enjoyed more, including art, photography and cottage conversion, which led to an interest in surveying. When they found out that her husband had leukaemia, Sarah's interest in environmental issues intensified and she became involved in debates about the relationship between radiation from nuclear fuel and leukaemia. After he died, she became more and more interested in environmental issues, and at the age of 43 went to university again to study science and the environment.

At university she took a variety of courses in different departments, particularly philosophy, sociology and environmental science. On each course she encountered slightly different varieties of academic discourse with their associated discourse conventions, including technical terminology, styles of argumentation and ways of establishing authority. One of the courses she took was called environmental ethics, run by the philosophy department. The assignment for this required her to choose a particular environmental problem and to discuss it from the point of view of philosophical theory. As you can imagine, her whole life-history shaped how she approached this task. Which environmental issue did she choose to apply philosophical reasoning to? The disposal of nuclear waste in Britain, of course. She was extremely well placed to see this issue from different perspectives, as she – unlike most students on the course – understood both the scientific issues and the perspectives of people working for

141

UKAEA, as well as knowing with intimate detail the arguments of the environmental pressure groups. She was familiar not only with the arguments of people on both sides, but also with their discourse types: the way in which they would talk and write about nuclear waste. On the other hand, you can imagine the difficulty she had approaching this 'objectively', attempting to weigh up the various arguments about 'disposal', when all she could think of was that nuclear waste should not exist at all, because of the harm she believed it caused. So she brought to the task several conflicting interests and beliefs, along with a plethora of different discourse types for writing about the topic.

Sarah's life-history also affected the process of writing this assignment. She came from a family that did not engage in 'academic discourse'. She loved books as objects of beauty, but she did not read a lot, and had begun reading academic articles only since starting university: at the age of 43. To put it rather startlingly, she was not socialised into academic clause structures. In so far as she was used to the literacy practices of education at all, she was used to writing as a scientist, not as a philosopher. Her experience of writing in science had been short lab. reports, whereas this essay was expected to be over 3,000 words of philosophical argument. In scientific writing she was used to a standard format of aims, method and results. However, she had been advised by philosophy lecturers that they wanted to know her position right from the beginning: 'We don't want detective stories in philosophy.'

Sarah's personal life-history before coming to university and since starting her course contained particular experiences, interpersonal involvement with particular people, opportunities for developing particular interests, values, beliefs and feelings about her own self-worth, and reasons for preferring some discourse conventions over others. She brought all these with her to the act of writing her assignment on environmental ethics. In the next section we use examples from this assignment to discuss how writers give particular impressions of themselves through the discourse conventions on which they draw.

THE DISCOURSAL SELF: SELF-REPRESENTATION IN THE TEXT

Writing not only conveys a message about content but also conveys a message about the writer. The term 'self-representation' refers to this process of conveying an impression of self to others through some form of social action.[3] This is not an option: whatever we do consciously or subconsciously makes a statement about our identity. Where language is concerned, it is important to recognise that people convey messages about their identity not only by talking or writing about themselves, but also through their practices and the discourse types they draw on. These sources of information about a person's identity are often in conflict. Even when we are not talking or writing about ourselves, we are indirectly 'saying' something about ourselves through the way in which we talk or write. We are calling this aspect of writer identity 'the discoursal self' because it is the identity that is conveyed by the writer's discourse practices. Our interest in this section is in how writers create impressions of themselves as they write. We first link self-representation to the aspects of writer identity we have already discussed, we then discuss the influence of the expected reader(s) on how writers portray themselves in their writing, and end the section by giving examples of the identity that Sarah constructed for herself through the discourse conventions she drew on when writing her essay.

Writers do not create impressions of themselves in a vacuum; they do so by drawing on the 'socially available subject positions' we discussed above. There is a range of abstract conventions – both discourse conventions and conventions for physical, mental and interpersonal literacy practices, as we mentioned above – that provide the 'building materials' for self-representation, and writers draw upon these in infinite combinations as they write real texts. Writers take on the identities inscribed in the particular conventions they draw on, and these conventions position them both in their own eyes and in the eyes of their readers. However, this process of drawing on conventions is not completely free-ranging. Which conventions people draw upon depends partly on their life-histories, experiences and affiliations to particular groups, and partly on the pressure to conform to the prestigious conventions for the type of writing in the institutional context. Access to resources for self-representation is facilitated or constrained by the writer's social history, as discussed in the previous section.

The conscious or usually subconscious selections that writers make from among possibilities for self-hood depend on their assessment of the characteristics of the immediate social context. This involves understanding both the purpose(s) for the particular writing they are engaged in (as we discussed in Chapter 5) and the nature of the reader–writer relationship they are entering into (as we discuss further in Chapter 7). Particularly, they have to make a judgement about the power relations between themselves and their readers. How writers present themselves in their writing is going to depend on whether it is necessary for them to maintain a good standing in the eyes of their readers, or whether they can afford to disregard the impressions of them that their readers might form. If it is necessary to create a good impression in the eyes of their particular readers, as it very often is – particularly for students writing academic assignments – they also have to predict what their readers value, in order to appear to 'belong to the same club'. They then position themselves in this minefield as best they can.

As a result of these conflicting considerations, self-presentation is not necessarily unitary or even coherent. Writers may shift from one subject position to another, creating multiple and possibly contradictory impressions of themselves, even within a single text. Writers often feel more comfortable with the subject positions they have constructed for themselves in some pieces of writing or parts of writing than in others. This sense of 'fit', of ownership, is perhaps what people mean when they talk about 'the real me'.

Writers consciously or subconsciously adjust the impression they convey to readers, according to their commitments and what is in their best interests. These two forces may be in conflict, especially in situations like writing an academic assignment for assessment purposes. Writers often find themselves attempting to inhabit subject positions with which they do not really identify, or feel ambivalent about. This can sometimes involve some quite deliberate deception, when a writer tries to appear to be the sort of person they are not. Our tutorial work with students has led us to believe that this is one of the reasons why writers get 'stuck' with writing: subconsciously they are worried as much about the impression they are giving of themselves as they are about the subject-matter they are writing about. Readers in turn form impressions of writers as they read, based on the experience they are bringing to the reading. Different readers will construct the same writer slightly differently, and these 'reader constructions' of writer identity may well differ from the impression the writer consciously or subconsciously wanted to convey. (We discuss this further in the next chapter; see also Hayes and others 1992.)

144

Writers convey messages about themselves both by the way in which they engage in the act of writing and by the discourse conventions they draw on. However, the impressions they create of themselves by their physical, mental and interpersonal literacy practices are fleeting, and many of them may not be observed, or may not be apparent from the final product. For example, a writer may spread her papers out all over the table, turn ideas round and round in her head, and keep phoning up her friends to discuss ideas, but none of these practices will be visible in the text, and only the friends on the end of the phone will have formed any impression of the writer from her actions. By contrast, the discourse conventions that they employ leave a permanent mark, and are particularly powerful means for self-representation to whoever reads the writing. Although we have so far been referring to self-representation through all writing practices, our examples are specifically about the impressions a writer creates of herself through the discourse conventions she draws on.

We illustrate the idea of self-representation by discussing some of the discourse types that Sarah was drawing on in the assignment we described above, and showing what sorts of identities they were setting up for her. Sarah was drawing on a variety of discourse types, partly because of her personal history, and partly because of the nature of the course she was on. Environmental studies is a new, multidisciplinary field, requiring students to participate in a wide variety of discourses, all of which position the user differently: imbuing her with interests, values, beliefs, knowledge-making practices and principles that are sometimes in conflict.

Firstly, throughout her essay she was drawing on the very broad discourse type that is sometimes called 'academic discourse' – something that is recognised as being in very general terms the way in which people talk and write in higher education. This discourse positions Sarah as a member of the academic community in general. To exemplify this, here are two sentences from the middle of her essay.

Extract 1 (lines 238–41): *an identity as a member of the academic community*

These are just a few areas of concern I identified. But they serve to illustrate the fact that there are many areas of uncertainty to prevent a reasonable consequential analysis of this method for disposal of radioactive waste.

145

There are many factors that make us recognise these thirty-eight words as belonging to 'academic discourse':

- The second sentence is one twenty-eight-word long clause.
- There is a twenty-three-word nominal group embedded in this sentence:

  the fact that there are many areas . . .

- There are many abstract nouns, several of them nominalisations of verbs or adjectives:

  areas, concern, fact, uncertainty, analysis, method, disposal, waste

- Most of the verbs are present tense relational processes, not material processes:

  are, serve, are,

These characteristics represent the dominant interests, knowledge-making and knowledge-telling practices of the academic community: avoiding reference to people, discussing abstract ideas, and compacting them into chunks that can be related to each other. This way of thinking has achieved high status in most industrialised and educated societies, and is believed to be a sign of intelligence. So using language in this way is highly prized, and confers status on those who can do it.

Sarah's identity is constructed by this discourse type throughout the assignment, but there are variations: what could be called sub-categories of 'academic discourse'. Firstly, she draws on the discourse of two very different disciplines: philosophy and natural science. Extract 2 is an example of what we suggest is the discourse of philosophy, positioning Sarah as a philosophy student.

Extract 2 (lines 284–8): *identity as a philosopher*

In particular, utilitarianism aims to promote the greatest happiness for the greatest number of people. This is a theory which adopts a single basic principle, as opposed to deontological theories which appeal to fundamental principles of what is right.

One recognisable characteristic of this discourse is its lexis:

utilitarianism; deontological; fundamental principles.

146

Another is that abstract concepts play major grammatical roles in clauses, acting as subjects and objects of verbs:

utilitarianism aims to promote . . . happiness
a theory . . . adopts . . . a . . . principle
theories . . . appeal . . . to fundamental principles

This discourse sets up an identity for those who enter into it of someone interested in 'playing with abstractions', of someone who thinks of abstract entities undertaking what might otherwise be thought to be human actions.

In another part of the assignment, however, Sarah positions herself as a scientist by drawing on the discourse of natural science. Extract 3 is an example.

Extract 3 (lines 121–9): *identity as a natural scientist*

The hazards of Radioactive waste
The main problem with all categories of radioactive waste is its potential hazard to the health of humans and other organisms. The characteristics of the waste which determine this hazard are the types of radiation emitted (alpha, beta or gamma) and its "half life", that is the time for the activity to have decreased by one half. The rate of decay varies widely from Argon 41, which has a half life of 100 minutes to Uranium 238 (the most common form of uranium in nature) which has a half-life of 4500 million years.

A striking feature of this discourse is that its 'objects of interest' are not human or abstract, but material. A particularly interesting example of this is the choice of the expression 'humans and other organisms', which marks the transition from argument about environmental ethics into scientific discourse. Other expressions that signal a focus on the material are 'types of radiation, Argon 41,' and 'uranium'. Another striking feature is that this discourse is full of numbers ('100 minutes, Uranium 238, 4500 million years') and numerical processes ('decreased by one half, rate of decay'). This discourse type sets up an identity for its user as someone who is interested in the physical aspect of human experience, and believes in quantification as the most significant knowledge-making process.

Academic discourses differ not only according to their content, but also according to the writer's relationship to the reader.

For example, in extract 1, Sarah wrote 'I identified', but in her draft version she had written 'were identified'. The change brings Sarah more into the picture, positioning her as taking more responsibility for the knowledge-making process, and recognising her own subjective role in it. Another example is in extract 2, where she gives a definition of utilitarianism. In a tape-recorded discussion about this assignment, she pointed out that if she were a well-known academic publishing a paper in a journal, she would not need to do this; in fact such a definition would seem odd in an academic article (although expected in a textbook). But because she is 'only' a student, she has to show that she knows what utilitarianism means.

Partly because of the nature of her assignment, and partly because of her own allegiances and life experiences, Sarah also drew on other discourse types that are not specific to the academic discourse community. Discourse types leak from one domain to another in many ways. Extracts 4–6 are examples.

Extract 4 (lines 20–35): *identity as an insider to the nuclear industry*

> It is the UK Government's responsibility to manage safely all radioactive waste and to this end they announced in July 1982 the formation of the Nuclear Industry Radioactive Waste Executive (NIREX) to represent the component parts of the U.K industry and provide a uniform approach to the management of low and intermediate level radioactive waste (LLW and ILW see note 1)
> ... NIREX proposed three alternative "deep disposal concepts" – basically all involving underground disposal and eventual sealing off after backfilling with a suitable grouting material. The important difference between these three concepts is their access arrangements: under land, under the seabed accessed by land or under the seabed and accessed by sea.

Extract 4 shares some characteristics with extract 1, such as long sentences, many abstract nouns, many of them nominalisations (for example 'responsibility', 'management', 'approach', 'arrange-ments') and present tense verbs. However, it differs in that it also contains past tense verbs, reporting the verbal actions of govern-ment bodies:

the UK Government announced . . .

NIREX proposed . . .

It also contains acronyms that are common to bureaucratic reports, such as UK and NIREX, and technical terminology: 'underground disposal', 'backfilling', 'grouting'. In the draft version of this essay Sarah had not included the final sentence of the extract. That is, she had behaved as an 'insider', assuming that her readers would know what these three alternative "deep disposal concepts" were. Even here, she does not explain the term 'backfilling', which would be common parlance within NIREX, but is not understood by the general public (if we are at all representative of 'the general public').

This bureaucratic/technical discourse of the nuclear fuel industry sets up an identity for Sarah as an objective reporter of the activities of the industry, and knowledgeable about the technical detail of the processes of "disposal". We want to make special mention of the quotation marks she put around the expression "deep disposal concepts". These are what are sometimes called 'scare quotes', signalling that she distances herself from this discourse, identifying it as NIREX's way of referring to the issues, and not an expression she is willing to adopt for herself. Had she used the expression without the scare quotes, she would be further identifying herself with the ideology of the nuclear fuel industry, which talks about 'disposal' as if it were possible and acceptable to think of 'disposing' nuclear waste: something that is highly contested in the debate about the environmental hazards of nuclear waste.

Extract 5 (lines 153–9): *identity as a participant in the public debate about nuclear waste disposal*

Consequently whatever method is chosen for managing waste, it must be reliable for many hundreds of thousands of years. It should provide conditions such that any subsequent release of radioactivity, in whatever form will not result in radiological risks to either present or future generations.

Extract 5 differs from academic discourse and from the bureaucratic technical discourse of extract 4 in its modality. The verb forms of all the main clauses are highly modalised:

149

it must be reliable
It should provide
will not result

These all make high value judgements about what should be done: the discourse of polemic persuasion, not of neutral reporting. This discourse type sets up a position for its user as someone with a strong opinion to uphold, and the right to express it.

Another noticeable characteristic of this extract is its stylistic techniques for persuading the reader. The weightiness of some of the expressions (almost clichés) makes the stipulations all the more imperative: 'for many hundreds of thousands of years, either present or future generations'. The alliteration of 'r' in 'reliable', 'release of radioactivity', 'result in radiological risks' gives the message an irresistible ring. This represents yet another discourse type that Sarah was drawing on, an almost literary discourse. Extract 6 is a further example of how Sarah draws on discourse practices and associated values from literary or 'creative' writing.

Extract 6 (lines 412–14): *identity as a creative writer*

under that sort of threat they might be well advised to, metaphorically speaking, lock the door and throw away the key.

This extract contains a metaphor drawn from everyday usage: 'lock the door and throw away the key'. Metaphors are normally associated with poems, novels and journalistic types of writing, not academic writing. Sarah likes imaginative, creative, artistic forms of expression, and by using a metaphor positions herself as someone who values aesthetic qualities. However, she does this very tentatively, announcing her move into this different discourse type with the words 'metaphorically speaking'.

Drawing on a particular discourse type positions the writer as someone who shares the interests, values and practices that under-pin it. When Roz talked to Sarah about the way in which her discourse choices positioned her, she was happy to own some of the impressions she was giving, and vehemently disowned others. For example, she said of extract 4 that she hated sounding like that, and would not want to write like that again. We interpret that as meaning that she disowned the identity set up for her by that discourse, and did not want the values, beliefs and practices associated with it to be imputed to her by anyone reading her writing.

Throughout this section we have kept shifting from writing about the discourse conventions to writing about the way in which they positioned Sarah. This is because of the dialectic relationship between the abstract subject positions that are made available by discourse conventions and the individual identities of real writers. Individual identities are nothing other than the material form of socially available subject positions, and subject positions do not exist other than in the instantiations of them in the form of the identities of real people. Applying this specifically to writing, the possibilities for self-hood that exist in discourse conventions manifest themselves only when actual writers employ them in actual texts.

In this section we have been discussing what we have elsewhere called 'the discoursal construction of identity'. To summarise, in all forms of social action people give an impression of themselves by the way they behave. Self-representation is about taking up available subject positions according to the particular exigencies of the immediate social situation. Here we have been concentrating on the way in which writers construct a 'discoursal self', portraying themselves through the discourse conventions they draw on intertextually. This construction of self is grounded in a difficult, usually subconscious, assessment of the competing ideologies and power relations in the immediate social context of writing. By accommodating to or resisting dominant positionings, writers participate in the struggle over which practices, discourses and associated subject positions will dominate in the future.

The aspect of writer identity that we have discussed in this section concerns the writer's 'voice' in the sense of the discoursal choices a writer makes when writing. The idea of 'voice' is very popular in discussion of writing and learning to write, but it amalgamates two aspects of the identity of a writer, which need to be disentangled. We want to differentiate two meanings of the writer's 'voice' – voice as *form*, and voice as *content*. One meaning of 'voice' is concerned with the *form* of language: the combination and range of discourse conventions with which the writer is comfortable, as we have been discussing in this section. There is no such thing as a personal 'voice' in this respect: just an affiliation to or unique selection among existing discourse conventions.[4] The other meaning of 'voice' is concerned with the *content* of language:

151

writers' expression of their own ideas and beliefs, which we discuss next.

THE SELF AS AUTHOR: THE WRITER'S SENSE OF AUTHORITY, AND AUTHORIAL PRESENCE IN THE TEXT[5]

This aspect of writer identity is more to do with writers having their 'own voice' in the sense of its content rather than its form. The writer's 'voice' in this sense means expressing their own ideas and beliefs. This is what people usually first think of as 'writer identity': whether the writer is present in the writing with a strong authorial voice or not: whether s/he is *saying* something.

One component of the self as author is the issue of how authoritative writers feel as they write. Many writers approach writing, particularly academic writing, without a sense that they have anything worth saying. They do not see it as their place to have a position to argue or an experience or idea worth communicating to others. Viewing oneself as an 'author' – feeling authoritative, and feeling the right to exert a presence in the text, is often related to the sense of power and status writers bring with them from their life-history. This sense of the right to authorship is, we suggest, often associated with the gender, class and ethnicity of the writer: white middle-class men are likely, for socio-historical reasons, to have a greater sense of authority than most black, working-class women.

The other component of the self as author is how, and how far, writers appear authoritative by establishing an authorial presence in their texts. We make this second component the starting point for our discussion, since it is the visible evidence of writers' feeling of authoritativeness and sense of themselves as authors. Some writers, in some types of writing, make their 'voice' in this sense heard more than others. Writers may put themselves at the centre of the writing, exerting control over it and establishing a presence within it. At the other extreme writers may relinquish control of the situation to other, named authorities, or to some abstract, impersonal source, or perhaps to the reader. Authoritativeness is sometimes condoned by the currently dominant discourse conventions, and sometimes not. Writers can accommodate to or resist the degree of authoritativeness that is sanctioned by the conventions for a particular type of writing.

The most obvious type of 'authorial presence', especially in academic writing, is the use of the first person: I, me, my. But it has other manifestations too, as we exemplify in this section. The overarching idea is that writers differ in how much they feel, and appear to be, in control of the act of writing: how much they feel themselves to be not just 'writers' but also 'authors' with the authority to say something.

If any aspect of the clover-leaf diagram could be treated separately from the others, this one might. It is the aspect of writer identity which has been studied and written about more than the other three (see, for example, Kaufer and Geisler 1989; Greene 1991; N. Hall 1989, and several studies of citation practices). However, we see this aspect of writer identity closely connected to the others, with the two components of it mapping roughly onto the two previous sections. Some genres set up more authoritative identities for writers – such as the academic journal article; other genres constrain writers to subordinate roles, or to excise themselves altogether – as in student essays. Some people's life-histories will have led them to feel relatively authoritative and powerful as authors; others less so. Some people are more inclined than others to assert their identity as authors, to give an impression of themselves as authoritative. The assertion of authorial presence is socially and discoursally constructed in the same way as representation of other aspects of identity.

In the rest of this section we give examples of ways in which writers do and do not exert their authorial presence in academic writing. We no longer draw our examples only from Sarah's writing, because this would not provide a wide range on the continuum from least to most authoritative. Our examples are therefore drawn from the writing of several mature students in higher education.

The first example is a sad story of opportunities for authorship, authoritativeness and authorial presence being passed over. Frances was taking an anthropology course and was set the assignment: *"There is no such thing as a free gift." Discuss.* She read this as a request to review the anthropological literature on the topic of gift-giving. Consequently most of her essay is like extract 7, presenting the insights of published authors such as Sahlins. There is no authorship role for Frances herself: her task is to report the contributions to knowledge of others more authoritative than herself.

Extract 7: Frances (lines 111–15) – *Anthropology*

> Balanced reciprocity as Sahlins sees it, characterises reciprocity that is prompt and equal, usually between people of the same generation.

Further, she did not take up an opportunity which, she later found out, was afforded by this assignment: to do a mini-ethnography of her own. While those students who were given first-class marks studied the gift-giving patterns in communities with which they were familiar, Frances referred to the Weardale community of her childhood only in passing. Extract 8 is the only place where she mentions Weardale: a topic on which she would indeed be an authority, and one which would, in fact, have made an excellent focus for the whole essay.[6] The chance of authorship is buried in hypotheticality, passives and modal verbs, and Frances has little presence in the essay.

Extract 8: Frances (lines 228–32) – *Anthropology*

> A similar picture could be built up if English people from close mining communities like the Weardale of my childhood was studied, for many of the reciprocal rights and obligations differed from but were as apparent as those in the Pakistani communities of today.

The next two extracts contrast different ways of dealing with personal experience as a source of authority. In extract 9, Angela is writing about the experience of mature undergraduate women, and clearly acknowledging and foregrounding her own membership of this group, thereby claiming a certain authority on the topic. The use of 'us, 'our' and 'we' places her as a central participant in what she is writing about.

Extract 9: Angela (lines 439–42) – *Independent Studies*

> As mature undergraduate women, most of us nearing the end of our time in higher education, with great effort and determination we have managed to struggle through, survive, and to some extent resist institutional pressures to 'conform'.

By contrast Donna, in extract 10, is referring to black women in the third person, not mentioning the fact that she herself belongs to this group. She actually attributes an understanding of black women to four published authorities, rather than claiming the authority of her own experience. We suggest that the decision to retreat from a position of personal authority may be associated with Donna's identity as a black woman. She feels that, in order to succeed in what she experiences as the white, patriarchal institution of academia, she must not 'rock the boat', but must conform to the dominant convention for student writing of respecting the wisdom of others.

Extract 10: Donna (lines 81–4) – *Independent Studies*

> Despite of such imagery, Black women have resisted these externally defined images of their social realities, that portray them as worthless, insignificant and inferior [Zhana: 1988; Bryan et al: 1985; Braxton et al: 1990; Collins: 1990].

As we mentioned above, a rather obvious way of claiming authorial presence is to use first person references. However, even this is not so simple as it might seem, because the nature of this claim to authorship depends on what, exactly, the 'I' is portrayed as doing. For example, in extract 11 John uses what is sometimes called the strategic 'I', referring to himself as the architect of the essay – hardly a very powerful role to lay claim to.

Extract 11: John (lines 3–4) – *Medical Ethics*

> I will answer this question by splitting the essay into four sections.

In extract 1, Sarah uses 'I' to refer to herself as the person who did the thinking behind what she is writing – a somewhat more powerful act than 'splitting the essay into four sections'. Extract 12 illustrates the first person being used for a much more powerful sort of authorial presence: Sarah is presenting herself as the author of the argument that runs through the main body of the essay.

Extract 12: Sarah (lines 472–5, i.e. last sentence)

> The main thrust of my argument has been to show that neither fact directed consequential theories nor fundamental principles provide the answer to the moral issues involved in this case.

These examples show that the first person 'I', 'me' or 'my' can introduce the author into the text, but there are considerable differences in the relative authoritativeness of specific instances.

In discussing extracts 7, 8 and 10 we have pointed out how attribution to other authorities and modal expressions can weaken the authoritativeness of the writer. By contrast, writers can show themselves as very authoritative by the use of unmodalised present tense assertions which give a sense of certainty, and the placing of value judgements. But for student writers there is a fine line between sounding appropriately authoritative and overstepping the limits of their authority. In extract 13 Valerie made her evaluation of Engels authoritatively.

Extract 13: Valerie (lines 155–6) – *Sociology and Communication Studies Link Course*

> But Engels was an inadequate observer, because of the way he viewed England from Berlin.

She had very clear reasons based on her reading and her own experience for making this assessment of him. However, her tutor deemed that she had overstepped the limits of her authority: who is a mere undergraduate to pronounce Engels to be an 'inadequate observer'? And Valerie had not learnt that a categorical statement like this, criticising such an internationally recognised social theorist, has to be thoroughly justified with extended argumentation. Extract 13 provoked the following annoyed response from the tutor in the margin, indicating that she had overstepped her authority. The capital letters reveal the tutor's annoyance:

> INADEQUATE? IN COMPARISON WITH WHAT OR WHOM?
> Engels' *Condition of the Working Class* (1944) is now regarded as a classic of urban description, after all.

Finally, extract 14 is an example of a student writer asserting her identity in relation to a quotation from a published authority. Cathy first passes judgement, based in strongly felt personal experience, on Rogers and Groombridge's position. Then after the quotation she weighs up the truth of what they say, bringing evidence to support her position. This is in stark contrast to the ways in which Frances (extract 7) and Donna (extract 10) appealed to other authors as the sources of ideas, without taking any stance towards them.

Extract 14: Cathy (lines 182–94) – *Educational Studies*

> However, this quote from 1976 Rogers and Groombridge takes the treatment of adult education to the extreme by implying that we should be wrapped in cotton wool
>> Adult learners have certain special needs. They are nervous, proud, touchy and humble; anxieties must be soothed, faces saved. They have short-term memory difficulties, must learn at their own pace, and will do better from written than from verbal explanations . . .
> On the one hand yes, 'second chance' students do need a different kind of help. This is because of the length of time they have been away from education. Many adults as I have said before now have few qualifications due to many things: they may not have got on well at school; they may have missed a lot due to family problems. Nevertheless, it is important that the help given is constructive.

Extracts 7–14 show student writers taking up very different positions as authors, ranging from Frances and Donna, who in various ways deny their roles as authorities and remove themselves from their writing, to John, Angela, Sarah, Valerie and Cathy, who in various ways do establish themselves as authors and bring their authorial presence into their writing. We want to emphasise the variety in this aspect of writer identity. Firstly, as the examples have shown, there are several different ways for writers to be, or appear to be, relatively authoritative and to bring their authorial presence into their writing. The textual features associated with establishing authorial presence include the following:

1 whether or not writers use the first person;
2 if writers do use the first person, whether it is for structuring the essay, for presenting personal experience, and/or for making statements of value or belief;
3 how writers position themselves in relation to other authorities;
4 the relative certainty with which they write: how far they use categorical modality, and how far they use modal verbs and adverbs;
5 the extent to which they claim authority for their personal experience;

6 the types of reporting verbs they use when referring to the work
of others; and

7 the extent to which they comment on and evaluate the work of
others.

Secondly, people vary in how consistent they are in conveying
authority in their writing. Although we think the extracts are to
some extent typical of the writers, how far they position themselves
as more or less authoritative varies considerably from section to
section, even from clause to clause in their writing. So Valerie, for
example, appears very authoritative in some places, and far less so
in others. On the other hand, some people, such as Cathy, are
fairly consistent about how strongly they establish their authorial
presence.

Authoritativeness is a personal characteristic which writers can
construct and convey through their discourse choices, just as
they may construct and convey their identities as feminists or
philosophers. However, authoritativeness is a special case because
it means establishing an identity as the author of the writing. We
therefore think it is useful to view it as a separate aspect of writer
identity in its own right.

CONCLUSION

In this chapter we have shown that acts of writing depend on the
multiple identities that writers bring to them, and that acts of
writing in themselves constitute an on-going struggle over possible
identities. We are claiming that writing is a political act in which
a writer aligns him/her self with ideological positions available
in the socio-cultural context, and takes up a position within the
relations of power in that context. We have suggested that
writers' class, gender, race and sexuality affect how they think
of themselves as writers; we would also suggest that these social
factors carry with them subject positions which writers may or may
not maintain in particular types of writing, depending on the
dominant conventions for that type of writing, and how far they
accommodate to or resist these conventions. We have proposed
four interrelated factors that contribute to the notion of 'writer
identity', as represented in the 'clover-leaf diagram' in Figure 6.1.
These factors take account both of the abstract way in which
discourse socially constructs or positions people, and of more

individual, interpersonal aspects of self-representation. We have also suggested that writers might contest the rules of appropriacy for different types of writing, taking opportunities where they can to assert their identity, and/or to promote writing conventions with which they would prefer to identify.

To summarise, the all-pervasive, 'abstract', social meaning of 'writer identity' is that conventions – including, specifically, discourse conventions – carry encoded within them particular subject positions – particular sets of values, practices and beliefs, and particular power relations – for the individuals who draw upon them. The other meanings of 'writer identity' apply to particular writers writing particular texts. Firstly, people bring with them to the act of writing a 'self' that has been shaped by their life-history up to that moment. This 'autobiographical self' relates to abstract subject positions, in that the 'selves' that writers bring to the act of writing have been shaped by the possibilities made available by the discourse conventions to which they have had access. Secondly, writers participate in the process of their own on-going identity construction in each new act of writing, creating a 'discoursal self': an impression of themselves through the discoursal choices they make from among available subject positions. These choices are usually subconscious, made in the tension between writers' current affiliations, allegiances and sense of self, and their sense of what will be in their best interests in the social context in which they are writing. However, some writers are acutely aware of these dilemmas of self-representation. Thirdly, writing is potentially a way of asserting the 'self as author', of saying things that matter to the writer. In our understanding, all this is going on simultaneously moment by moment, word by word, as a writer puts pen to paper and makes decisions about lexical choice, syntactic structure, discourse organisation and, in the case of multilingual students, which of their languages to write in.

All our examples have been from the experience and writing of a small group of British mature students. However, we believe that all four of these aspects of writer identity apply to any writer of any age undertaking any type of writing in any cultural context. There is little research paying attention to these aspects of writer identity, and we recommend further studies, focusing on different types of writer and/or different types of writing. We have indicated the complexity of these issues of identity for adults writing in their first language; how much greater this must be for adults writing in a language other than their first. Further, we believe that the account we have given here of 'writer identity' could be generalised to apply to the issues of subject positioning and identity formation in a broader sense which are of interest to many social scientists. How far are the aspects of *writer* identity which we have described also aspects of identity *in general*?

7

THE ROLE OF THE READER
IN WRITING

INTRODUCTION

In Chapter 3 we identified ourselves with the view that writing is embedded in its social context. We expanded on what this means, distinguishing between 'context of situation' and 'cultural context', following Halliday (1985). One important element in the 'context of situation' for writing is the reader(s). Researchers in the past fifteen years have taken a lot of interest in the role of the reader(s) in shaping writing – see, for example, Britton and others (1975), Kroll (1984), Nystrand (1986) and Kirsch and Roen (1990). Current models of the writing process include 'thinking about the reader' as one element in the process, as we showed in Chapter 4. Books about the teaching of writing mention 'considering the reader' as important – see, for example, Byrne (1988), Hedge (1988), National Writing Project (1989) and Waters and Waters (1995).

In this chapter we draw on the work of the linguists Halliday, and Fowler and his colleagues at the University of East Anglia, and of the sociologist of culture Stuart Hall, in order to explore the role of the reader in writing. First we discuss two interrelated meanings of 'considering the reader', and the way in which discourse conventions (i.e. influences from the context of culture) lead writers to construct readers in particular ways. We then discuss writers' responsibility to their readers to make clear their own positions and attitudes and the strength of their commitment to their ideas, and we present some of the linguistic realisations of this responsibility. In the next section we discuss the dynamic nature of the writer–reader relationship and focus on the significance of reader decoding positions. We argue that it is important to recognise the

161

relative power relations between writer and reader: the way in which readers usually view the writers of published writing as more powerful than themselves, whereas teachers view student writers as less powerful than themselves. We conclude the chapter with an example of two different readings of the same text which illustrate the point that no matter how carefully the writer attempts to position his/her readers, they do not all necessarily accept this positioning, thus demonstrating that there is no automatic fit between writer intentions and reader uptake.

WHAT IS THE WRITER–READER RELATIONSHIP?

In Chapter 1 we introduced Halliday's identification of three macro-functions of language:

1 the ideational
2 the interpersonal
3 the textual

We think this is a useful way of thinking about language because it allows us to distinguish between the way in which the writer/speaker relates to the world of ideas, or the propositional content of texts (1), how s/he relates to the receiver(s) of those ideas (2), and the way in which the writer/speaker organises these into a cohesive stretch of discourse (3). In this section we focus on the interpersonal function of language in written discourse, which is what we are referring to as the writer–reader (W–R) relationship. Fowler and colleagues (1979) call this function of language 'modality'. Adapting what they say to refer specifically to writing:

> [It covers linguistic constructions] which express writers' attitudes towards [themselves], towards their readers and towards their subject matter; [writers'] social and economic relationships with the people they address and the actions which are performed via language (ordering, accusing, promising, pleading, etc.).
>
> (Fowler and others 1979: 200)

Fairclough (1992a: 64 ff.) expands on Halliday's interpersonal function and separates it out into two distinct but inter-related functions: the 'identity' function and the 'relational' function. The 'identity' function refers to how discourse contributes to the construction of social identities or subject positions for both

162

the writer and the reader. The 'relational' function refers to the discursive construction of social relations between people. This means that readers are reading three types of message from the writer's text in addition to the events, objects, ideas and opinions that are written about (the ideational message). Firstly, they are developing a sense of the writer's identity – her/his views, attitudes, writing and thinking style, intellectual abilities – as we discussed in the previous chapter. Secondly, they are reading a message about themselves: what sort of person they are expected to be as a reader of this text. Thirdly, they are reading a message about their relative power and status in relation to the writer.

An important aspect of Halliday's theory is that the three macro-functions of language operate simultaneously. This means that the interpersonal function – for our purposes the W–R relationship – is not an optional extra: it is an integral part of all writing. In real life writers scarcely ever write anything without considering who is going to read it, and what identity they will be constructing for themselves in relation to those readers. When writers get stuck it is just as likely to be caused by the complexity of the W–R relationship as by the content of what they are writing. At times consciously and at others unconsciously, writers are aware of the different dimension of this relationship, and this can have an inhibitory effect on them. We therefore believe it is essential to have a clear view of the W–R relationship in order to understand fully what is involved in writing. In Chapter 6 we discussed writers' concerns about the impressions they create of themselves; in the next section we discuss how the reader affects the decisions that writers take when writing.

CONSIDERING THE READER

The formulation of the above title captures two separate but related aspects of the role of the reader in writing; the first is that writers need to bear in mind who their reader is, and the second refers to ways of writing the text that are helpful to the reader in negotiating the text.

Thinking about who the reader is

Widdowson (1983: 44) refers to the internal dialogue between the reader and the writer, and Nystrand (1986) refers to the same thing as 'reciprocity'. Because the reader is not present and is often unknown, the writer has to make constant judgements about what the reader knows, how much to take for granted (presuppose) and how much to make explicit, etc. This constitutes one of the biggest stumbling blocks for students when they are writing coursework for their lecturers. They generally know who their reader/assessor will be and this leads to a number of difficult issues for the writers. Firstly, the genre itself is a hybrid one – part writing to explore and exchange ideas, part writing to show understanding of what has been learned – and this is the source of many problems over how to think about the reader. One common worry is: How much detail of explanation is necessary? Students assume that their reader will know more about the topic than they do. As a consequence, lecturers complain that they are often not explicit enough in the explanations of the points they are making or in laying out what they assume to be common ground. They frequently do not explain how they arrived at the argument they put forward or what its implications might be, assuming that these will be obvious. This is often a problem for the lecturer reader: the reader has to work hard to second-guess the writer's understandings; the reader cannot judge the thought processes – the way of thinking the discipline – of the writer; consequently, the reader feels frustrated because s/he would like to know more.

Secondly, because of the power relations in which the writing of coursework is embedded, students often feel that they have to write what they think the lecturer is expecting to hear. This often leads to conflict over what to include or not to include, how far to go in disagreeing with positions set out by the lecturer in lectures and seminars or perceived from the reading list as the 'orthodox' views on the topic. This conflict has direct consequences for the style of writing. If a writer wants to take issue with a particular point of view expressed by the lecturer reader, s/he has to think very carefully about the wording of that disagreement. The onus is always on the dissenter to argue a tighter case than those who go along with the orthodox views.

The building of the 'dialogue' between writer and reader is frequently referred to in the literature on writing, but there is one essential part of this dialogue that is mostly neglected: the ideological dimension; that is, the values and beliefs of the participants which are rooted in their socio-political identity. Wallace (1986: 40) refers to the fact that writers make assumptions about their readers and give their readers' identities. In building the dialogue with readers, writers in all genres often take for granted that readers are going to share their beliefs and values. In textbooks and newspaper articles, for example, one way in which writers signal that they assume a shared point of view is by using the pronoun 'we'. In this way they position their readers as consenting, part of an 'usness' that is hard to resist (see Chapter 2) because of the relative powerlessness of the general reader. This is borne out by our work with students in higher education; in fact, they often adopt this technique in their own assignment writing because they believe it will be more 'persuasive' of their readers.

If writers are writing something to persuade a group of potentially resistant readers over to their point of view, they will need to treat the dialogue with their readers differently from the way in which they would construct it with a potentially assenting audience. This is also true for writers who are not quite sure who their readers will be or what their response is going to be. All these conditions apply to the writing of Trevor Griffiths. In a conversation about his television play *Country* (1988b), he talked about the devices that a play uses to encourage people to join or separate from the play, making the audience ask itself questions about whether it wants to conjoin with it or feel alienated by it, and making them constantly interrogate the text in an active way.

One of the ways in which he 'dialogues' with his audience in *The Gulf Between Us* (see the example at the end of this chapter) is by reminding them of and demolishing the various arguments that have been used in the public domain to justify the Gulf war. He draws readers into the text by exploiting their ability to recognise 'intertextuality' between texts. He makes it the audience's responsibility to come up with other arguments if they are still resisting his tightly argued logic. In this play he works with what he expects his audience to be familiar with, and then forces them to confront that familiarity (see section 1 of the analysis of different readers' responses at the end of this chapter).

Talking again about his television play *Country* (1988b), Trevor focused on another aspect of intertextuality, namely the choice of actors, as a way of exploiting audience/reader familiarity:

there is something interesting about what actors and actresses carry, what charge they carry, which is partly to

165

do with all the roles that summate inside an audience's reception. An excellent example of casting for me is Wendy Hiller. She made a major reputation on T.V. playing Queen Mary, so I wanted that fake authenticity, that charge that it carries with it. I wanted the audience to feel that they were OK with this woman, that they knew her, that they liked her, and then little by little everything peels away and you begin to see naked self interest and a kind of toughness that is very unpleasant.

In other plays, such as *The Party* (1974), he uses dialectics to present opposing arguments and ways of understanding left-wing politics in the wake of the student uprising in France in May 1968, obliging his audience to confront the arguments and then make up their own minds. Griffiths recognises that there are different ways of looking at the issues and these are the central theme and the dramatic pivot of the play. In *Comedians* (1976), Griffiths works with the kind of humour that is dominant in many working-class clubs, and which will be familiar to most of his audience through popular comedians in clubs and on television, in order to explore with the audience the woman-hating and racist nature of much of that humour.

Thinking about the reader means recognising that readers will interpret what is written according to diverse ideological perspectives. As we show at the end of this chapter, writers cannot take for granted that readers are going to accept unproblematically the script with which they present readers.

Being considerate towards the reader

By 'being considerate towards the reader' we mean that writers have to take care that the way in which they write makes the task of reading as easy and as interesting as possible. How this is done will in part depend upon the genre of the writing. In the context of writing a play for the stage, the writer is writing for the producer, the director, the leading actor who will read the play in advance of it being produced, and for eventual audiences 'out there in the dark'. As Griffiths says:

> In my case I want the reader to be able to have a dramatic experience of the text through reading. It's like, you know, producing your first audience, and so on the page you need

to surprise, to stimulate, to intrigue, to weave the reader's attention into the piece that you're writing to get the reader on the journey.

(Griffiths 1993)

In writing plays the writer has to construct the play, its plot and themes and its characters in such a way that the audience will want to stay with it, get engaged in it and its meanings, but also be entertained by it and the drama of it. For example, decisions about how much to tell the audience at the beginning, to get them hooked, are important. Part of the enjoyment of watching/ reading a play is anticipating how things are going to work out, how the story is going to develop, so the writer must not give too much away too soon. In academic writing, on the other hand, it is an important part of being considerate towards the reader that the writer share the conclusion with the writer at the beginning. This is so that the reader can measure what the writer says against the signalled intentions and does not have to struggle too much to work out what those intentions were. Uncertainty and ambiguity are less tolerated in factual and argumentative writing than in fiction.

In more general terms, 'being considerate' towards the reader also includes things like making sure that handwriting is legible, that spelling follows the conventional rules, that syntax is that of standardised written English, that language choices are 'appropriate' to the type of writing and that there is 'appropriate' signposting of intentions, connections between ideas and across the text. But as we have said elsewhere (Chapter 8), the conventions and norms of what is appropriate are socio-cultural constructs (see also Fairclough 1992c), and not everyone learns to operate these conventions, or wants to adopt them. So a broader and more complex interpretation of the notion of being considerate to the reader is needed. This includes, we believe, paying close attention to the potential disaffection of the reader because of the unquestioning adoption of conventions that have long been established but that can in fact be highly offensive. Readers may be disaffected in any, or all, of three ways, as outlined below.

The way in which the reader is positioned

A writer positions readers by the language choices s/he makes. An example of this is that if a writer uses predominantly factive modality (unmodified simple present tense or past tense that is presenting what s/he writes as 'the truth') s/he positions the reader into acceptance of this 'truth'. Student readers or less experienced readers are particularly vulnerable to this positioning because of the power relations between themselves and the perceived 'authorities' that they are reading. Being considerate to the reader involves making space for the readers' own intentions and interpretations.

Expressions like 'if we look at X we find that Y', which are common in textbooks and newspaper editorials, are another example of this kind of positioning.

Readers from other cultures sometimes feel that the British academic practice of writers frequently signposting their intentions and connections between their ideas positions the reader as a 'poor reader', treating the reader 'as an idiot'. (This is the response we got from, for example, a French student and also from a Greek student in workshops we ran in 1996 on Dissertation Writing.) So being considerate towards the reader involves drawing the difficult and fine line between being helpful and being patronising.

The way in which the world is represented

Writers appear to be imposing a view of the world on readers. An obvious example is the use of sexist language and any language that presents powerless groups of people in a stereotyped and/or unfavourable light. By using racist language in its articles, *The Sun* newspaper positions its readers as xenophobic; it presupposes a homogeneous monoethnic readership with a shared ideology that imagines 'the other' as enemy.

Writers often impose a particular view by presenting only one side on complex issues – or, more typically, two sides, which masquerades as fair writing, when in fact many more sides to the argument often exist but are excluded for convenience of argument or ideology: closure rather than openness. Being considerate to the reader involves reconsidering stereotyped representations of the world and of social identities and relations within it.

The way in which the writer presents him/herself

Writers construct, or mask, their own identity as they write, which in turn affects the reader. Being considerate to the reader includes writers being more honest about their own positions when they are writing, rather than adopting the questionable conventional practices of so-called objectivity, typical of journalism and so-called factual writing. Deborah Cameron, a feminist linguist, argues for a greater sense of responsibility towards the reader in academic writing: writers taking responsibility for their own ideas and positions and showing respect for their reader, which includes giving the reader space (Cameron 1985).

THE WRITER'S RESPONSIBILITY TO THE READER

By 'responsibility to the reader' we mean the decisions that writers take in order to show (or hide) their own views and attitudes – taking responsibility for the ideas they are expressing and not, for example, hiding behind expressions such as 'it is widely believed that' in academic writing. Writers occasionally make their own position explicit to readers. For example, Cameron (1985) makes very explicit to the reader what her own feminist standpoint is in a preface entitled 'On Demystification' (an extract is reproduced on the next page). She criticises what she considers to be bad academic practices that mystify the reader. She sets out to create a different, more transparent relationship with her readers. She does this in a number of ways, but in particular she tries to make it very clear what her own opinions are. In other words, she tries not to disguise 'opinion' as 'fact' by using impersonal so-called objective language, as is common in much academic writing.

The extract from Cameron's book is, we think, a good example of a writer taking very clear responsibility for the opinions that she is expressing (for other examples of feminist positions on this, see Mills and others 1989, and Skeggs (ed.) 1995). She has drawn upon some of the conventions in academic writing in a creative way and has made a conscious decision to challenge the dominant practice of depersonalising ideas. This decision is the result of a strong commitment to the concepts of academic responsibility, democracy and feminism. This strong commitment is revealed by the language choices that she makes in the preface itself, such as the use of the pronoun 'I' to make it clear that she takes responsibility for the ideas that she is putting forward (not hiding behind the academic 'we' that is often used in single-authored writing).

169

Intellectual mystification occurs when a writer, to put herself in a position of authority, denies the reader sufficient resources to understand and dispute what she says. It can be done in a number of ways.

For example, the writer may leave unexplained and taken for granted the conceptual framework she is working in, or may present it as a given rather than something open to question. Or she may depersonalise herself, hiding behind the spurious authority of an 'objective commentator' by not making it clear where she stands, politically and intellectually, in relation to the ideas she discusses.

In this book, therefore, I have tried to spell out even the most basic assumptions behind the theories I deal with, and to provide enough background to suggest how they may be called into question themselves. I have been at pains to make clear what my own opinions are, and to present the opinions of others scrupulously. To do this I have used a lot of quotation – which allows my subjects to some extent to speak for themselves – and it is important that the reader scrutinise that quotation carefully.

Another important source of mystification in academic writing is the language used. . . .

In this book I have attempted a relatively simple style. . . .

I have avoided language that conceals the presence of the writer and the process of writing. The word *I* appears frequently, and at many points I indicate exactly what argument I am trying to put forward. The aim here is to give the reader every opportunity of saying to herself, 'hold on a minute, that doesn't follow', or 'but what about x?' or 'I can't accept that'. In other words, the reader is encouraged to be an active maker of her own ideas in relation to this book, and not simply a passive consumer of other people's.

I have also avoided offensive and sexist language. . . . Most sex-indefinite and generic references in this book will be *she* and *her*. If there are any men reading who feel uneasy about being excluded, or not addressed, they may care to consider that women get this feeling within minutes of opening the vast majority of books, and to reflect on the effect it has.

An extract from 'On Dymystification', the Preface to Feminism and Linguistic Theory (Cameron 1985: vii–ix)

Cameron constructs a particular social relationship with her readers by her use of the pronoun 'she' as the generic. This is done, we believe, both in order not to offend women readers and to demonstrate to those men who find it offensive how women have felt about the traditional use of 'he' as a generic. She makes extensive use of quotations so that the readers themselves can check whether they agree or not with her interpretations. We suggest that Cameron is constructing her readers either as women who will share her ideological presuppositions about, for example, language and gender issues and feminist views on the construction of knowledge, or as men who either share or have to rethink their attitudes to these issues.

We now identify some of the linguistic realisations of writers taking responsibility for their ideas. Texts are more or less authoritative, more or less believable, in part because of the language choices that writers make in connection with the certainty of their assertions. This aspect of language is called 'modality' by linguists such as Halliday and Fowler, and it is central to the writer–reader relationship. There have been various attempts to categorise the linguistic devices that writers can draw on in order to show – or hide – the strength of commitment to their ideas (e.g. Fowler and others 1979, Thompson and Ye 1991). Based upon these and our own work in this area we propose the following categories:

1 *modal adverbs*
   e.g perhaps, decidedly, questionably
   Ex: 'The nurses' decision to go on strike was *unquestionably* irresponsible.'
2 *evaluative adjectives/adjectivals*
   e.g. sort of, undeniable, plausible, tentative
   Ex: 'There is *undeniable* evidence that insider dealing has taken place.'
3 *modal auxiliaries*
   e.g. can/could, may, must
   Ex: 'Smoking *can* cause cancer.'
4 *lexical verbs*
   e.g. think, suppose, suggest, agree, realise
   Ex: 'These results *suggest* the following conclusions.'
5 *context-dependent nouns*
   (nouns that summarise and categorise previous text)
   e.g. difficulty, problem, factor, comment, view, variable, issue, explanation

Ex: 'In his speech the German Speaker recalled the events leading up to Kristallnacht and appeared to justify them. This *issue* has deeply angered many Germans and the Speaker has resigned.'

6 *passivisation*

e.g. compare 'It *is* widely *believed* that . . . '
with   'I believe that . . . '

7 *appeals to authority*

e.g. quoting, paraphrasing and attributing
Ex: *Kress* argues that . . .

8 *lexical choice*

e.g. compare 'collateral damage'
with   'civilian deaths'

Fowler and colleagues argued that such features are particularly revealing of the underlying ideology of the text. The term 'ideology' is here used in the sense of 'a systematic body of ideas, organized from a particular view' (Kress and Hodge 1979: 6). Writers intentionally or unintentionally show the reader through their language choices how far they subscribe to particular views, how certain they are of what they are saying, and also how subjective or objective a view of knowledge they have. Giving careful thought to the use of these devices is part of the writer's responsibility to the reader.

Checklists of this kind can be useful instruments in language awareness-raising (Clark and Ivanič 1991; Clark and others 1991). However, they can be criticised (Clark 1984) on the grounds that they seem to presuppose that the writer's intentions override the reader's interpretations. That is, they embody a deterministic view of the relationship between writer and reader and of the production therefore of meaning. They are rather mechanistic and do not direct attention to what happens at the interface between reader and text. Texts are 'multi-meaninged' (Vološinov 1973), that is, open to interpretation (see also Fairclough 1996) and require an alternative, dynamic view of the writer–reader relationship, situated within structural relations of power. In the next section we will try to explain this by looking at the writer–reader relationship from the point of view of writer control and reader compliance or resistance, within a wider view of text as socially produced and interpreted.

WRITING AND CONTROL

We suggest that writers with positions of prestige or power in society, and who represent and reproduce the dominant views and beliefs in that society, constantly draw on the presuppositions or assumptions of the dominant ideologies and assume them to be natural. These views and assumptions are presented to the reader as 'common sense', and they are difficult to resist. One way to understand what this means and how it works is to refer to the concept of 'script' (Schank and Abelson 1977). Scripts are mental representations of stereotyped events, social subjects, objects, etc. Associated with these scripts are the ways of wording them (appropriate vocabulary, metaphor, etc.). Most people share certain scripts because they are conventions that they learn, often unconsciously, through schooling, through their families and through other socialising institutions. However, some social groups have different scripts for the same event. For example, Deborah Cameron resists the dominant masculine script for how to be an academic writer, and the corresponding discourse choices she makes demonstrate that. Social groups struggle for their mental representations of events to become accepted as the 'best' ones, and in that sense we can say that scripts are ideologically constructed and are a site of struggle.

Because readers do not necessarily share the same scripts as the writers they read, writer control over the reader is not straight-forward or unproblematic. In the previous section we mentioned the checklist of features that Fowler and others produced to show how writers could control their readers through language choice. We suggested, however, as they also recognise in later work, that this list by itself ran the risk of describing the writer–reader relationship in an over-mechanical or deterministic way. Applying this list uncritically inevitably leads to the notion of a passive reader who plays no role in the construction of the meaning of the text. A great deal of work on the dynamic nature of reading and the role of the reader has been done (see Wallace 1992a among others). It is now widely recognised that different social groups experience the world differently, and so often interpret it and word it differently. These different interpretations of the world lead to what Vološinov (1973) calls a 'struggle over meaning': a struggle, that is, over whose meaning prevails.

The most obvious examples of the 'struggle over meaning' are

173

words like 'terrorist' and 'freedom fighter', where the choice of word to refer to the same person or group will depend upon the writer/speaker's attitude towards the action of that person/group. Texts become an 'arena of struggle', and the resolutions of the struggle over meaning between writer and reader depend, as Hall (1980) argues, on the decoding positions of the reader as much as on the encoding position of the writer.

Hall refers to 'three hypothetical positions' for decoding (same book: 136 ff.): these positions may vary with the same reader within one text or from one text to another. For example, a reader may start reading a text from one 'position' but gradually shift to another/ others. Although these refer to reading positions, and are not directly related to the act of writing, we explain them below because they help to demonstrate that the writer–reader relationship is not one of straightforward control between the powerful writer and the less powerful reader (see also Fairclough 1996 for more details on the issue of the openness of texts and interpretation).

The hegemonic decoding position

This means that the reader decodes the message written in terms of the view of the world in which it has been encoded. That is, the reader is 'operating inside the dominant code' and shares the writer's underlying assumptions or what Hall calls the 'ideological presuppositions'. These are the linked, but unstated, taken-for-granted propositions that have to be believed to be true before the stated proposition can be accepted as true. These underlying assumptions are part of the commonly agreed beliefs and values that bind together into one seemingly homogeneous society social groups that actually have conflicting interests (see Chapter 2 in this volume). By incorporating these beliefs and values into their writing and taking them for granted, that is not making them overt, writers draw and position the reader into a complicit acceptance of those values.

The negotiated decoding position

In this position, the reader acknowledges the legitimacy of the position of the writer and shares it in principle, but contests the position in relation to his/her own self or challenges the domain of application. The reader is full of contradictions in this position, as different subject positions or identities are called up by the text colliding with his/her varied experience.

The oppositional decoding position

In this mode the reader does not share the beliefs and values expressed or presupposed by the writer, but rejects them and reinterprets what s/he reads according to his/her own set of beliefs and values. For example, where a text in a national newspaper sympathetic to the government refers to 'the national interest', the reader who does not share the same political viewpoint or indeed the same pretence of a 'united' and 'unitary' country may read it as 'class interest', or as 'the interest of a particular group'.

This approach undermines the notion of the automatic fit between writer intentions and reader meanings, or textual determinism, where the reader has little or no power over meaning. At the same time it shows how important the concept of ideological presupposition is in determining just how much control writers have over their readers. When writers draw on presumed commonly agreed beliefs and values in writing and do not make them explicit or do not open them up to challenge by the reader, they are potentially reinforcing them in the minds of the readers. This in part explains how dominant ideas remain dominant and how hegemony is maintained. If we return to Hall, and our argument in Chapter 2, the important thing to recognise is that the dominant, or hegemonic, positions are more frequently expressed than oppositional ones – particularly in writing – and the likelihood of readers decoding from an oppositional position is consequently greatly reduced. As we showed in Chapter 2, in Britain the majority of newspapers usually represent the point of view of the powerful groups, and so there is often a lack of easily available alternative sources of information or of different models of society. (See Fairclough 1996 for a fuller discussion of heterogeneity of texts and openness of interpretation; epistemological relativism versus judgemental relativism.) For example, in the academic context, most textbooks are written from within the acceptable parameters of the discipline. It consequently becomes very difficult for the reader to have a different point of view.

Romy did some research (Clark 1984) to try to find out what people say about a given text and what they point to in it when they try to explain or justify their own particular interpretations of it. The research was carried out as part of her study of reader response to press coverage of a controversial issue: 'Jubilant bosses, jubilant miners, or, what the papers say'. It appeared, from this research, that readers quite easily recognise surface features, such as nouns and adjectives, as carrying a 'point of view', but find it very hard to recognise 'deeper' features and their significance. In addition, despite considerable expressed scepticism about the press and its 'truthfulness', the readers in this study seemed to believe that the representation of events in the texts provided were just 'descriptions', therefore true. Lexical features (nouns, lexical verbs and adjectives) were the most common feature mentioned, and in Figure 7.1 we show the full list of the things that eight people mentioned. (The actual terminology, e.g. 'lexical item', was not used with the informants, but they were asked to point to bits of text that they found significant. The responses were subsequently categorised in the terms shown in the table.) None of the readers pointed to any 'deeper' features as indicating point of view, truthfulness, or strength of commitment, such as modality, transitivity, transformations, ideological presuppositions, intertextuality, etc. (see Clark 1993b and 1995 for a discussion of these).

One of the findings of this small study was that the majority of the readers found it extremely difficult to recognise and discuss the effects of language use in the construction of meaning and reader positioning. It is very hard for most people to unpack the ideological presuppositions and other significant discoursal features of written text in order to arrive at a critical reading. Only those readers who had clear alternative sources of information and experience were able to both recognise and challenge the position set up in one of the texts that told the story from the dominant point of view. These findings are confirmed by our teaching experience, which is why we believe Critical Language Awareness work is so important (see, for example, Ivanič 1988; Janks 1993a; Wallace 1992b; Clark 1992, 1993b, 1995), as we discuss in Chapter 9.

In academic writing, the control is reversed. When students are writing academic assignments it is the reader (i.e. the teacher) who has more institutional power. Just as established authors have higher status than the majority of their readers, so teacher readers

Items	Subjects								
	4	*8*	*5*	*6*	*2*	*3*	*7*	*1*	*total*
Lexical	13	21	10	10	12	18	3	2	89
Figures	3	5	5	4	1				18
Naming	2	4	6	4	1				17
Textual	4	1	2	3					10
Dialect	4		1	1	1				7
Metaphor	5				1				6
Weighting	1		1			1	2		5
Omission		1	1		3				5
Implication	2		1		1				4
Verb forms					1	1			2
Attribution					1				1
Total	34	32	27	22	21	21	5	2	164

Figure 7.1 The number of times different textual features were identified as responsible for communicating points of view
Source: Clark 1984: 51

in the academic context have higher status than the students whose writing they read. In addition to the power that all readers have to make their own meanings as they read, teacher readers also have the additional power to assess and give grades. This is important because it means that student writers have a different sense of responsibility and commitment from 'real' writers. They often assume that they have nothing to contribute to their reader's knowledge, and therefore have no personal involvement in what they are writing.

This question of the relative control over meaning that the writer and the reader exercise is crucial and leads us to the final part of this chapter: the reader's prerogative.

YES, BUT . . . THE READER'S PREROGATIVE

We end this chapter with some extracts from two readings of the same text which illustrate the different decoding positions we outlined above. The text is an extract from Trevor Griffith's play *The Gulf Between Us: The Truth and Other Fictions* (Griffiths 1992) and is reproduced below, with line numbers for easy reference. The extract comes towards the end of the second act of the play. Dr Aziz is an education administrator in an unspecified country in the Gulf. A bomb has destroyed a shrine sheltering children from a creche for which she is responsible. The mothers, off stage, are calling out their children's names. Aziz has just found the charred remains of the children. The extract is the final part of her (two-page) speech after this discovery.

DR AZIZ: (*To sky*) I have travelled in your countries, taken   1
food in your homes, shared feelings and hopes, thought
of you as brothers and sisters in the long struggle for
human dignity. And I have seen you, Mr President, with
your sensitive expression and sorrowing eyes on my   5
television screen . . . And I had forgotten, what you will
not acknowledge but the world knows, that yours is
a country forged and shaped in brutal genocide, the
destruction of whole peoples, lives, customs, beliefs,
men, women and children who had learned respect for   10
the place that nourished them, who had learned to
tread gently on this good earth . . .

A WOMAN'S VOICE: (*A child's name*) Ghazi.

DR AZIZ: (*To sky still*) You destroy your past with these
acts. Your future too. Wars only have beginnings. No   15
endings.

ANOTHER VOICE: (*Another child*) Samzi.

DR AZIZ: What kind of world have you in mind, Mr
President, Mr Prime Minister, Mr Secretary-General,
what kind of world do you work to preserve, where   20
a mere 20 per cent on your side of this tiny planet
take and hold and consume a full 80 per cent of its
bounty? Tell me, please. I would know this. I would
know this . . .

VOICE: (*Name*) Nidal.   25
(*She looks down again at the charcoal figure.*)
DR AZIZ: Qassem. Nidal. Four years one month. Hard of
  hearing. I will pray to my God for you, child. (*She looks
  up again.*) And what will you say to yours? No no no,
  please, this will not be justified by invoking the evil   30
  of my rulers or the unavoidability of your 'collateral
  damage', gentlemen. This world is full of evil rule, look
  at those you bought or bribed or bullied to give you
  houseroom here, look at those you would restore to
  their thrones, and tell me how we are worse. As for the   35
  unavoidable, how stupid, how very stupid you must
  think us, to imagine a decent human being believing
  you for one second, when you have told us and you
  have shown us your ability to tell the time on a child's
  wristwatch from one hundred miles, the side a woman   40
  parts her hair, the stubble on a man's face. We have a
  holy place, a place of worship, a place your cameras tell
  every day is filled with children. And you send a missile,
  not a wayward falling bomb, to burn it up . . . In the
  name of God? In the name of humankind? In the   45
  name of . . .
A FINAL VOICE: Suad.

An extract from 'The Gulf Between Us: The truth and other fictions'
(Griffiths 1992: 48–9)

Two readers responded independently to the text. One reader
(Romy) read it in a predominantly hegemonic decoding position,
that is, within the same ideological code as the playwright's – as
confirmed by the writer's comments on her reading. The other
reader (Roz) read the text in a predominantly oppositional position, that is, not sharing the writer's ideological presuppositions.
Both readers focused independently on the same features of the
text for their comments but responded differently to these (for
details of the methodology see Clark 1993a). In Figure 7.2 we give
some of their responses to this extract to illustrate the differences
between the readings. The bold numbers 1–4 signal sets of
comments by the two readers and the author which are referring

more or less to the same part of the text, and/or to the same aspects of it. The first column contains Romy's comments on the text, with line numbers to indicate which lines of the extract are being referred to, and headings to indicate which linguistic features of the text she is commenting on. The middle column contains Griffiths' responses to Romy's reading. Roz's comments are in the last column, also with headings.

This example of different readings illustrates the point that however carefully a writer tries to put a particular understanding of an issue to readers, or to an audience, the readers will accept or resist that understanding by activating their own ideologies and experiences. Griffiths' final comments in a sense acknowledge this. To sum up our view, we want to argue that where ideologies and/or experiences coincide there is likely to be little reader resistance; where the reader/audience is less committed to a pre-existing point of view or is unsure of what their position is and is more disposed to listen to the arguments, and where the arguments convince, there may be some shifting of position; but where the clash of ideologies and experience is great, the resistance is more likely to be complete.

Romy: a reader who shares the ideological presuppositions of the author	Trevor Griffiths: the author of the play	Roz: a reader who does not share the ideological presuppositions of the author
1.	1.	1.
intertextuality		
lines 29–32 This is an interesting example of intertextuality. Aziz pre-empts attempts by the audience reader to justify the war using the main arguments used by Bush et al and rehearsed in the media . . . which you, through Aziz, and I do not share. But it is an important bit of dialogue for the audience reader to engage in and the point is reinforced by reference to the contradictory nature of the justificatory accounts. The repetition of the adjective 'stupid' would make an opposi-	Yes, what I'm actually doing, I suppose, what's actually happening – and it's good you brought the audience in there – she returns to the sky to whom she's addressing this. In a way, by addressing Bush and Perez de Cuellar and with 'what will you say to yours?' I think the audience takes it that she's addressing them, particularly as she's speaking out across the audience. As the audience begins to gather its responses, it's almost as if she hears them and she's heard Bush and says: Don't use those	*Pronouns 'we' and 'you' positioning the reader* I felt an undercurrent of annoyance at the 'we' and 'you' being partly individuals, and partly 'we the Iraqi people in general' which includes the rulers. The same is true of 'you' on the other side. Of course this is absolutely intended, but 'you' is sometimes somebody on stage, and sometimes people in the audience.
line 36 tional reader very uncomfortable, I should think, because s/he would have to shake off the adjective 'stupid'.	arguments [for example about the unavoidability of] collateral damage we've already heard in the first act.	

Romy: a reader who shares the ideological presuppositions of the author	Trevor Griffiths: the author of the play	Roz: a reader who does not share the ideological presuppositions of the author
2.	**2.**	**2.**
ideological presuppositions I share all Aziz's presuppositions about the Allied countries fighting the war, and am (your) persuaded by her arguments.	that's right . . . [and what she's saying is] please don't talk about how evil my rulers are as the justification of killing children and do not talk about the unavoidability of this. She's developing the argument: first of all the 'world is full of evil rule', you've only got to look at those you now fight this war alongside, 'those you bribed and bullied to give you house room' and those you would 'restore to their thrones and tell me how they are worse.' She's not saying that we're not as bad, she's saying: tell me how we're worse that you've singled us out for this. And that's about evil rulers.	[this is] very striking because I do invoke the evil of Aziz's rulers as certainly as deserving of the blame for what happened as anybody else. So this is very different from anything else, which is telling me that my political view will not be justified, not saying why. It just dismisses it. [*Interviewer: What about the bit of text that follows?*] 'This world is full of evil.' I suppose this could be why it's not satisfactory to invoke *just* the evil rulers [as a justification] maybe, but certainly not enough to tell me I'm wrong to involve the evil rulers as part of the blame.
lines 6–12 and 18–24		
lines 29–46	this bit in particular reinforces my identification with her position. The logic is presented as unarguable-against, and I agree	
		Pronouns 'we' and 'you' positioning the reader 'look at those you bought or

Romy: a reader who shares the ideological presuppositions of the author	*Trevor Griffiths: the author of the play*	*Roz: a reader who does not share the ideological presuppositions of the author*
		bribed': I can't tell who the 'you' is there but I feel uncomfortable with it. I feel that 'you' is 'me' and I don't necessarily want to be associated with whoever bribed or bullied so I'm not totally accepting that … then 'tell me how we are worse': because 'we' has been used so often to mean Dr Aziz and mothers and children, that 'we' is very annoying to me. It asks me to say of course you, Aziz, the children and mothers aren't worse, but I think your ruler is worse and it doesn't allow me to make that distinction. It's part of the heart-string plucking.
3.	**3.**	**3.**
intertextuality the term 'collateral damage' was used a lot in the media.	Now, as to these unavoidable collateral damages, well let's think about it. We're not talking	*intertextuality not recognised* I don't know why 'collateral damage' is in scare quotes:
lines 31–32		

Romy: a reader who shares the ideological presuppositions of the author	Trevor Griffiths: the author of the play	Roz: a reader who does not share the ideological presuppositions of the author	Ideological presuppositions / reading position
	about a wayward falling bomb here where you cannot precisely pinpoint [the target], we're talking about a thing which is laser guided and which comes precisely to its target. At least, that is what you [the US] have told us for many years now.	I didn't recognise it.... You say two things but because I do invoke the evil of the rulers it suggests that I've got to be positioned into this as well ... thinking that the collateral damage was unavoidable....	I'm inclined to believe, in spite of all the apparent technical wonder, that one or two things which I abhor *were* unavoidable. So I *am* that 'decent human being', but the text is telling me I'm *not* for being inclined to believe that.... I'm not totally taken in by arguments [of unavoidability] nor am I hardly swayed at all by his sort of
4.	4.	4.	4.
lines 35–41 TV in particular has made much of the precision bombing.	That's right, so you meant to bomb a holy place, that's what you're saying, and you meant to bomb it, presumably because you believed it was being used for our defence in the war. But if you knew that, if you knew that there were soldiers using this place you had to know that there were children and mothers and that's precisely the case of the air raid shelter [in Baghdad]. They may well have seen soldiers using that		

Romy: a reader who shares the ideological presuppositions of the author	Trevor Griffiths: the author of the play	Roz: a reader who does not share the ideological presuppositions of the author
	place. They could not *not* have seen hundreds of civilians going into that place as well. So I just give my logic. But if they're [the audience] still resisting me at the end they've got to come up with something different [from the argument that the war was unavoidable or that Saddam was like Hitler and so had to be punished]; they won't accept the adjective 'stupid'.	rhetoric that it was avoidable, therefore on purpose, therefore an evil act by people who are enemies of all decent thinking people. I don't accept that.

Figure 7.2 Different readings of the extract from *The Gulf Between Us: The Truth and Other Fictions*
Source: Clark 1993a: 203–5

CONCLUSION

In this chapter we explored the complex relationship between the writer and the reader. We first used Halliday's framework to explain the role of the writer–reader relationship in writing. We distinguished between two inter-related meanings of 'considering the reader' which we had identified as a key component of the writing process in Chapter 4: bearing in mind the reader while writing, and being considerate towards the reader. We listed some of the linguistic devices available to writers for establishing their relationship with their readers. We elaborated on both the writer's responsibilities to the reader and the reader's rights in responding to the writer. We then examined the relative power relations between writer and reader and the crucial role of ideology in the relationship between intended meanings and reader interpretations. We concluded the chapter with an extended example of two different readings of the same text, which demonstrates that ideology is the key factor in that relationship.

We have emphasised the view that the writer–reader relationship is not an optional extra, but an ingredient that cannot be neglected when describing writing and considering how to teach it. We believe that 'the right to write' includes the right to develop a role as a writer in relation to a range of readers. It involves not only establishing your own identity as a writer, but also recognising your reader(s)' right to respond critically to what you have written. It involves learning how to take responsibility for the position of relative power a writer usually has in relation to readers. It involves recognising the crucial difference between writing as a student for a reader who will also be your assessor, and writing in most other settings. Finally, it involves developing the confidence to take a stand against the pressure some readers exert on writers to conform to particular conventions.

8

ISSUES OF CORRECTNESS AND STANDARDISATION IN WRITING

INTRODUCTION

In this chapter we discuss the key political issue of standardisation as it concerns written language, arguing that the insistence on 'correctness' in spelling, punctuation and sentence structure has a disciplinary, normative and discriminatory role in social life.[1] Conventional spelling and punctuation particularly have the symbolic function of representing social acceptability and educational achievement rather than having intrinsic value in their own right. We are claiming that the moral hysteria that surrounds these issues is misplaced and extremely damaging. It condemns those who have difficulty with mechanical aspects of written language, and it places teachers in the impossible position of having to perpetuate the hold these beliefs have over society in order to ensure the life-chances of those they are teaching.

Arguments about correctness and standards frequently erupt in the media in Britain and, according to people we meet from other countries, almost everywhere in the world. The most recent example in the UK at the time of writing is Melanie Phillips (1996) who claims that children are being betrayed by lack of attention to spelling and grammar. Cameron in her book entitled *Verbal Hygiene* (1995) makes a detailed analysis of the political underpinnings of what she calls 'The great grammar crusade' in British educational politics between 1987 and 1994. This was a period of conservative rule during which politicians, journalists, employers, members of the public quoted in the media and even Prince Charles referred to 'grammar' and 'grammar teaching' as 'a problem'. They claimed, and found statistics and stories to provide evidence, that people were failing to conform to 'the rules of grammar', and that permissive teaching methods were responsible for this state of affairs. Cameron spells out in detail how these 'rules of grammar' came to symbolise a whole interconnected set of conservative values and standards:

> conservatives use 'grammar' as the metaphorical correlate for a cluster of related political and moral terms: *order, tradition, authority, hierarchy* and *rules.*

> (Cameron 1995: 95)

and

> Grammar was made to symbolize various things for its conservative proponents: a commitment to traditional values as a basis for social order, to 'standards' and 'discipline' in the classroom, to moral certainties rather than moral relativism and to cultural homogeneity rather than pluralism.

> (same book: 111)

She argues that this symbolism lies at the heart of the 'moral panic' that evolved during this period over the 'state of linguistic emergency' (p. 89) about low standards of grammar usage and grammar teaching. Her argument is important because it explains why there is from time to time so much fuss about a small set of grammatical features which are claimed to characterise 'correct English' – a tiny fraction of all the grammatical features of the English language as a whole.

In political movements such as 'the great grammar crusade', the symbolic significance of grammar at a subconscious level is usually compounded by fundamental misunderstandings about language: about the role of context in shaping language use, about the relationship between function and form, about the relationship between identity and language use, and about the nature of language change. Firstly, they do not take account of the role of context, purpose, social identities and social relations in language use. We have already discussed how every instance of language use has its own particular configuration of production conditions (see Chapter 4), its own purposes (see Chapter 5), and is affected by the identity of its writers and readers (see Chapters 6 and 7). It is these that shape the way in which the grammatical resources of the language are used, not some criterion of 'correctness' based on one particular type of language use. Secondly, those who complain about falling standards are resistant to language change, assuming that forms should not change over time; holding, for example, to outmoded spellings such as 'all right' as if it is intrinsically better than the increasingly used 'alright'.

We suggest that written language plays a particular part in such campaigns for standardisation, correctness and grammar teaching. Those proclaiming that standards are falling are often referring to the spelling, punctuation and sentence structure of a limited range of *written* types of language. Consequently, written language often has a normative, disciplinary and discriminatory role in social life. Conventions for written language act as the arbiter for correctness in spoken language. Only writing in a particular handwriting, particular spelling, particular grammar and lexis has high status. Adherence to standard conventions in these technical aspects of written language has come to be used as a criterion for assessing people's intelligence and even moral worth. This often has a gatekeeping function, as we discussed in Chapter 5 (see also Cook-Gumperz 1986 for this argument).

In the rest of this chapter we first comment on the way in which aspects of writing are used to police the way in which people speak, and then discuss issues of correctness and standardisation in relation to handwriting, spelling, punctuation and grammar in writing.

WRITTEN LANGUAGE AS THE ARBITER OF STANDARDS

Many in 'the complaint tradition' treat the written form of the language as if it were the ideal form of spoken language. Those who harp on about what they claim to be 'grammatical correctness' in spoken English often say such things as

'pronounce it as it is spelt',
'use proper sentences',
'no double negatives',
'subjects and verbs must agree',
'no recapitulatory pronouns',
'don't end a sentence with a preposition'.

They assume that standards of pronunciation can be judged by how close it is to spelling, and that standards of spoken sentence structure can be judged by how close it is to the sort of sentence structure to be found in academic writing. Neither of these positions is tenable from the perspective of linguistics. Phonology, morphology and the history of English show that the relationship between sound and symbol in English is extremely complex. In all languages, the faster we talk, the more the phonetic and graphic representations of words diverge. Pronunciation can be judged only according to the purposes and circumstances of its use, including what identities speakers intend to maintain and project, in the particular social setting in which they are speaking.

Insisting on 'correct' ways of speaking that are modelled on written language is linked to the obsession with preserving a 'standard English', since many aspects of written English are already standardised. Particularly, the spelling of 90 per cent of English words has, according to Gerry Knowles (personal communication), been relatively standardised since the revolutionary decades (1640–60), when correct spelling of English words became a part of the cult of Englishness in the court of 'Queen Bess', in opposition to all things Catholic, and therefore Latin. (Discussion of the effects of the revolutionary decades on the English language can be found in Knowles forthcoming.) Fortunately, it is easy to upset those who want to insist on particular pronunciations by appealing to the conventions of written language. For example, the spelling of the words 'any' and 'many' do not phonetically represent the variety of English spoken by the middle class of south-east England, but the variety spoken by natives of Dublin. Similarly, the spelling of the word 'bath' most closely represents the variety of English spoken in south-west England, and that of 'book' represents Lancashire English. Consequently, those who do want to appeal to the conventions of written English as the arbiter of pronunciation soon find themselves in a quandary as to whose pronunciation they are advocating.

What counts as a complete sentence in continuous prose, and the attendant punctuation conventions, are more or less standardised, although the punctuation of complex clause relations defies standardisation, as we discuss later. But a whole tradition of linguistic theory, represented by the work of Chomsky (for example, 1965), underpins the belief that there are grammatical structures that are 'correct': a highly developed and still dominant approach to the study of language involves using intuitive judgements of acceptability of grammatical structures. The structures that these linguists study are often far removed from those used in speech or in most writing, but they do represent a statement that the language consists of a repertoire of acceptable structures, and that there are other structures that are unacceptable. So in this respect, there is a tradition of linguistic theory which fuels lay beliefs about correctness, and it is easy to move from this position into viewing written language as a criterion by which to judge the grammaticality of speech. In many types of writing – those involving the use of continuous prose – grammatical structures are usually presented in full, and so they are closer than those found in most speech to those recognised as part of the repertoire of the language. This provides the 'complainers' with a powerful argument for demanding that people should 'speak more like they write'. However, in this they do not have backing from linguists. Most linguists would agree that the cognitive processing involved in the production of speech and writing is different; many go further and point out major differences in social function and social context which affect syntax, emphasising differences within speech and within writing as well as differences between them.

Finally, there are some prescriptions, which 'complainers' want to import from written to spoken language, that are not essential characteristics of written language in the first place, as we argue later. In all these ways, and more, written forms of English have been appealed to as a way of insisting on adherence to a spoken 'standard'. We hope that, in this section, we have gone some way towards debunking the belief that it is possible to do this. Just because written English has become more standardised than spoken English has, that is no reason to require the spoken to conform to the written. Further, we suggest that we should hold the standardisation of *written* English up for critical scrutiny, and not necessarily conform to the dominant conventions. In the following sections we examine the issue of correctness and the effects of standardisation in relation to different aspects of written language.

HANDWRITING

Handwriting is the most physical part of writing, the most connected to the body rather than the mind of the writer. It is consequently part of what Bourdieu (1977) calls the 'habitus': the bodily disposition of a person (as discussed in Chapter 2). This perhaps explains its potency and the passionate responses it evokes. It is subject to significant social judgements, it is a means of discipline and control in society in general and in the education system, and it is woven into people's sense of their personal identity.

The value-laden expression 'good writing' is more often used to mean neat handwriting than anything to do with meaning. Having 'good writing' in this sense has powerful social meanings. Stories are rife about employers who ask applications for employment to be handwritten, and then make a preliminary short-list based entirely on the 'look' of the handwriting before even reading the content. We have noticed that adults receiving letters from children comment first, and perhaps only, on how neatly it has been written, rather than what it says. We have experienced people making assessments of other people's social status on the basis of their handwriting: treating someone as socially inferior if their writing is untidy in a particular way, or if it is 'too neat'. Neat handwriting is taken to be a token of good work habits, respect for persons, an attention to detail, and generally a 'proper' attitude to life. Paradoxically, and interestingly, extremely untidy handwriting, almost illegible, is taken to be a sign of 'character' or importance: doctors, academics and others of high social standing are generally admired for having idiosyncratic hand-writing (more of this below). But awkward handwriting, laboured, yet with uneven size and spacing, irregular slant of ascenders and descenders, and crossing out is seen as a mark of sloppiness and lack of discipline – just as Cameron was arguing in relation to particular grammatical usages.

We suggest that this belief is very salient in British society, and it both affects and is maintained by practices within the education system. There is an enormous emphasis on neat handwriting in primary education. Children's work is often evaluated in terms of how neatly it has been written. They are frequently reprimanded for untidy handwriting, and comments on handwriting are all too easily and often extended to comments on the child's moral character. While there is no point in championing 'untidy' writing, we would nevertheless want to question this constant emphasis on neatness, sometimes in preference to emphasis on other aspects of writing development. Neatness of handwriting becomes a part of a whole network of bodily regulations within the authoritative context of the school, along with sitting, moving and talking in particular ways. We suggest that over-frequent insistence on neat handwriting – and sometimes on a particular style of handwriting – is in danger of having a homogenising effect on the population and creating docile citizens: a political objective to which nobody would want to admit.

Fortunately, these stipulations are not universally adhered to: the resistant, non-conformist spirit is alive and well where handwriting is concerned. Nevertheless, in combination with other regulatory practices in the classroom, undue attention to neat handwriting can contribute to children growing up to believe that political life is just to do with respecting or resisting authority, rather than active participation in shaping the circumstances that affect them. Teachers are held in a double bind by social attitudes to handwriting: if they do not insist on neatness, they may be in danger of failing to prepare children for the reality that life chances may depend on neat handwriting; but if they do insist on neatness, they are likely to be perpetuating the very attitudes that lead to this inequity, and subjecting children to unnecessary, even damaging, discipline and control, possibly at the expense of fostering other, more empowering aspects of learning to write.

Views on what is proper or acceptable handwriting are subjective and culturally determined: people will differ in what they consider to be good handwriting. This is well illustrated by the way in which it is often possible to tell the nationality of a writer from their handwriting. Differences in handwriting from one nationality to another often contribute to people's sense of national identity, and its opposite face: prejudice and xenophobia. Yet there can be no objective basis for calling one style of handwriting better than another. Even when some criteria for good handwriting have been agreed, meeting them is a matter of degree: someone's handwriting cannot unequivocally be judged correct or incorrect. Teachers who impose what they consider acceptable handwriting styles need to recognise this, and perhaps use it as a basis for critical discussion of the issues associated with neatness that we are raising here.

We suggest that neat handwriting is not actually a mark of respect, good working habits and attention to detail, but simply a by-product of a smooth ride through the education system. Those who have no difficulty with spelling often develop a fluent, and therefore neat, handwriting style independently of any other qualities. By contrast, those who have suffered any serious set-back in relation to basic literacy, particularly people who are constantly worried about whether they are spelling every word correctly, usually have great difficulty with handwriting. Ironically, the very insistence on correctness and neatness is likely to exacerbate the situation, since a fear of making mistakes causes physical tension, which has negative effects on handwriting. Those whose self-confidence with writing has been dented are likely to have untidy handwriting in spite of, almost because of, their most conscientious and determined efforts. When physical tension sets in, their handwriting starts to screw up, literally: their hand movements become cramped; holding the pen feels awkward; the hand gets sweaty and does not travel smoothly from left to right. And as a result their ascenders and descenders are at irregular angles; letters do not flow, but come out at different widths and are inconsistently joined to each other; mistakes of letter formation compound with spelling errors and lead to endless crossings out. We want to suggest that, far from signifying those negative moral qualities that are associated with it, untidy handwriting is often a consequence of extreme efforts to please.

In spite of the educational pressure towards neatness and a relatively homogeneous style of handwriting, people who learn to write without difficulty develop a wide variety of styles. Handwriting is potentially a mark of identity, which explains why teenagers, in Britain at any rate, spend hours trying out their signature, and changing it every week. But by the time they are adults, a distinction develops between the majority who write in more regular styles, and the few who develop distinctive styles of their own. We suggest the privilege of using handwriting as a mark of 'character' is ultimately reserved for those who write confidently from a position of social power. For people who enjoy high social prestige, untidiness is taken to symbolise not sloppiness and a lack of respect, but busy-ness and importance.

Although we know of no research on this topic, we suggest that there is an interesting gender distinction in people's expectations about handwriting. People tend to expect women to have neat handwriting, conforming to the sorts of patterns taught at school, and men to have more idiosyncratic handwriting. It is common to hear such comments as 'He's got very neat handwriting for a man' or, looking at rather irregular handwriting: 'I'm surprised a woman wrote that: it looks like a man's handwriting.' Teachers often comment on the fact that girls learn what they teach about handwriting easily, whereas boys do not. There may be some biological base in this: girls' fine motor skills may develop earlier than boys', or boys may biologically be more resistant to conformism of this sort than girls. But we suggest that the difference is socially constructed: society expects males to be full of character and breaking new ground, whereas females are expected to be more compliant. Girls might be more used than boys to being policed from an early age about neat behaviour in general, and so be patient and painstaking in achieving the neatness required at school. Judging by the handwriting that the two of us have seen in examination papers in a wide variety of educational settings over a period of twenty-five years, there is widespread conformity to these stereotypes.

It is interesting how typewriting/word-processing erases the mark of identity from writing. Some people in some situations avoid typing for this reason: they do not want to seem impersonal. The opposite is also common: some people in some situations choose to type because they are not confident about the identity their handwriting would convey, and prefer to hide it. For people with access to modern word-processors, this distinction breaks down to some extent: the variety of fonts and other layout features available means that typewriting can have almost as much of a personal character to it as handwriting. But typing is always at one remove from the body, the actual person of the writer, and for this reason employers will continue to use handwriting as a screening device, as we discussed above.

We have discussed issues of standardisation, correctness and neatness in handwriting in some detail, partly because we have not seen this issue addressed elsewhere, and we believe it to be an important aspect of the politics of writing. We go on to discuss standardisation and correctness in relation to spelling, punctuation and sentence structure, drawing out similarities and differences between these aspects of writing and what we have said about handwriting.

SPELLING[2]

Like handwriting, spelling is used as a basis for making broad and damaging social judgements. Unconventional spelling can be enough to lose an applicant a job, to get a lower grade for a piece of work at school or even in higher education, to make some people dismiss the writer as 'illiterate'. Spelling is often equated with education: we have heard people refer to others as 'uneducated' if they make a spelling mistake.

Spelling differs from handwriting in that the requirement to adhere to spelling conventions applies to all social groups: prestigious people have no special prerogative allowing them to spell creatively, as they have for untidy handwriting. Poets, pop groups and writers of advertisements can and do use spelling creatively to make particular points and achieve particular effects, but these are characteristics of the type of writing they are doing, rather than the people they are. They would be expected to use conventional spelling on application forms and in business letters, just like everyone else. However, people in authoritative positions can and often do escape from the pressure of being judged on the basis of their spelling by employing clerical staff to deal with spelling and other low-level aspects of writing. This points up the inconsistency in using correct spelling as the arbiter of 'literacy': those who are high-powered users of literacy reserve their energies for the other, more important aspects of it.

Many people are obsessed with correctness of spelling to the exclusion of any other aspect of writing. This is because, unlike handwriting, punctuation or 'grammar', spelling *can* be unequivocally judged right or wrong. Since the publication and wide availability of comprehensive and consistent dictionaries (that is, since Johnson's dictionary of British English in 1755 and Webster's of American English in 1783), it has been possible to appeal to a dictionary for arbitration as to whether a spelling is correct or incorrect. By contrast, good handwriting is a matter of degree, as we discussed above; punctuation and grammar, while possible to judge right or wrong according to conventions, cannot be disentangled from choices of wording, and each application of the conventions is to some extent unique. So spelling is an obvious weapon for those who want to discriminate between 'good' and 'bad' writing, the 'literate' and the 'illiterate'. As we argue in detail in the rest of this section, we believe that using ability to spell according to the conventions as a discriminatory device is linguistically untenable and socially and politically unacceptable. Firstly, there is nothing sacrosanct about the spellings catalogued in the dictionary. Secondly, there is not a consistent relationship between the sounds of words and the letters used to represent them, particularly in the English language. Thirdly, spelling is a mechanical capability which is independent of intelligence, efficiency, creativity and other, more important aspects of literacy and education.

There is nothing sacrosanct about the spellings in the dictionary

It was not always possible to have recourse to a dictionary in order to judge a spelling right or wrong. To use the English language as our example, before the revolutionary decades in the mid-seventeenth century it was accepted that the same word could be spelt in a variety of ways, all of which were recognisable as the intended word, as can be plainly seen in manuscripts written before that time. With no ultimate authority as to how a word should be spelt, the concept of 'correct spelling' was much more flexible, and could not be used as a means of discriminating between people. It is interesting to speculate why spelling did become standardised in Britain in the mid-seventeenth century. Why could we not continue with the practice of spelling words in a variety of ways? Could it be that literacy was spreading to a larger and larger proportion of the population, and those in prestigious positions needed new grounds on which to claim the ignorance of those they viewed as their inferiors? If so, a dictionary which turned spelling into a criterion for literacy was extremely useful. We suggest that there is no intrinsic reason why words should always be spelt in the same way, just as there is no reason why they should always be pronounced in the same way.

Further, the ways in which words are spelt in the dictionary are not established as correct by any defensible criteria but are simply Johnson's personal selections among a range of possible alternatives when he published the first comprehensive dictionary of the language in 1755. Many of the choices he made are arbitrary, and some are inconsistent. For example, no appeal to logic or etymology explains why *clean* is spelt in this way: the choice of 'ean' as opposed to, say, 'een', 'eane' or 'ene' is arbitrary, representing a particular moment in the history of the spelling of the word, which originated from Old English *cl óe ne*, and had been spelt *clene* and *cleane* within the 100 years before Johnson's dictionary, and *cleene* not long before that (according to the *Oxford English Dictionary*). Some spellings that were set in stone in Johnson's dictionary are totally inconsistent, the most obvious example of which is the fact that *receipt* is spelt with a 'p', whereas *deceit* and *conceit* are not. All three words are noun forms of verbs that end in '-ceive', and have cognate nouns ending in '-eption', and are derived from variations of the Latin verb *-cipio, -cipere, -cepi -ceptum*. While etymologists can usually justify the conventional form of a word by appeal to its origins, or by appeal to the set of conventions that Johnson set in stone, there is no intrinsic reason why a particular sound or sound sequence should be represented by a particular symbol or symbol sequence. Comparing English to other languages provides the proof of this.

Spelling is not a correct representation of correct pronunciation

Those who are determined to find ways of branding others as inferior on the grounds of spelling correctness often maintain that you should spell words the way you pronounce them – often the same people who insist that words should be pronounced as they are spelt, which we discussed above. The 'spell as you pronounce, pronounce as you spell' argument is a vicious circle based on complete ignorance of the linguistic characteristics of spoken and written language and the relationship between them. A good English language example of this from the spelling perspective (as opposed to the pronunciation perspective we discussed above) is that many people spell *might have* as 'might of'. Appealing to 'correct pronunciation' here is quite erroneous: there are virtually no linguistic contexts in which anyone says / m a ɪ t h a v / . The phonetic representation of the normal pronunciation of this expression in virtually all contexts is / m a ɪ t ə v / : the word 'have' is pronounced in the way 'of' is usually pronounced, because, as the second word in a verb complex, it is phonetically reduced. Those who make this particular spelling mistake are actually following the dictum 'spell as you pronounce', and it is not coming up with the goods.

The 'spell as you pronounce' dictum falls short for at least half the words of the English language for two linguistic reasons:

1 English is thought to have the most irregular alphabetic spelling system of all languages. It is more regular than any non-alphabetic system: it is not necessary to learn each word of English separately as in Chinese. However, it is not simply a set of sound-symbol correspondences as Italian or Czech spelling is: there are several graphic representations of some sounds, and several different sounds represented by some letters or letter

combinations. English spelling is also affected by patterns related to word structure, word class and the historical origin of words. It would take a book to explain all the spelling systems operating in English; Albrow (1972) is a useful source for this information, and Vallins (1965) describes the relationship between spellings and word origins. The point here is that English spelling is enormously complex: there are approximately 364 ways of spelling the 44 sounds in the language.

2 English pronunciation is highly reduced. Most words of more than one syllable have one or more vowels reduced to the schwa sound (represented phonetically as /ə/). So, for example, in the word *occasion*, the vowels in the first and last syllables cannot be heard as an *o*, but sound /ə/.

While the argument that it is erroneous to insist on spelling as you pronounce is particularly relevant to the spelling of English, it also applies in varying degrees to other languages. Further, pronunciation in all languages varies according to context, varying according to the relationship between the speakers, the nature and purpose of the message, whereas spelling is constant across contexts, and does not carry markers of emotion and urgency. Evidence for this can be seen particularly in close friends' letters to each other, particularly young people, and those communicating on the Internet. Unconventional spellings are often used to represent characteristics that would be carried by pronunciation, particularly prosody, in spoken language. For example, in an e-mail message that Roz recently sent, she wrote 'meeeeting' to represent the way she would have pronounced it to indicate how long and boring it was. So insisting on 'spelling as you pronounce' leads to *un*conventional spelling, not so-called 'correct' spelling.

Spelling ability is not related to other aspects of literacy and education

Being able to spell according to the conventions depends on certain motor functions in the brain, the main one being 'visual memory' – that is, the ability to remember visual patterns. The majority of people – approximately 70 per cent – have an excellent visual memory, and acquire a visual image of most of the spellings they need along with other aspects of their development between the ages of 5 and 15. Other psycho-motor factors are involved in spelling too: auditory memory (ability to remember sound patterns), kinaesthetic memory (ability to remember movements, so that handwriting can help with remembering spellings), and the co-ordination among these sensory inputs. These are physical characteristics of the brain, and not directly related to intelligence or any other cognitive aspects of the brain concerned with the more important matters of communication and content in writing. This is dramatically illustrated by the case of a young woman Roz knew who had had a terrible road accident that damaged her brain, after which she forgot everything she knew. Through painstaking tutoring she learned to read aloud and to spell again perfectly, but she did not understand anything she read, and she did not have any knowledge or ideas to write with her perfect spelling. She had lost the part of her brain that contained 'intelligence', but had not lost the part that contained the motor functions required for learning spellings.

Fortunately there are two trends that are helping people to recognise that spelling is merely a mechanical matter, independent of other aspects of literacy. Firstly, increasingly sophisticated word-processors are able to take over responsibility for a lot of the fine detail of spelling. This means that those who have access to such technology can concentrate on more important matters such as the content of their writing: they do not need to pay so much attention to correct spelling as the machine will do 90 per cent of the work for them. This provides a useful argument against treating the ability to spell as a gatekeeping device. If a machine can do it, surely it is not an essential criterion in selecting the right person for a job.

Secondly, and far more significant for the majority of people, teachers in primary schools are no longer treating spelling as a prerequisite for writing. Most teachers of young children work with a theory of 'emergent spelling', recognising that the majority of children will discover conventional spelling through a process of hypothesis forming and testing over a period of about five years (the classic work on this is Read 1986; others include Hall 1987 Barton 1994). The most important thing teachers can do to foster the learning of spelling by this method is to keep children 'hooked on writing', rather than reprimanding them for all their errors. This approach is sufficient for most children to learn to spell all the words they need in their writing. We suggest that the reason why some children with good visual memories do not 'pick up' spelling is that they do not have enough sense of self-worth or motivation to write, rather than that they need more spellings tested and corrected. Our experience of working with adults with spelling difficulties convinces us that even those who do not have adequate visual memory for 'acquiring' spelling in this way will benefit from this approach; they must not become alienated from the activity of writing, or any amount of extra support with learning spelling will be useless.

In spite of these persuasive arguments against putting such a premium on correct spelling, it is still taken by most to be the primary factor in distinguishing 'literacy' from 'illiteracy'. Correct spelling is one of the cluster of aspects of language that has acquired the moral symbolism discussed by Cameron. Spelling according to the conventions becomes associated, consciously or subconsciously, with behaving in an orderly manner, in accordance with rules and with respect for authority. Not being able to spell attracts disapproval with these moral overtones, and hence bars the way to educational and employment opportunities. We have found university lecturers particularly guilty of dismissing the worth of their students in this way, having heard them say such things as 'They can't even spell "criteria"', and write on students' work such comments as 'Haven't you got a dictionary?'.

We suggest that the insistence on correct spelling, like insistence on neat handwriting, is part of a wider ideological tendency towards regulation, conformity and subjection of people to authority. If people are kept busy learning spellings, they will not have time for other, more subversive activities, including literate activities such as stating their views and claiming their rights in writing. As with handwriting, schools are under pressure to act as executors of this covert policy, being required by the National Curriculum orders and examination board criteria to insist on correct spelling as a prerequisite for educational success. Teachers are put in the invidious position of having to prioritise spelling when their understanding of literacy development tells them that other things are more important. As a result many children learn little about writing other than that they are 'no good at it', and are alienated from it long before they are old enough to use it for any form of social action.

As we argued in relation to handwriting, people who persist in trying to learn to write, in studying, and/or in trying to get or hold down a job in spite of difficulties with spelling, far from being

201

careless and disrespectful, actually display laudable moral qualities: patience, persistence, and determination to overcome obstacles. If some people's lives are made miserable by insistence on conforming to what is recognised to be in many cases an arbitrary norm, should we not consider having a less punitive attitude to spelling? Would we not be better, perhaps, to return to the state of affairs that existed before 1640, when it was the norm to have several alternative spellings for the same word in circulation?

There have been some tentative and not very successful movements in this direction. There is, from time to time, a new movement for spelling reform. In the nineteenth century George Bernard Shaw proposed a simplified spelling of English (for details, see Stubbs 1980: 80). Recently, The Simplified Spelling Society has proposed 'Cut Spelling', a system for making the spelling of English more economical and regular (see Upward 1988). Both of these advocate a simpler relationship between sound and symbol for English spelling, and the 'cut spelling' movement recommends more flexibility over what counts as 'correct'. However, these movements have not met with much public enthusiasm, and it is worth asking why. What have people got invested in maintaining a set of spelling conventions that are very difficult to learn and, to some extent, have to be learned by rote? The most common argument is that the range and complexity of English spelling represents the rich and glorious history of the language. To change this would be to lose an essential part of our tradition. This is a conservative, or perhaps *pre*servative, view that is hard to dismiss, reminiscent of the desire of the French to insulate their language from sociohistorical influences, as represented by the existence of the *Academie Française*. But we suggest that this argument hides a more pernicious tendency for those who do acquire the conventions of spelling to protect something that has the function of discriminating in their favour. If people cannot claim superiority over others by showing how they can spell better than them, they may not have other means of doing so. Further, the ideological function of insisting on correct spelling which we discussed above – the function of regulating persons through conformity to authoritative rules – may contribute to the failure of spelling reform movements.

There are other social changes that may dent the apparently impermeable hold that correct spelling has on the majority of people. Firstly, there is the increasing use of spell-checkers (which we have already mentioned) as a physical separation of the mechanical process of spelling from other, more important aspects of writing. We see this as a positive development in that it is harder to maintain that people should be judged by their spelling when it is possible to get a machine to do it for them. Secondly, widespread publicity about the existence and nature of dyslexia means that unconventional spelling is not so stigmatised as it used to be (see Miles 1983, Ellis 1993 and Fawcett and Nicholson 1994 for information about dyslexia). If someone over the age of 8 uses extremely bizarre spelling it is less likely than it used to be that they will be punished or derided, and more likely that someone will say, in a hushed voice, 'S/he might be dyslexic'. This understanding is not so forthcoming for people who experience mild difficulty with spelling: they still attract accusations of carelessness. Thirdly, some people who have suffered discrimination on the grounds of difficulty with spelling have been brave enough to be militant about it. We know of people who have been assertive about their rights as people suffering from the disability of dyslexia. They have insisted that spelling should not be used as a criterion for judging their eligibility for higher education, and have appealed when they thought their work has been negatively evaluated on the grounds of spelling. Each person who stands up for their rights in this way contributes a little in the fight to diminish the hold that spelling correctness has over the education establishment, even if moral righteousness about correct spelling is rife in society at large.

To summarise, we are arguing that the over-insistence on correct spelling may be counter-productive. It attaches the stigma of illiteracy to what is nothing more than a mechanical feat of memory. There is no inherent value in the particular way of spelling immortalised in dictionaries. Rather, the need for people to spell according to the established conventions is socially constructed, perhaps even ideologically motivated, as we have argued here. However, understanding this does not solve anything for teachers. They still have to decide how to negotiate the tension between insisting on correct spelling in order to provide learners with access to the privileges that are attached to it, and not insisting on it for the reasons we have outlined here.

PUNCTUATION[3]

Punctuation is often believed to be like spelling in that it can to a large extent be judged 'correct' or 'incorrect' by a set of rules, and consequently is another aspect of written language that is frequently used as a basis for passing social judgements on people and for discriminating among people for educational qualifications and employment opportunities. People have been complaining about standards of punctuation for a couple of centuries (see Hall 1996a for an overview). Conventional punctuation, like conventional spelling, has the symbolic function of standing for an acceptable standard of literacy and education. A small number of unconventional uses of punctuation can make the crucial difference between a grade C and a grade D in GCSE English examinations. Adults often mention being 'no good at punctuation' among the factors that can lead to their own and other people's perception that they are generally 'bad at writing' (for examples, see Robinson 1996).

In this section we argue that the so-called rules of punctuation, like the set of correct spellings in the dictionary and beliefs about what constitutes good handwriting, do not have any intrinsic merit. We also argue that punctuation is very different from spelling in that every decision about how to apply the so-called rules depends on the particular wording that is to be punctuated, and is therefore unique. People can learn to punctuate only through long-term experience in using written language for purposeful meaning-making: it is not a simple question of the rote learning and mechanical application of rules. Those rules-of-thumb that are commonly offered are inadequate explanations for how punctuation works; the factors affecting punctuation are interrelated in complex ways, and there is often just as much logic in alternative explanations. These arguments present a serious challenge to the premium placed on conventional punctuation, and throw into question the widespread practice of using ability to punctuate 'correctly' as a gatekeeping device.

Questioning the premium put on 'correct punctuation'

Firstly, punctuation is not even an essential feature of written language. Early scripts did not use punctuation at all, since it was invented only relatively recently in the history of writing. For example, classical Latin was written without word breaks, let alone punctuation. The North American poet ee cummings does not use punctuation, preferring to leave the chunking and emphasis of his words to the reader. He thereby makes a statement about the way in which our arbitrary conventions privilege some aspects of the message and demote others. Children when they first start to write do not use punctuation until they are explicitly told to do so. It does not perform any essential function for them; they write and read what they have written quite fluently and happily without needing punctuation (see Hall 1996a for discussion of this point).

Punctuation conventions are culturally evolved aids to meaning-making which members of a particular culture have in common, and use as a resource for communicating through written language. However, the particular set of conventions that constitute the 'rules' of punctuation for any culture are nothing other than 'conventions', and are not based on any permanent or universal principles of language.[4] These conventions do not transfer across languages and cultures, and they have evolved and are still evolving over time. Some languages use more punctuation than English, for example, German, and some languages use less than English, for example, Chinese. We have found that when, for example, Greek students write in English, they put in more commas than we are used to, chunking meaning in a way that makes it hard for us to follow. The punctuation of English has also evolved over time: the conventions were very different 400 years ago, and noticeably different only 100 years ago (see Parkes 1992 for a detailed discussion of the history of punctuation, and Crystal 1987 for an overview). Punctuation conventions, not being fixed in a dictionary like spelling, are liable to change in the future, and indeed are currently in a state of flux. A particular case is that in US English the colon is more commonly followed by a capital letter, whereas in British English it is commonly followed by a lower-case letter.

It is commonly believed that the punctuation of English is 'logical', as if there is some inherent necessity to use the marks the way we do. However, the main features in the punctuation system (full stops and commas) merely single out some linguistic features – clause boundaries – for special marking rather than others. Further, punctuation is not like spelling in that one set of punctuation conventions does not apply to all types of writing, whereas all types of writing do draw on the same stock of spellings. The way in which punctuation is used differs from one genre to another, and

205

the emergence of new genres to serve new social needs brings with it the need to develop genre-specific punctuation conventions. New communications technology is leading people to invent new devices for marking written language in order to achieve the immediacy of face-to-face interaction. All these factors lead us to argue that, while punctuation conventions can be useful, the conventions themselves have no intrinsic virtue and hence adhering to them should not be treated as a marker of ability.

Nevertheless, the conventions are now an established, if changing, part of the meaning-making system available for use in writing. We now discuss what is involved in punctuating according to these conventions, showing that punctuating and learning to punctuate are not as easy as is often assumed by the literate majority.

Why learning to punctuate is different from learning to spell

Neat handwriting and conventional spelling are more mechanical aspects of writing which most people can produce by painstaking effort, but punctuation is different. On the one hand, punctuation seems like a tiny, insignificant element in the whole complex of what is involved in learning to write. There are only a small number of punctuation marks, they are not hard to spell, they do not seem essential for conveying meaning, and they are just there to help to break the writing up into smaller chunks. Consequently they should be extremely easy to learn to use. But to every learner writer's annoyance, these few little marks are by no means easy to use according to the accepted conventions. There are no straightforward rules that operate consistently and according to any immediately transparent logic, and the stigma attached to not using the punctuation marks in the accepted way seems out of all proportion with their apparent value to meaning-making. These so-called rules are not amenable either to rote learning or easy application. The problem is that, whereas the spelling of a word remains the same every time you use it, many punctuation rules work differently every time you use them. Once you have learned a spelling you just repeat it, but once you have learned a punctuation rule, such as 'end a sentence with a full stop', you have to apply it afresh to every set of meanings you want to put into writing. Thus each decision as to what counts as a sentence is unique.

We argued that spelling and handwriting are annoying distractions from the real business of writing for communicative purposes, but this argument does not apply to punctuation, except perhaps for very young learners. If punctuation has any intrinsic function, it is to contribute to the way in which written language communicates. Although many young children punctuate by adding in the marks after writing, for fluent writers, deciding how to punctuate is integrally bound up with meaning-making. The writer is constantly making on-line decisions about how to chunk meanings, which to treat in complete sentences, which to treat in main or dependent clauses, and which to embed in other phrases, what to emphasise, what to treat as an aside, or as an addition. All these decisions have consequences for punctuation. The need to punctuate often also contributes to the process of meaning-making, in that if a writer is aware that 'a sentence has gone on too long', s/he goes back to reword into smaller, more punctuatable units, and so often improves the process-ability of the message. People who write extensively often talk about using punctuation 'creatively': how the difference between one punctuation mark and another adds a subtle nuance to their meaning. (For an interesting discussion of how fluent writers make punctuation choices, see Nash 1986.) A group of students on an Access to Higher Education course talked of using punctuation 'like voice in speech . . . to create significant meaning changes'.

For those who do become confident, self-motivated writers, there is a constant interplay between learning to use writing for new social (including educational) purposes, learning new ways of exploiting the syntax of the language, and learning new subtleties of punctuation. For the majority, however, the way in which punctuation is dependent on meaning is more a cause of difficulty than of delight. Most children do not, for the sorts of social and political reasons discussed in Chapter 2, see themselves as meaning-makers, or as having the authority to use writing for purposes of their own. For someone who is not writing with a sense of authority and voice, who does not write as a 'meaning-maker' but as a failure in the school system and a subordinate in the social system, punctuation becomes a mystery rather than a resource. We suggest that teachers who are helping children develop a sense of self-worth and a sense of identity as meaning-makers, and who are giving them experience of social purposes for writing, are doing far more for children's ability to punctuate than those who are concentrating on rules and exercises.

The limitations of standard explanations for how punctuation works

In spite of well-intentioned efforts to elucidate the system, many textbooks and teachers offer misleading explanations for how punctuation works which cause as many punctuation mistakes as they cure. Recent research has accumulated evidence that both teachers and textbooks often provide partial or muddled guidelines on how to punctuate (see Robinson 1996). These explanations do not withstand the test of time, and many adults are left clinging to inadequate, unitary explanations for how punctuation works, believing that punctuation is an unprincipled, arbitrary process, that the rules of punctuation do not work, so they are not worth attending to, and/or that the system is too complicated for them to learn. In these respects, adult learners often have a good deal to *un*learn about how punctuation works before they can develop the necessary tolerance of uncertainty and openness to complexity that underpin the development of flexible strategies for punctuating. Here we discuss briefly the types of explanation that are commonly offered for how punctuation works, showing how each is inadequate if taken in isolation from the others, and how any adequate explanation has to take into account the complex ways in which all these considerations interact with each other (for more detailed discussion, see Ivanič 1996; Hall and Ivanič 1996).

Many teachers and exercises focus on the technical requirement that there must be a full stop at the end of a sentence. While this may successfully introduce young learners to full stops, it does not help them to know how much of their own writing counts as a 'sentence', as soon as they begin writing more than one. The real difficulty is knowing how to use full stops for sentence *division*, rather than sentence *ending*. Unfortunately, in many cases no further advice is offered. The rule: 'put a full stop at the end of a sentence' is supposed to explain everything (see Hall 1996b). While the real criterion for what counts as 'the end of a sentence' must be a syntactic one, many people who attempt to give a further explanation do so in terms of pausing or meaning.

A very common way of explaining punctuation is that it marks 'pauses'. However, the punctuation of written English does not coincide exactly with the tone units of the language. This has been recognised by some linguists, for example:

Rhythm and intonation are roughly indicated by punctuation and capitalization, but too much is left out and what is put in suffers from a confusion of two aims: the representations of the breaks that we hear and the divisions that logical-minded persons sometimes insist that we write – the two usually agree, but not always.

(Bolinger and Sears 1981: 277)

Many teachers give advice like 'put a full stop when you pause' without realising that this could be misleading. In the study we mentioned above (Ivanič 1996), 50 per cent of adult students' decisions about where to place full stops based on this criterion were wrong. In fact, when writers read over their own work to check it, they often run sentences together when they are about the same topic. This makes pausing, or any other appeal to 'sound', a particularly unreliable criterion for judging where to put full stops.

Another common explanation for full stops is that they mark 'the end of a complete idea'. But punctuation does not map on to meaning units of written English in any systematic way. People often choose to write two or more sentences on the same sub-topic in a paragraph. This is illustrated in the three samples below, which are based on the actual composition of a student writer.

1 The mower used to slide about when I went up the steep slope. This caused my lines to be crooked.
2 The mower used to slide about when I went up the steep slope, which caused my lines to be crooked.
3 My lines were crooked because the mower used to slide about when I went up the steep slope.

The writer actually chose the first wording, but did not use any punctuation before 'this', on the grounds that he had not finished what he was writing on this topic. Thus the full stop does *not* mark the end of a complete idea, but a syntactic division within it. The same information can be written as either one or two sentences, depending on the grammatical wording the writer chooses, and there are several possible choices of sentence structure for any idea. Punctuation depends not on the meaning units, but on the way in which a writer selects a grammatical structure for her/his configuration of meanings.

While a system of punctuation could, in principle, be devised to mark prosody or meaning, the main punctuation conventions of English and of most other languages (full stops and commas) have evolved to mark syntactic structure. The actual judgement we make about where to put a full stop or a comma is guided by our conscious or unconscious awareness of the constituent structure of what we are writing: of divisions between different types of clauses. Making this judgement depends on knowledge of such things as which conjunctions signal the beginning of a subordinate clause, which sorts of verbs count as a finite verb and which do not, the difference between relative and other types of pronoun, and the way in which some clauses can be embedded within others. Explanations that draw attention to these matters are more likely to be reliable than the others we have discussed, but they are much more difficult to give, especially to writers who do not know the metalanguage that such explanations would use. Teachers understandably avoid these sorts of explanations, either because they are not themselves consciously aware enough of them to discuss them explicitly, or because they do not want to muddle learners with over-technical detail. But the truth is that, in order to operate the punctuation conventions perfectly, everyone *must* acquire at least an intuitive knowledge of these syntactic considerations (see Hall 1996b and articles in Hall and Robinson 1996 for suggestions as to how this can be achieved).

There is a great deal of overlap between prosodic, semantic and syntactic considerations. The syntax, semantics and prosody of a message are all subject to a larger psychological consideration of how much the human mind can process in one chunk. While the final decision as to how to punctuate writing depends on its syntax, the choice of that particular syntax depends on the meaning the writer is trying to convey. The resources of prosody would also be drawn upon to convey that meaning in spoken language, and they, too, interact with the syntax. Consequently, most people assume that they are putting full stops 'where they pause' or 'at the end of a complete idea', and pass on this sort of explanation to learners. But these explanations actually leave a lot for learners to figure out for themselves. Punctuation is actually a much more complex process than most people assume, with syntactic, semantic and prosodic considerations inter-related. To some extent this is an advantage, since understanding one of these factors can act as a platform for developing an understanding of the others, but to some extent it is a disadvantage, as this overlap means that there is no simple, straightforward set of guidelines to learn, or to teach.

In spite of all these questions about the nature of punctuation and the process of punctuating, people continue to use so-called 'correct punctuation' as a criterion for making educational and social judgements about people: a practice we consider to be ill-informed and unjust. Again, teachers are caught in a double-bind: if they do not devote a lot of attention to teaching the accepted conventions, they may be denying their learners access to employment and educational opportunities, and may be exposing them to the danger of being labelled 'illiterate'; but by accepting the social pressure to insist on these conventions, they are party to the process of entrenching their symbolic value.

GRAMMAR

Under this broad heading we discuss issues of correctness and standardisation concerning forms of words (particularly forms of verbs and different uses of the ending -s), the construction of negatives, and sentence structure.

The question of what is considered to be standard English grammar, and the issues surrounding its use and its place in education, have been widely discussed by sociolinguists (see DES 1989; Milroy and Milroy 1985, 1993; Stubbs 1986; Stubbs and Hillier 1983; Romaine 1994; Trudgill 1975; Wardhaugh 1992).[5] These and other authors draw attention to the fact that there is nothing intrinsically preferable about the grammar of 'standard English': it is just one variety among many that has become privileged in the course of 500 years of socio-economic history. We suggest that the term 'standard English' is misleading, suggesting that it is a variety of the language from which others have in some way deviated. From here onwards we refer to it as 'standardised' English, to emphasise that its privileged position is the result of an ideologically shaped process, not an objective fact.

Most discussions of standardised English and correct grammar revolve around a small number of specific features:

- the use of *ain't* vs. the use of *isn't* or *haven't*
- the use of multiple vs. single negatives

211

- the past and present forms of a small number of common, irregular verbs, particularly *come/came, give/gave*
- the singular and plural forms of a small number of common, irregular verbs, particularly *be/is/are, was/were*
- whether it is necessary to mark the plural of regular verbs with *-ed*
- the use of particular forms of pronouns and determiners (for example *he/him/his, they/them/their*) and of personal pronouns functioning as subject or object (for example *we/us*)
- whether it is necessary to mark plural nouns with an *-s*
- whether it is necessary to mark the agreement of verbs with singular and plural subjects

Most sociolinguists explain that the grammar of spoken varieties of English differs in one or more of these respects, and that these varieties constitute valid linguistic systems in their own right. However, those who mention written English tend to treat it as a single, homogeneous variety, which should use only the standardised options from these grammatical alternatives. Stubbs (1986) recommends that the standardised grammatical forms should be taught, as they are part and parcel of what it means to learn to write; Trudgill takes the position that 'there is much less psychological involvement with the written language than the spoken' (1975: 80), and therefore it is not damaging to learners' identities to be required to use the standardised forms in writing, even though it may be damaging to be required to use them in speech. However, students report that the standardised English they learn for educational purposes interferes with other types of writing, such as letters to family and friends, and they feel uncomfortable with this.

The general belief that the standardised grammatical forms must be used in written English lies behind the practice of using written language as the arbiter of standards for spoken language, as we discussed earlier in this chapter. There, we condemned this practice, but we would like to go further, arguing that there is nothing sacrosanct about this particular set of grammatical conventions, even for written language. The socio-economic forces that privileged particular grammatical options for speech are also responsible for associating written language with the statusful variety of English. It is the social history of this variety, and not intrinsic merit, that privileges these particular forms. We therefore argue that judging people's writing by the extent to which they use the standardised grammatical forms is unjust. Teaching these forms may be a social necessity, in the sense that people in positions of status and power are going to continue to privilege the standardised grammatical forms. However, it is not justified by appeals to logic or linguistic correctness.

A particular case of grammatical form that applies to written language but not spoken language is the use of the apostrophe. It is rarely mentioned as an aspect of grammar: the apostrophe is actually a punctuation mark that is used to indicate genitive case. In spoken language this feature is not distinguished: genitive singular, genitive plural and other plural cases of nouns all sound exactly the same, with the morpheme / s / added to the root word. However, the convention of using the apostrophe to mark the genitive forms in written language has evolved. It is now, we suggest, in the process of being dropped from the conventions of written language too, having no essential communicative function: meaning is not enhanced or clarified by its use. Genitives are increasingly seen in public uses of written language without the apostrophe. However, in spite of the fact that it is such an insubstantial, insignificant and obsolete feature, it is frequently used as a basis for making demeaning remarks about people. Missing an apostrophe, though actually a part of linguistic change, still provokes ridicule from people in gatekeeping positions in employment and education. The 'grocer's apostrophe' – the use of an apostrophe where it is not needed in lists of fruit on sale – is an extremely patronising expression, implying that grocers, and anyone else who uses apostrophes where they are not needed, are illiterate. We suggest that insisting on the conventional use of apostrophes is part of a desperate attempt to hold on to an outdated linguistic form as a means of discriminating against people, and actually demeans the people who *make* these judgements more than those who are the butt of them.

Another aspect of grammar that is used for making judgements about writing is the completeness of grammatical structures. This issue is closely related to the way in which punctuation is used, as discussed in the previous section. Judgements are often made about people's writing on the basis of whether they write 'in complete sentences'. We suggest that such judgements are the consequence of a limited view of the nature of writing. Firstly, those proclaiming that standards of grammar are falling are often referring to the sentence structure and punctuation of a limited range of types of writing. They are holding up the characteristics of certain genres that have a very limited role in social life, such as school essays, as their models for writing of a high standard (and, by extension, as models for language use in general). Yet, as we have argued earlier in this book, this is not the sort of writing that is relevant to the lives of the majority of the population. Secondly, the idea of whole sentences and correct grammar is bound up with a narrow view of how thought must be represented. The conventions for what counts as completeness of sentence structure have developed alongside a linear view of rational thought, but other ways of communicating ideas are possible. For example, -ing clauses are considered to be incomplete, yet they are used in spoken language and in poetry for expressing ideas in looser relationships to one another, and the connections can be easily inferred. And the increasing use of hypertext on computers is fast rendering linear representation of ideas obsolete. Thirdly, long-turn writing is bound up with a monologic, individualistic rather than a dialogic, collaborative view of the construction of knowledge. The convention that writing must be in complete sentences is associated with the production of stand-alone texts, where all the thinking is done by an isolated individual. In many types of writing, particularly e-mail, writers can take over from each other in mid-sentence, changing the grammatical construction as might happen in an interruption in spoken interaction. We are not arguing that there is no place for writing in complete sentences; but we are arguing that there are several reasons for demoting the completeness of sentence structure as a criterion on which to make judgements about standards of literacy.

CONCLUSION

People often use the term 'uneducated' to describe someone who puts apostrophes in the wrong place, or spells 'accommodation' with only one 'm'. Employers often dismiss (sometimes literally!) people with the remark 'S/he doesn't even know what a sentence is'. It is these physical aspects of writing that are far more subject to value judgements than anything to do with content, structure or style. Ironically, the relatively trivial aspects of writing are the very ones that are used as the main criteria of quality, probably because they are so easy to recognise. This leads to the widespread practice of making judgements on the basis of the testable aspects of writing rather than the communicative aspects.

The really valuable aspect of writing – the choice of wording to create meaning – is not so easy to recognise. Writing in your own way for your own purposes is not highly valued, actually often criticised. This depends on who you are: the few who have been elevated to the status of 'writer' in society do have the freedom to write in idiosyncratic ways (as we discussed in Chapter 2), and their work is praised as 'original' and 'creative'. But for the majority of people, the only criterion for judging their writing is its conformity to conventions, and originality or idiosyncrasy is censured.

We are arguing that writing can and does serve lots of functions without any need for punctilious attention to correctness. So why should there be such moral outrage, conservative hysteria and panic about the use of a few conventional forms? We suggest that this obsession with correctness is constructed by schooling and bureaucratic practices, but fuelled by those who see 'falling standards in education' as the root cause of all society's moral ills, and is therefore part of the wider debate about what kind of society we want. Insistence on correctness has a regulatory function in that it limits both the possibilities and the desire of many ordinary people to use writing to express their views. It also has a reproductive function in that it maintains particular forms as markers of prestige to discriminate between those who use them and those who do not.

Recognising these tendencies, however, does not lead to any easy solutions for educators. Firstly, they are caught in the vicious circle whereby teaching the conventions increases their learners' life-chances but at the same time perpetuates this spurious value system, as we have been arguing throughout this chapter. Secondly, as has been powerfully argued by Delpit (1988) and Ellsworth (1989), teachers do not do their students any favours by telling them that the conventions that are privileged by society are merely symbolic and have no intrinsic value. Learners must know the social consequences of not adhering to these conventions. But they may find it easier to ape these conventions for their own purposes if they engage in critical discussion about the tensions between their desire for success and the demand that they conform to the conventions, perhaps compromising their own identity in doing so (see particularly Ivanič 1988 for this argument). It may be possible to engage in 'power dressing' without sacrificing 'empowerment', and such learners may find ways of contributing to changing these socially divisive practices in the future.

9

SOCIAL AND EDUCATIONAL IMPLICATIONS OF OUR VIEW OF WRITING

INTRODUCTION

One of the major implications of what we have said about writing is that it is crucial for a popular democracy to create the circumstances in which as many people as possible contribute actively and on equal terms to the creation and circulation of meanings. In this final chapter we try to suggest some ways in which these circumstances might be encouraged, looking at some of the issues concerning access to the important public spaces for communicating meanings, focusing on the media in general and on publishing. These aspects of the broader socio-political environment affect the conditions that we believe are necessary for the realisation of the pedagogical principles that we propose. We then look at the possible ways of encouraging learner writers at various stages of their learning experience in formal educational settings to see writing as less of a chore and more of an exciting possibility for them to engage in the wider 'ideological activity' of society, as Kress calls it (1982: 10).

SOCIO-INSTITUTIONAL IMPLICATIONS

Participatory democracy

In a critique of British democracy, McLennan refers to the growing sense that the national parliament is extremely unwieldy and distant from the daily concerns of the majority of the voters (McLennan 1984: 248) and the widespread disaffection from electoral activity. He concludes that more local forms and forums of decision-making are necessary. As we have already mentioned in Chapters 1 and 2, we as authors do not always agree on the political means for achieving such changes. Possible ways might include the devolution of power to national assemblies in Scotland and Wales, devolved regional and local government with more powers than at present and the setting up of a network of neighbourhood councils and workplace committees alongside the more traditional 'single issue' political organisations. (This kind of widespread, local-scale devolution has been very successful in central Italy, particularly in the cities of Bologna and Rome.)

McLennan's views have important implications for the politics of writing in terms of widening participation in decision-making for 'ordinary' people. Participation in the decision-making processes involves engagement in a wide range of literacy practices in order to circulate ideas and get things done. They include writing up proposals and making suggestions for policy, writing letters, drafting new laws, writing speeches, taking minutes of meetings of all sorts which are part of the process of social participation.

A radical politics is needed, capable of taking a leading role in enabling people to work together to find solutions to issues of common concern. At the moment, the balance of power is firmly tipped in favour of the interests of the powerful, wealth-owning members of society rather than the wealth-creating, the dispossessed and marginalised. In our view, this hegemony should be challenged and broken down, and decision-making should be devolved to the people whom the decisions will affect. Such radical changes in the organisation of the democratic process would involve transformations in the way in which ideas are produced, circulated and consumed; the creation of a new vision of the public sphere, wide-ranging media reform and changes in educational purposes, content and methods. Such a radical politics would contribute to shaping what Williams called 'an educated and participating democracy' (1989: 37), in which all contribute to the determining of a 'common culture' and in which writing plays a central role (as we discussed in Chapter 2). He explains that:

> a common culture is in no sense the idea of a simply consenting, and certainly not, a conforming society [but] a common determination of meanings by all the people, acting sometimes as individuals, sometimes as groups, in a process which has no particular end, and which can never be supposed at any time to have finally realized itself, to have become complete.
>
> (same page)

In the next section we return to the media and their pivotal role in democracy.

Democratisation of the media

In Chapter 2 we argued that the mainstream media in general, and the press in particular, play a central role in constructing and maintaining hegemony. We also discussed the extreme narrowness of ownership of the press in Britain and the consequent difficulty of access to alternative accounts of the world and relationships within it. Britain has a press where 'ordinary' people's lives, experiences and points of view are generally marginalised as 'human interest' stories: 'ordinary' people are never the expert (see Fairclough 1995) but used to illustrate dominant prejudices (e.g. single mothers, unemployed youths, football 'hooligans'). It is a press that deeply alienates the majority of people and treats them as 'receivers' of information (i.e. the role of the media is to give 'information' to the public) and not as participants in a national forum of ideas. This is a press that is set up, as Williams argued:

> for the few communicating to the many, disregarding the contribution of those who are not seen as communicators but merely as communicable to.
>
> (Williams 1989: 36)

In late twentieth-century capitalist countries, social and economic life is increasingly market driven, the media are increasingly deregulated and globalised with an increasingly narrow cross-media ownership. Against this background, it is important to imagine how democratisation of the ownership of titles and better financial facilities for other forms of ownership of titles (e.g. co-operatives) and their circulation and distribution might be pursued. In that spirit, we try to outline an alternative way of looking at the media and their role in a democratic society.

We find the critique of the traditional perspective on the role of the media and the alternative perspective put forward by Curran (1991) an exciting contribution to rethinking the media. He takes as his starting point an early work by Habermas (translated in 1989) in which he traces the development of what he calls the 'bourgeois public sphere' – a public space between the economy and the state in which public opinion was formed and 'popular' supervision of the government was established – from the seventeenth century to the first half of the nineteenth century (Curran 1991: 83). The independent media played a crucial role in providing a public forum for debate until the public sphere became dominated by an expanded state and organised economic interests. The media then became less 'a conduit for rational-critical debate' (same page) and more and more a manipulator of mass opinion. Curran argues that it is possible, building on Habermas's study, to envisage a public sphere where access to relevant information affecting the public good is widely available, where discussion is free and open, and where all the participants in the public debate are equal. This public space would provide people with the opportunity to determine collectively through rational debate the ways in which they want society to develop. The media would facilitate this process by providing an arena and by 'reconstituting private citizens as a public body in the form of public opinion' (same page).

The problem, as Curran says, is how to re-establish this public sphere in an era of mass politics in a highly articulated and organised capitalist society. Through a thorough critique of the traditional perspectives on the democratic role of the media in modern society (the media as public watchdog, as consumer representation, as provider of information, as regulated by professional responsibility), he puts forward ways of rethinking the media. He argues firstly that the public dialogue should be based on a diversity of values and perspectives. The plurality of understandings generated by and in the media should:

> enable individuals to reinterpret their social experience and question the assumptions and ideas of the dominant culture . . . and to decide for themselves how best to safeguard and advance their welfare in collective as well as individual terms, and to set in the balance rival definitions of the public interest.
>
> (same book: 103)

He argues further that this would be emancipatory and empowering: 'giving people the right to define their normative vision of the world and their place in it through access to alternative perspectives on society' (same page).

Curran's view of the media as an agency of representation goes beyond simply disseminating diverse opinion in the public sphere. The media system should assist collective organisations and aid them in registering effective protest and in developing and promulgating alternatives. That is, the media should help to 'create the conditions in which alternative viewpoints and perspectives are brought fully into play' (same page).

He suggests that one way forward is to visualise the public sphere as a core surrounded by satellite networks and organised groupings. The core public sphere is where all interests intersect with one another in trying to reach agreement or compromise on the future directions of society. This core would be fed by a number of 'umbilical cords that connect it to the life force of civil society': different interpretive communities, different organised groupings, different cultures and different social strata with distinctive interests and social experiences (same page).

Finally, Curran argues that the media should assist in:

> the realization of the common objectives of society through agreement or compromise between conflicting interests. The media should contribute to this process by facilitating democratic procedures for resolving conflict and defining collectively agreed aims.
>
> (same book: 104)

This could include in-depth briefing of the public about the political choices involved in elections; giving proper publicity to the activities, programmes and thinking of organised groups, in addition to the formal processes of government and party opposition; by staging public dialogue in which diverse interests participate on equal terms; and by providing an adequate way for people to engage in wider public discourse. Although Curran is referring specifically to television, we believe that the same kinds of principles are particularly applicable to print media, given the advantages writing has in terms of cheap production, permanency and in-depth treatment of topics which can be read and re-read.

The vision outlined above would go some way to redressing what Williams described as the 'shocking' exclusion of the majority of people from contributing to a 'common culture' (1989: 35) and to establishing what he called an 'educated and participating democracy' (as quoted above). Such a vision is of course in conflict with the present social structures, the existing media system, organised interests and the function of the media as agencies of social integration and control. It would require a different legal framework, different patterns of ownership with funding made available to support alternative forms of ownership, and access to the technical means of production that, in our view, goes way beyond, for example, the limited and often patronising attempts at 'open access' television that exist in the UK today. In our view, wider access would have to include space for ordinary people to engage in public debate through writing in a wide variety of forms for print and broadcast media. This could be done, for example, by opening up the national and local newspapers and journals to ideas from 'ordinary' people, and not just in the Letters page. This would help prevent 'ordinary' people's writing being marginalised in small-circulation papers or journals, as happens at the moment.

Utopia? Unthinkable? We believe it is important to think through and fight for alternative ways of thinking about society and its institutions. Now more than ever we need Gramsci's 'pessimism of the intellect and optimism of the will' (1978: 213); that is, we need to understand the real difficulties that stand in the way of change but at the same time develop the political will that can mobilise popular support for those changes.

Ideas are circulated not only through the media, of course, but through all kinds of writing, including fiction. Most ordinary people are also denied access to this kind of writing, and so we now look at publishing and the circulation of published writing.

Popular publishing

We argued in Chapter 2 that the vast majority of people do not engage in the sort of writing that has prestige, that gets published and/or influences the way in which society develops. In this section we will ignore mainstream publishing and look specifically at the role of community publishing in encouraging 'ordinary' people to write and publish poetry, stories, autobiographies and local histories. We describe some examples of good practice in this field as an example of what might be further encouraged, developed and supported in the future.

In the 1960s and 1970s there was a flourishing of local political activity, and some of this led to an interest in writing and publishing the experiences of individuals and collectivities at grass roots level. A variety of local publishing ventures grew up from a variety of origins (WEA groups, local campaigns, etc.). In 1976, representatives of eight such community publishing groups met in London for discussions, and there the Federation of Worker

Writers and Community Publishers was born (Morley and Worpole 1982: 2). In spite of increasing difficulties with funding such work, 'The Federation' still exists, though with diminished and to some extent changed membership, and meets on a regular basis.[1]

Gregory (1984, 1991) has traced the origins of community publishing. He describes one of the widely proclaimed purposes of community publication as:

> to redress a class/historical balance of access to writing and print: to encourage 'ordinary' people to present themselves rather than being represented and misrepresented.

To take one example of a community publisher, Commonword Writers' Workshop in Manchester,[2] began in 1977 as an oral history group. In its own words it is:

> a non-profit making community publishing co-operative, producing books by writers in the North West, and supporting and developing their work. In this way Commonword brings new writing to a wide audience. . . .
>
> In general, Commonword seeks to encourage the creative writing and publishing of the diverse groups in society who have lacked, or been excluded from, the means of expression through the written word. Working class writers, black writers, women and lesbians and gay men all too often fall into this category.
>
> To give writers the opportunity to develop their work in an informal setting, Commonword offers a variety of writers' workshops, such as Womanswrite, The Monday Night Group, and Northern Gay Writers.
>
> (Commonword, 1988: 79)

In addition to writers' workshops and publishing, Commonword offers a manuscript reading service that gives constructive feedback to writers and provides information and advice on local facilities. Crocus books, the imprint of Commonword, publishes books of professional quality and at low prices compared with mainstream publishing. The work of other community publishers is documented and discussed in Worpole 1977 and in several contributions to Mace 1995.

Gregory (1991: 130) sets the success of community publishing, as clearly documented in a range of experiences and outcomes, in the context of participants' previous educational experience of writing. Many talked about their schooling in terms of failure and disaffection, and Gregory argues that:

> [s]chooling may have acted as often to control literacy as to expand it, and, for many participants in community writing and publishing activity, literacy had at school been taught as a technology detached from experience. Disillusioned with its meagre contributions to their lives, they had staged a tactical withdrawal from it.
>
> (same book: 131)

In evaluating the educational processes as well as the products of community publishing, Gregory relates these to Freire's view of literacy as the foundation of the 'pedagogy of the oppressed' and to Gramsci's principle that working-class people should submit their thought to the discipline of the written word – to gain the precision necessary to engage in debate with intellectuals (Gramsci 1971: 29, quoted in Gregory 1991: 133). In words that echo those of Williams, this submission of thought to the written word enables 'those to become producers of print who have hitherto been . . . consumers only' (Williams 1989: 133).

The potential of community publishing for enabling the marginalised and excluded to represent themselves, their experiences and their points of view, and of turning writing into action, were and are enormous. Unfortunately, the political and economic climate in the late 1980s and 1990s is such that the material conditions for it to flourish and expand are greatly weakened. Local authorities and other grant-giving bodies are themselves under pressure. Some of the original ventures, such as the Centerprise Publishing Project (London) have folded. Centerprise Publishing was wound up in 1994 for mainly economic reasons: booksellers were not selling the publications; limited resources could no longer be tied up in the time-consuming publishing activity; desk-top publishing was providing an alternative outlet. They now have their own small imprints with other book publishers and the operation continues as a bookshop. Gatehouse Books, based in Manchester, has continued to act as a community publisher of books by and for adult learners since November 1977. It is under constant threat of closure and, as well as constantly having to justify their funding from Manchester City Council and the North West Arts Board, has to engage in other fund-raising activities in order to publish its books.

At the same time, alternative bookshops – such as Collets in London – are closing down, too, with the result that there are fewer retailing outlets for writing published by community publishers. The scrapping of the net book agreement on retail prices has meant that large chains and stores, such as Dillons and WH Smiths are able to sell large quantities of stock at lower prices, threatening the existence of small bookshops who do not sell enough books to cut their prices. A near-monopoly situation is also arising through mergers and the concentration of cross-media ownership.

Books that are published by community publishers have small circulations and narrow distribution compared with mainstream books, and their influence is therefore limited. But community publishing has provided, and is still struggling to provide, an important arena for ideas to be debated in print by those individuals and collectivities who do not usually get the chance. Encouragement of such ventures and the creation of the material conditions for them to develop and expand – including a re-examination of the way in which publishing as a whole operates – would be an act of political imagination, a step in the direction of the 'participating democracy' envisaged by Williams, and an enrichment of us all.

The Internet: the technological democratisation of the circulation of meanings?

Old technology requires people to go through complex bureaucratic procedures to get something published or broadcast. A particular feature of this system is that it involves gatekeepers – guardians of appropriacy and relevance – at each stage deciding what will and what will not get published and disseminated. The development of the Internet has changed this. Very recently, software has become available for anyone with a computer and a modem to make their own contributions to the World Wide Web. This means that anyone can write something, using computer resources for combining text, layout features, graphics and hypertext, and make it globally accessible to anyone else who has access to a computer that is hooked up to the Internet. In this way 'ordinary' people can publish their writing without asking any permission and without going through any intermediaries: it reaches the public sphere immediately. Even better, the Internet is 'crawled' by automatic indexing systems, or 'search engines' as

225

they are called, which allow a user to find entries on a chosen topic written by anybody, anywhere in the world. It is not necessary to know an author's name, or have heard of their publication, in order to be connected to it. This makes ordinary people's writing more likely to be read, since it will be brought to the attention of those who are interested in its content.

However, it would be naive to see the Internet as the answer to achieving a participatory democracy. Firstly, while the Internet does facilitate the circulation of messages, this is cut off from any real power and from the decision-making activities of society, and could easily remain just what it is: meanings floating in cyberspace. Circulation of information does not, of itself, lead to more partici- pation in social and political life.

Secondly, access to the technology for using the Internet is limited, in spite of what many in the field of information tech- nology claim. The majority of people in the world, and even the majority of people in highly industrialised countries, do not have their own computers or access to the Internet. These facilities are increasingly available in educational institutions in industrialised countries, but relatively few people have the sense of themselves as meaning-makers that is required to make use of them. An impor- tant educational implication of this is that learning to write should not consist of merely learning to conform to certain conventions of accuracy and appropriacy, but that it should focus on devel- oping a sense of authorship, and viewing writing as a means for making and communicating meanings that matter. This is the topic of the rest of this chapter.

EDUCATIONAL IMPLICATIONS

In Chapter 2 we argued that the institution of education, as one of the prime 'ideological state apparatuses', to use Althusser's term (1971), contributes to the reproduction (or desired trans- formation) of class, gender and ethnic relations. We also claimed that current literacy practices in schools have as one of their outcomes the exclusion of the many from contributing to the 'wider ideological activity' of society.

Changes in education are dependent on and reflect what is happening in the wider society; education is not a politically or morally neutral institution. Changes in education by themselves, as the British experience of the last thirty years shows, do not eradicate the inequities of an unequal society. (According to Herzberg 1991 this is also true of the US.) Despite these limitations on what it can achieve, education is always an important site of struggle; as we argued in Chapter 2, it is one of the key institutions of civil society in which the struggle for cultural hegemony and the reproduction of class, gender and ethnic relations is played out (see, for example, Gibson's review of feminist critiques of schooling and gender, 1986: 157–8).

In this section we first discuss the aims of a critical pedagogy, which does not take for granted the ideologies and power relations in which the lives of learners are enmeshed, and then outline some pedagogic principles implied by taking account of the politics of writing and treating writing as a social practice.

Critical pedagogy

The aim of education should be to create a climate in which it is possible to think and talk and write 'a language of hope and trans-formation for those struggling in the present for a better future' (Giroux 1989: 151). To achieve this, education must enable a critical (that is, questioning) exploration of how ideology, culture and power work within late capitalism to limit, disorganise and marginalise more radical positions which represent the everyday experiences and common-sense perceptions of individuals and oppressed groups. In other words, it would involve exposing the *partiality* of accounts of the world, its events and its social relations.

Freire (1972) has dramatically shown that literacy is not simply a technical skill to be acquired but an essential basis for political and cultural action to achieve emancipation. Educators need to build on his insights and help people develop an understanding of themselves not only as socially constituted subjects but also as agents for their own and society's transformation.

Roger Simon says:

> An education that empowers for possibility must raise ques-tions of how we can work for the reconstruction of social imagination in the service of human freedom. What notions of knowing and what forms of learning will support this? I think the project of possibility requires an education rooted in a view of human freedom as the understanding of necessity and the transformation of necessity. This is the pedagogy we

require, one whose standards and achievement objectives are determined in relation to goals of critique and the enhancement of social imagination. Teaching and learning must be linked to the goal of educating students to take risks, to struggle with ongoing relations of power . . . and to envisage versions of a world which . . . is 'not yet' – in order to be able to alter the grounds on which life is lived.

(quoted in Giroux 1989: 166–7)

Alternatively as Gramsci argued in 1916 in response to a debate on the working class and culture, in words that are still relevant today:

critique implies . . . self-consciousness . . . [c]onsciousness of a self which is opposed to others, which is differentiated and, once having set itself a goal, can judge facts and events other than in themselves or for themselves but also in so far as they tend to drive history forward or backward. To know oneself, to be master of oneself, to distinguish oneself, to free oneself from a state of chaos, to exist as an element of order – but of one's own order and one's own discipline in striving for an ideal. And we cannot be successful in this unless we also know others, their history, the successive efforts they have made to be what they are . . . without losing sight of the ultimate aim: to know oneself better through others and to know others better through oneself.

(Gramsci 1977: 13)

We believe that writing could play a large part in enabling such a critique as he describes to take place. As we discussed in Chapters 4 and 5, writers understand themselves and what they think through the very act of writing. Writing at school and in other educational settings can (and should) provide opportunities for exploring one's own world and that of others.

In the kind of emancipatory literacy project we have described, teachers would take on the role of 'transformative intellectuals' (Giroux 1989: 170). But as Giroux also recognises, this is possible only if the ideological and material conditions permit this. Educational reform, as we argued at the outset of this section, cannot be separated from the wider struggle to radically reform the basic structures and relationships of society. Emancipatory literacy needs wider emancipatory politics and emancipatory politics needs emancipatory literacy. Only then does Williams' dream of an 'emancipatory democracy' (1989: 38), where all are truly free to contribute to the common process of participation in the creation of meanings and values, as we outlined in Chapter 2, have a chance of being realised.

Teaching and learning in schools in Britain in the 1990s is in the ever-tightening grip of centralisation, regulation and codification by a national curriculum, forms of assessment and prescribed syllabuses (Sealey 1996 provides a powerful critique of the ideologies implicit in these policies). There are also signs as we write that methods of teaching will be increasingly regulated: the Secretary of State for Education has just (September 1996) announced the introduction of a national curriculum for teacher training, imposing for the first time approved teaching methods. All of this means that there is less space, literally and ideologically, for teachers to engage in what Giroux (1989; after Freire) calls 'emancipatory literacy' and for what we call 'critical language awareness' (which we discuss further below). However, we believe that if real democracy is to flourish it is ever more urgent that future citizens be properly and critically equipped to take as full a part as possible in political and cultural life as well as in economic life. The development of a critical awareness of the world, and of the possibilities for changing it, ought to be the main objective of all education. In the next section we give some examples of how this might be done in practice and draw up a set of pedagogic principles based on the arguments we have presented in the book.

The teaching of writing: pedagogic principles and practice

Even to talk about 'learning to write' separately from 'writing' contradicts the view of writing we have been presenting here. If writing is embedded in its socio-political context, then every time someone writes in a new context, or for a different purpose or a different reader in a familiar context, there must be some learning involved alongside the writing. There is no such thing as a point at which someone has finished learning to write: learning to write is a life-long process. Although this life-long, situated learning is perhaps the most important way of learning to write, it is not our focus in this section. Here we are specifically concerned with what teachers can do when faced with the task of facilitating or augmenting the learning that takes place outside the classroom.

We have already emphasised, particularly in Chapter 8, that teachers of writing are held in a double-bind: on the one hand it would be in their learners' interests if they could help them to conform to the expectations of society; on the other hand, by doing so they are reproducing the ideologies and inequities of society. Further, the majority of learners have a love–hate relationship with writing, sensing its necessity for access to life-chances, yet often feeling alienated from its forms and purposes. We can offer no solutions to these dilemmas, although we hope that making them explicit is more help than sweeping them under the carpet.

In this section, we outline a set of principles for the teaching of writing that we have evolved in response to our developing understanding of the issues we have raised in this book. We do not claim originality for these pedagogic principles; our aim is simply to bring together recommendations for the teaching of writing that are in line with the view of writing we have set out, including recommendations we ourselves have made at greater length elsewhere, and to endorse principles underlying existing good practice. We separate the principles out under headings for the purposes of presentation but they are in reality all closely interrelated. Our examples come from the learning and teaching of academic writing although we believe that the principles we discuss apply to the learning of all kinds of writing.

Take a Critical Language Awareness (CLA) approach to the teaching of writing

This principle is an umbrella to many of the others. CLA-raising involves developing learners' explicit knowledge of the sorts of issues we have been exploring in this book. In an article that we both contributed to (Clark and others 1991: 52) we argued that CLA work contributes:

> to help children develop not only operational and descriptive knowledge of the linguistic practices of their world, but also a critical awareness of how these practices are shaped by, and shape, social relationships and relationships of power.

CLA is relevant to – we would say, essential for – all age groups and all aspects of language. Those of us who have developed the concept of CLA have explored the possibilities of including CLA-raising in a wide variety of forms of language education (see Ivanič 1988; Fairclough 1992b; Janks 1993b, 1995, 1996; Pardoe 1994b; Wallace 1992b). Here we are concerned specifically with its role in learning to write. CLA-raising focuses on the critical discussion of discourse choices and the way in which they position language users. In relation to writing, it means recognising that writing in a particular way means appearing to be a certain type of person; that is, writers need to be aware that their discoursal choices construct an image of themselves and that they need to take control over this as much as they can, *not* so that they can deceive their readers but so that they do not betray themselves. CLA also involves action as a result of awareness. It is based on a view of language in which discourses influence what people say and write or how they interpret, but are open to contestation and change. Learners should be encouraged to make choices as they write that will align them with social and political values, beliefs and practices to which they are committed, if necessary opposing privileged conventions for the genre and thereby contributing to discoursal and social change.

In discussing pedagogic principles for the learning and teaching of writing in the following sections, we stick closely to the order of the earlier chapters in the book. We are considering all three dimensions of writing-as-language that are represented by Fairclough's diagram, as we introduced it in Chapter 1. We start by recommending the raising of critical awareness about issues of power in the socio-political context – the outer layer of the diagram – and work inwards towards raising critical awareness of aspects of the text itself.

Raise consciousness about issues of power and status in relation to writing

The concept of power in the context of writing has several meanings. Above all, as we argued in Chapter 2, it means that writing has the power to reproduce ideologies and make them available for broader consumption. Learner writers should not be acculturated unquestioningly into the ideologies that support particular social orders. Rather, pedagogy should bring to the surface the issue of which values and beliefs are embedded in certain writing practices, discourses and genres, and what alternatives there might be (see Brodkey 1987; Bizzell 1992; Clark 1992). Secondly, having an identity as a writer has status in society. Learner writers need to become conscious of this symbolic power attached to writing, and be prepared to fight for it, or fight against it, as necessary. Thirdly, in order to write, a writer must have a sense of personal power or authoritativeness. So learner writers need to be encouraged to think of themselves as people who have the power and authority to be an author, and that what they write will be valued for what they say and not just treated as practice in 'good' grammar or spelling (see Mace 1992, Chapter 5, and Mace 1995).

Discuss differences between speaking and writing

In Chapter 3 we discussed the way in which most writing differs from speaking in that the writer and the reader do not share the same physical context, and in Chapter 4 we discussed the differences between writing and speaking as mental processes of language production. In our experience, adults who are learning to write find it useful to discuss these differences explicitly, and to recognise that writing is not just a question of putting into physical form the words that they say (for a detailed discussion of this type of language awareness, see Wendy Moss 1995). We suggest that some exploration of these issues with children may also help them with learning to write. However, in classrooms most of the writing the children do is for their teacher to read, and therefore it does not allow them to experience the lack of shared physical context which makes writing different from speaking. We suggest, firstly, that teachers take up all possible opportunities for children to write for readers other than themselves so that they are communicating across contexts and, secondly, that writing at home and in the community (as described in Chapter 3) becomes an explicit subject for discussion in school.

Raise consciousness about how writing is embedded in social context

As part of the wider consciousness-raising about the process of writing, students should be helped to understand how no act of writing takes place in a social vacuum (see Flynn 1991 for a critique of pedagogy that does not pay attention to this). This involves paying attention to both the social context of situation and the context of culture, as discussed in Chapter 3. Treating writing as a 'decontextualised', neutral technology does not prepare students for the real demands that are placed on them when they write in everyday life. Further, it robs writing of its social power which is what makes it really worth learning.

It is difficult to deal with this aspect of writing if learning to write is limited to the context of the English lesson. In our experience students can increase their understanding of the effect of context if writing from other contexts can be brought into the classroom for discussion. This includes writing across the curriculum in school or university. In the teaching of academic writing, raising consciousness about the social context of writing includes exploring with students the nature of the discourse community they are working in, what its dominant genres and discourses are, the reasons for and effects of the existing dominant conventions and how they, the students, feel about them. One useful exercise in this connection is to examine critically with the students an assignment and the lecturer's feedback to explore how the lecturer contributes in the feedback to the construction of what is acceptable and what is not.

Demystify writing processes and practices

In Chapter 4 we argued that it is important to understand what goes on, cognitively, emotionally and physically, when writers write and we presented our view of the writing process. The immediate implication of that chapter is that it is important to share insights about the processes and practices of writing with learner writers as soon as possible and to let them voice their worries about them. We have developed a way of doing that with a task that enables the students to examine the process and practices involved in writing and to reflect critically on their previous experiences and attitudes towards writing. The task is based on the key components of the process of writing we identified in Chapter 4. Each of the components is written on a piece of card. Students work in small groups, each with a pack of cards. They discuss each component in turn, trying to figure out what each one means, any problems that it might cause and any ideas for overcoming the difficulties. The students are encouraged to reflect constantly on their past experiences and their expectations about future writing needs and demands. In the second phase of the task, the students try to arrange the cards in such a way as to represent what they think the process of writing really looks like, rather than what they have been taught that it should look like. The different representations are then compared and discussed, and finally the teacher encourages

233

the whole group to consider what they have learned from the exercise and what implications there are for their future writing (see Ivanič and Clark 1991 for a full account of this activity).

Another way of demystifying the writing process and its associated practices is to try to open up the process of writing and to introduce a more interactive approach during the drafting process. One way of doing this is to encourage more collaborative practices among the learner writers. Collaboration can range from brainstorming ideas at the beginning of a task, through reading and commenting on each others' drafts, to composing together at the word-processor. Collaboration can be in pairs or in groups and the writing outcomes can be graded accordingly.

One of the most mystifying aspects of writing for assessment, in school or in higher education, is the grading system. Students often complain that they do not understand why they have received the grade that they have – whether it is good or bad. So it is vital that feedback on writing is seen as part of the learning process and not just a question of giving a grade. Writers need to understand why what they have written is considered good or interesting as well as why it is considered less so (see Clark and others 1994 for examples of different feedback practices and for more discussion of this aspect of helping writers to improve their writing).

Allow time for thinking, discussing and drafting in order to engage with meaning

We have stressed throughout the book that writing is a thinking process and that much of what writers think becomes clear only through and in the act of writing. This implies that they cannot plan rigorously in detail what they want to say in advance of the actual writing. While planning is useful as a way of getting into the writing, getting started, learner writers need to be aware that sticking too rigidly to a plan may be costly in terms of lost creativity. They may be sacrificing the development of new ideas. The implication of this is that writers need time and encouragement to draft, discuss and redraft their work. They cannot be expected to hand in a 'perfect' piece of work at the end of one short classroom session, or one homework period. This expectation only encourages learner writers to see themselves as 'failures' because they cannot do what is expected, rather than come to an understanding that it is the writing process itself that is complex, difficult and takes time.

It is important to encourage students who are writing academic assignments with a deadline to start writing much earlier than they deem necessary, not to wait until they think they know what they are going to write.

Ensure that writing in pedagogic settings has a communicative purpose

People learn most about writing when they are doing it for real purposes. The problem with practice activities such as those found in many writing textbooks is that they are decontextualised, fragmentary and not for a real purpose or for a real reader. This means that the tasks do not adequately prepare the students for the real world they are about to enter or have just entered and the students have little interest invested in the outcome. We have argued elsewhere (1991), with respect to the context of English for Academic Purposes (EAP) teaching, that students need to be engaged in creating meaningful, purposeful texts. In a university Academic Support Programme such as the one we are involved in it is possible and essential – in our view – to work on real tasks that the students have to do for their departments, such as assignment, report and dissertation-writing. These are assessed in the normal way by subject tutors. When learner writers are able to work on writing that has a real purpose they have a context in which to figure out the important issues such as the readership (see Chapter 7), genre and discourse conventions and, crucially, to engage in writing as meaning-making, rather than as an exercise.

In other educational settings it may not be easy to engage learners in real tasks all the time; nevertheless in our view it is possible to set 'realistic' writing tasks that have purposes beyond that of practising formal accuracy. For example, in some schools project work is widely encouraged. Involving pupils in local community issues and encouraging writing tasks that are relevant to the lives of the pupils in that community would provide purpose and meaning, and an opportunity to engage in the kind of critique we envisage. Another type of purposeful task is to involve pupils in writing their own family history, researching and recording significant episodes in the lives of family members (see Clark and others 1991 for a detailed description of the aims and procedures for such an activity). There are many suggestions for purposeful writing activities in Hall 1989 and The National Writing Project 1989–90.

Discuss the relationship between context, purpose and form

People who are learning to write particular types of writing need the opportunity to explore the links between situation, purpose and form that seem so self-evident to those who have more experience of the situation. As we argued at the end of Chapter 5, these links are not straightforward, and cannot be learned as a set of prescriptions. In most types of writing there are tensions between different purposes which have consequences for the structure and wording of the writing. In our experience, explicit discussion of these tensions helps people to gain control over writing. In academic writing, students' own, often subconscious, self-generated purposes may be at odds with those of the tutor and need to be identified and explored (this point is discussed in detail in Pardoe 1994a).

Raise awareness about the importance of identity in all types of writing

Writers come to writing with different configurations of cultural and linguistic capital (see Chapter 2). Learner writers who have not had the life-chances that provide the cultural and linguistic capital that is prized in their socio-political context need to be helped to become aware of the socio-economic structures and processes that determine those life-chances and determine what is prized and what is not. This is important, so that learner writers do not feel failures and do not blame themselves for not being able to write in ways that they are being asked to do at school, say, or at university.

Writing can produce an 'identity crisis' which is a major stumbling block. Writers may have to make choices about writing in a particular language or variety of language, or about adopting certain discourses or genres, which mean sacrificing other aspects of their identity, as we described in Chapter 6. In the university context, our experience is that for many students, 'improving' their writing involves complex issues of identity and socio-political allegiances. For example, one student writer felt that by taking on some of the values of academic writing (and talking) – such as standardised forms of English, 'big' words and academic jargon – she was betraying her home community: working-class Afro-Caribbean. She was torn between wanting to do well at university and not wanting to cut herself off from her roots. This aspect of writing should not be ignored in teaching; on the contrary, we believe it is a fundamental issue for explicit examination. Such consciousness-raising could take the form of whole class discussion and/or one to one discussion as part of the feedback on the particular person's writing (see Clark 1992; Ivanič and Clark 1991; also pedagogical implications at the end of Ivanič 1994a, 1995 and forthcoming).

In Chapter 6 we also argued that writing conveys direct and indirect messages to the reader about the writer. This occurs not only through the content engaged in but also because of the forms – linguistic, discoursal and generic – that the writer has adopted. Learner writers need to be helped to develop awareness of the ways in which these aspects of writing affect the writer–reader relationship and the perception that the reader may have of the writer. This awareness can help the writer either to avoid mis-representing him/herself or to give the kind of image of self that s/he is happy with. The choices that the writer has to learn to make include deciding whether to accommodate to or resist the perceived values and expectations of form and content of the reader – where known – or those of a particular institution. They also include weighing up the risks involved in flouting these values and expectations. This is why it is important for learner writers to be engaged in real writing because only then do these kinds of choices have any real meaning. But this provides also an opportunity for writers to contribute to new ways of writing in their disciplines: to make a contribution to ideological activity, particularly when they challenge the existing orthodoxies of their field rather than just reproduce them.

Pay attention to the role of the reader in writing

The writer–reader relationship is not an optional extra: it is present in any naturally occurring act of writing. Yet one of the reasons why writing is difficult, we have suggested, is that the reader is not physically present and able to give ongoing feedback. Teachers of writing can help learners by making the reader a reality.

Learner writers can write only for the *actual* reader of their writing, and not for a pretended reader. Ideally this means finding readers for the writing other than the 'English teacher'. There are many examples of good practice in this respect, particularly in primary education. Many are described in a National Writing Project publication (1990), and in Hall (1989). Examples are writing for a class newspaper or school magazine, writing stories for younger children, writing to pen-friends, either by conventional mail or by e-mail hook-up. Adult basic education has taken this principle seriously and there have been many publications by first-time writers, usually through community publishing networks such as the Gatehouse Project and Centerprise Publications, as discussed above.

Another way of providing 'real readers' for learner writers is to bring their writing across the curriculum into the English class. We have taken this approach to providing language support in higher education, as we described above when discussing the need for a real communicative purpose. The fact that the reader is the subject tutor, and that the assessment will count towards the students' final degree, means that all the decisions the writers make are 'for real', with real consequences. These decisions include the sort of relationship the writer establishes with the reader and the judgements s/he makes about this relationship.

However, it is not always possible to arrange for all writing to have a real reader. An alternative is to ensure that the English teacher, and other learners in the class, are 'reading for real'. Learners have interesting things to say! In spite of the enormous pressure of work, the enormous amount they have to read each week, many English teachers manage to respond to their students' writing as readers, not just as assessors. Teachers often find that, once the pressure to assess – to 'mark' or 'grade' – is taken off them, they can respond to the writing out of interest in its content. This may sound like a small change in method. In fact it embodies a quite different view of the nature of writing and learning to write. English classes can be arranged around a principle of 'story exchange' and 'information exchange', in which everything everyone writes is displayed, circulated and responded to not only by the teacher but also by other learners.

One way of helping learners to focus more closely on the writer–reader relationship is through collaborative writing. An intermediate writer–reader relationship will actually be built into the writing process. Collaborators are able to provide the 'dialogue' for each other that single authors have to create for themselves. This means that while drafting a piece of writing, each collaborator is constantly having to think about how readers will respond, because s/he knows the other collaborator(s) will be looking at the drafts. When the collaborators meet, their discussion of the draft anticipates potential reader responses to it. We have encouraged collaborative writing of various sorts in academic writing. This includes students both helping each other with their own individual assignments and writing joint assignments. Students say that in early drafts they find they are writing with their student colleagues in mind: conscious of how they will react to what they have written. In the final drafts, however, they start discussing together whether any changes need to be made in view of the fact that the assignment will be read (and assessed) by a subject tutor. The issue of the writer–reader relationship arises naturally in collaborative writing workshops of this type.

Take a critical approach to correctness and appropriacy

In Chapter 8 we discussed the way in which questions of formal accuracy are fundamentally linked to issues of class and power. It is often the case – and will increasingly be so in the UK because of the emphasis on 'accuracy' in the National Curriculum and associated testing – that writing in school is judged primarily on its formal aspects: spelling, punctuation and syntax. Yet conventional spelling, punctuation and grammar are nothing more than surface, mechanical aspects of writing, and to emphasise these is to neglect the teaching of writing as meaning-making, and as a means of social action. The argument that children are being betrayed by lack of attention to spelling and grammar is extremely misleading. Focusing more and more on these aspects of writing can only perpetuate inequalities, since the ability to use writing powerfully will remain exclusively with those who acquire it outside school. Further, using the mechanical aspects of writing as the main criterion for literacy and educational success militates against those who, however hard they and their teachers try, do not pick up these conventions easily, thus contributing to the exclusion of many from mainstream ideological activity in terms of written circulation of ideas. It is therefore essential to make content rather than form the primary focus in the teaching of writing.

Because the mechanical aspects of writing can be labelled 'correct' or 'incorrect', however, they are used as gatekeeping devices, and consequently teachers cannot disregard them. It is widely recognised that these conventions are more likely to be learned by engaging in purposeful and interesting activities that involve writing rather than by being drilled. We fully endorse the widespread practice in primary and adult education of allowing conventional spelling, grammar and punctuation to emerge through frequent opportunities for using writing meaningfully. However, we suggest that this can be combined with critical discussion about the conventions, and that critical discussion about them is more helpful than insistence on them. In our experience, an understanding of the social and historical basis for conventions, along the lines we presented in Chapter 8, helps to engender control over them (see Ivanič 1988). An example of materials that are designed to stimulate critical discussion of this sort is *Language and Power* (Harris and others 1990). However, materials provide only half the solution, and a more challenging task for teachers is to know enough about these conventions to be able to explain the difficulties that learners are encountering with them as they arise.

The same applies to the models of appropriateness that form the basis of teaching writing in the National Curriculum (Fairclough 1992c). Prescriptions as to what are and are not appropriate ways of writing in particular circumstances act as social constraints on the writer, and people need to learn to interact with and react to those constraints in many different ways, depending on their ideological positioning and the reader–writer power relations involved in the act of writing (see Chapter 7 for further discussion of this). It is not simply a matter of the writer recognising the normative social constraints, but rather of negotiating a position on those constraints and acting accordingly. We believe that it is essential for teachers to help people learning to write at all levels to question these views of appropriateness and to develop a critical social awareness of the way in which they are socially and historically constructed.

There is a difficult tension between, on the one hand, enabling learner writers to access the powerful forms of language and writing so that they develop the cultural capital that is perceived as necessary for success in education and in the world beyond school or university, and, on the other hand, opening up for them the possibility of challenging those prescriptions (see the debate in Reid and Hudson 1996). We experience exactly this tension in providing support for writing in Higher Education (as described in Clark 1992). In our view, explicit discussion of the social origins of conventions for correctness and appropriacy can help to address this tension. On the one hand, such discussion can reduce the extent to which alienation blocks learners from acquiring the conventions by making the reasons for their alienation apparent. On the other hand, it can provide the basis on which they can, when the risk is not too high, contribute to the ideological work of challenging and changing conventions that work to the detriment of values, beliefs and social groups and ideas with which they identify.

CONCLUSION

In this chapter we have drawn together the major implications, as we see them, of the view of writing as a social practice that we have set out in earlier chapters. We have argued that writing plays a central role in the circulation and consumption of ideas and, for that reason, in the development of democracy. We first examined some of the political implications and argued for the development of a devolved, participatory democracy, which would enable ordinary people to participate more directly in decision-making about how society should develop. We then suggested changes in the patterns of ownership and organisation of the print media and argued for greater encouragement of projects, such as community publishing, that would allow more ordinary people to engage in public debate through writing. We proposed a set of pedagogic principles to guide the teaching of writing. We also suggest that the view of writing presented in this book and the pedagogic principles arising from it lend weight to the argument that research on writing and on learning to write must be conducted in natural contexts (Clark and Ivanič 1991; Newkirk 1991).

We suggest that a writing pedagogy that is informed by the principles outlined in this chapter would not alienate the majority of people from writing but could, perhaps, excite them and help them to see the tremendous possibilities that writing offers them (not just 'others'), in terms of engagement with ideas and actively participating in social, cultural and political life.

NOTES

INTRODUCTION

1 The use of the term 'discourse' rather than 'language' in this broad way is in itself a site of ideological struggle. We would prefer to reclaim the terms 'language' and 'linguistic' to represent the whole socially constructed act of language use, with all its ideological underpinnings and consequences. To use the words 'language' and 'linguistic' in this way would be to claim that there is no such thing as language, or the study of language, without a social dimension: to contest the very idea that it is possible to think of language in a neutral way. However, for the purposes of this book, we need a way of distinguishing between discourse as a whole and the actual linguistic features of written text. We are therefore rather reluctantly reserving the terms 'language' and 'linguistic' to refer to the latter.
2 The word 'voice(s)' is used by Bakhtin (1981, 1986) and Wertsch (1991) in the same way as we are using the term 'discourse type'.

WRITING, POLITICS AND POWER

1 For an analysis of how the meanings constructed in the press go beyond representations of the world, and include constructions of social relations and social identities, see Fairclough 1995, especially Chapter 7.
2 The Conservative government published its new proposals for media ownership on 23 May 1995. These proposals encourage further concentration of cross-media ownership.
3 The Calcutt Committee was set up by the government in 1990 to examine the issue of privacy and the press. It recommended self-regulation by the press, and the Press Complaints Commission was set up as a result in 1991 (for a discussion of this see McNair 1994).

   The 'd' notice system refers to the practice whereby the Ministry of Defence – hence the 'd' – briefs journalists and controls the kind of information given out.

   The 'lobby' system is a similar practice, operated by government ministries. Journalists accredited to the 'lobby' receive unattributable briefings from government 'sources'. See the Introduction to *War and Peace News* (Glasgow University Media Group, 1985a) for a description of how the lobby system works.

4 The *Belgrano* was an Argentinean ship sunk by a British ship during the Falklands/Malvinas War. There was a lot of controversy surrounding the decision to torpedo the ship, which resulted in a large number of Argentinean deaths, as it emerged that the *Belgrano* was sailing outside the exclusion zone away from the islands, not inside, as claimed by Mrs Thatcher in parliament. The Minister of Defence resigned over the affair.

5 Currently (while writing this chapter in 1996) on British television (four channels): four hospital dramas, two vet dramas, four police dramas, six soaps and a number of thriller movies.

6 Williams used the past tense because he was referring to the debate about culture that had been going on in the 1950s and 1960s.

WRITING AND SOCIAL CONTEXT

1 'Drownings': during the 'Terror', men, women and children in Nantes were taken out in boats and drowned in an attempt to quash dissent.

WRITING PROCESSES AND PRACTICES

1 This insight comes from Greg Myers in discussions we have had with him of the Hayes and Flower model.

2 This list grew out of discussions in The Teaching of Writing Research and Development Group at Lancaster University.

3 This quotation was first published in Clark and Ivanič 1991.

4 Transcription conventions:
[ ]: words added to aid comprehension;
punctuation: my chunking based on tapescript;
false starts, hesitations and repetitions are omitted.

WHY WRITE? PURPOSES FOR WRITING

1 Jilly Cooper is an English writer of popular, 'blockbuster' novels.

2 The Mass-Observation Archive holds a collection of writings by volunteer writers from a wide variety of backgrounds about their experience of everyday life. The earliest material covers the period 1937–mid 1950s, and the later material covers 1981 to the pesent day. The Archive is housed in The Library, University of Sussex, Brighton, BN1 9QL, and its work has been documented by Dorothy Sheridan (see Sheridan 1993, 1996; Sheridan and others forthcoming).

3 This play was never actually produced, but was published in *Collected Plays for T.V.* (Griffiths 1988a).

4 This was a play for television about a woman with breast cancer. It was

transmitted to an estimated audience of 11 million people. The author received 180 personal letters and over 1,800 letters were received by the *Sunday People* newspaper from readers writing about their experiences of mastectomy (see the preface to the play in Griffiths, 1988c: 129).

5 In this section we are drawing substantially on insights made by Simon Pardoe (1994a, 1997), and we are grateful for his comments on an earlier draft of the section.

WRITER IDENTITY

1 This chapter is a reworking of an article originally published in *Prospect: The Australian Journal of TESOL* 10.1 (Ivanič 1995) and we are grateful to the editor for permission to reprint it in its revised form here. The issues in it are discussed in more depth in Ivanič forthcoming.
2 See note 2 on Chapter 1.
3 The idea of self-representation originates in the work of Goffman (1959, re-issued by Penguin, 1969 and 1981), and has been developed from the point of view of writing by Cherry (1988) and Ivanič (1994, and forthcoming).
4 This argument is powerfully developed by Hashimoto (1987).
5 We are grateful to Theresa Lillis for insights that have helped us with the rewriting of this section.
6 Frances has shown how she could have done this in her own account of this experience under her real name as part of a collaborative article in the *RaPAL Bulletin* (Ivanič and others 1996).

ISSUES OF CORRECTNESS AND STANDARDISATION IN WRITING

1 We are grateful for valuable feedback on this chapter from Catherine Macrae, Team leader for the City of Edinburgh Council Adult Education Team and literacy researcher.
2 Many of the issues raised in this section originated in discussions with Wendy Moss, Lecturer at the City Lit. Training Unit, London.
3 We are grateful for valuable feedback on this section from Nigel Hall, reader in Literacy Education at Manchester Metropolitan University, and Jonathan Culpeper, lecturer in the Department of Modern English Language, Lancaster University.
4 For a complete outline of current punctuation conventions for English see *The Comprehensive Grammar of the English Language* (Second Edition) Appendix III (Quirk and others 1985).
5 We are grateful to Sarah Moss for providing an excellent review of these sources in 'Standard and non-standard language in the English education system', 1996, a dissertation for the course Language and Education, in the Department of Linguistics and Modern English Language, Lancaster University.

SOCIAL AND EDUCATIONAL IMPLICATIONS OF OUR VIEW OF WRITING

1 For details, contact the Secretary, currently Tom Woodin, Gatehouse Books, Hulme Centre, Hulme Walk, Manchester, M15 5FQ. Gatehouse Books is a founder member of the Federation of Worker Writers and Community Publishers, and will always be a good point of contact.
2 For details, contact Commonword, Cheetwood House, 21 Newton Street, Manchester M1 1FZ.

BIBLIOGRAPHY

Albrow, K. (1972) *The English Writing System: Notes Towards a Description*, London: Longman, for The Schools Council.

Althusser, L. (1971) 'Ideology and ideological state apparatuses' in L. Althusser (ed.) *Lenin and Philosophy and Other Essays*, trans. B. Brewster, London: New Left Books.

Bakhtin, M.M. (1981) 'Discourse in the novel' (first published in 1929) in M. Holquist (ed.) *The Dialogic Imagination*, trans. C. Emerson and M. Holquist, Austin: University of Texas Press.

—— (1986) 'The problem of speech genres' and 'The problem of the text in linguistics, philology, and the human sciences: An experiment in philosophical analysis', in C. Emerson and M. Holquist (eds) *Bakhtin: Speech Genres and Other Late Essays*, trans. V. McGee, Austin: University of Texas Press.

Barnes, D. (1988) 'The politics of oracy', in M. MacLure and others (eds) *Oracy Matters*, Milton Keynes: Open University Press.

Bartholomae, D. (1985) 'Inventing the university', in M. Rose (ed.) *When a Writer Can't Write*, New York: Guilford Press.

Barton, D. (1994) *Literacy: An Introduction to the Ecology of Written Communication*, Oxford: Blackwell.

Barton, D. and Hamilton, M. (1996) 'Social and cognitive factors in the historical development of writing', in A. Lock and C. Peters (eds) *Handbook of Human Symbolic Evolution*, Oxford: Oxford University Press.

—— (forthcoming) *Local Literacies*, London: Routledge.

Barton, D. and Ivanič, R. (eds) (1991) *Writing in the Community*, Newbury Park, CA: Sage Publications.

Barton, D. and Padmore, S. (1991) 'Roles, networks and values in everyday writing', in D. Barton and R. Ivanič (eds) *Writing in the Community*, Newbury Park, CA: Sage Publications.

Barton, D., Hamilton, M., Ivanič, R., Ormerod, F., Padmore, S., Pardoe, S. and Rimmershaw, R. (1993) 'Photographing literacy practices', *Changing English* 1,1: 127–40.

Beach, R. and Bridwell, L. (1984) *New Directions in Composition Research*, New York: Guilford Press.

Bell, A. (1991) *The Language of the News Media*, Oxford: Blackwell.

Benn, C. and Chitty, C. (1996) *30 Years On. Is Comprehensive Education Alive and Well or Struggling to Survive?* London: Fulton.

Bennett, S. (1994) *Theatre Audiences: A Theory of Production and Reception,* London: Routledge.

Bennett, T. (1982) 'Media, "reality", signification', in M. Gurevitch, T. Bennett, J. Curran and J. Wollacott (eds) *Culture, Society and the Media,* London: Methuen.

Bernstein, B. (1990) *The Structuring of Pedagogic Discourse: Class, Codes and Control, Volume IV,* London: Routledge.

Biber, D. (1988) *Variation Across Speech and Writing,* Cambridge: Cambridge University Press.

Bizzell, P. (1992) *Academic Discourse and Critical Consciousness,* Pittsburgh, PA: University of Pittsburgh Press.

Bolinger, D. and Sears, D. (1981) *Aspects of Language* (Third edition), New York: Harcourt, Brace/Jovanovitch.

Bourdieu, P. (1977) *Outline of a Theory of Practice,* Cambridge: Cambridge University Press.

—— (1984) *Distinction,* London: Routledge.

—— (1991) *Language and Symbolic Power,* edited by J. Thompson, Cambridge, MA: Polity Press.

Bourdieu, P. and Passeron, J.C. (1977) *Reproduction in Education, Society and Culture,* Newbury Park, CA: Sage Publications.

Britton, J. (1970) *Language and Learning,* Harmondsworth: Penguin.

—— (1983) 'Shaping at the point of utterance', in A. Freedman, I. Pringle and J. Yalden (eds) *Learning to Write: First Language/Second Language,* London: Longman.

Britton, J., Burgess, T., Martin, N., McLeod, A. and Rosen, H. (1975) *The Development of Writing Abilities (11–18),* London: Macmillan.

Brodkey, L. (1987) *Academic Writing as a Social Practice,* Philadelphia, PA: Temple University Press.

Bullock, R. and Trimbur, J. (eds) (1991) *The Politics of Writing Instruction: Postsecondary,* Portsmouth, NH: Heinemann.

Byrne, D. (1988) *Teaching Writing Skills,* London: Longman.

Cameron, D. (1985), *Feminism and Linguistic Theory,* London: Macmillan.

—— (1995) *Verbal Hygiene,* London: Routledge.

Chase, G. (1988) 'Accommodation, resistance and the politics of student writing', *College Composition and Communication* 39,1: 13–22.

Cherry, R. (1988) '*Ethos* versus persona: self-representation in written discourse', *Written Communication* 5,3: 251–76.

Chomsky, N. (1965) *Aspects of the Theory of Syntax,* Cambridge, MA: Massachusetts Institute of Technology Press.

Clark, R. (1984) 'Jubilant bosses, jubilant miners: or what the papers say', unpublished MA dissertation, Department of Linguistics and Modern English Language, Lancaster University.

—— (1992) 'Principles and practice of CLA in the classroom', in N. Fairclough (ed.) *Critical Language Awareness,* London: Longman.

—— (1993a) 'Developing critical literacy: The gulf between them: the truth and other media fictions', *Changing English* 1,1: 192–217.

—— (1993b) 'Developing practices of resistance: Critical reading for

247

students of politics', in D. Graddol, L. Thompson and M. Bryam (eds) *Language and Culture*, Clevedon: Multilingual Matters.

—— (1995) 'Developing critical reading practices', *Prospect: The Journal of Australian TESOL* 10,2: 65–81.

—— (1997) 'Weaving the web: Conversations with Trevor Griffiths', Centre for Language in Social Life Working Paper Series No. 83, Lancaster: Department of Linguistics and Modern English Language.

—— (forthcoming) 'From text to performance: Interpretation or traduction? Trevor Griffiths' *Fatherland*, as directed by Ken Loach', to appear in *Language and Literature*.

Clark, R. and Ivanič, R. (1991) 'Consciousness-raising about the writing process', in P. Garrett and C. James (eds) *Language Awareness in the Classroom*, London: Longman.

—— (forthcoming) 'Critical discourse analysis and educational change', in L. van Lier (ed.) *Encyclopedia of Language and Education, Volume 6: Knowledge about Language*, Dordrecht: Kluwer.

Clark, R., Ivanič, R. and Rimmershaw, R. (1994) 'What am I supposed to make of this?', *Centre for Research in Language Education Working Paper Series, no. 22*, Lancaster University: Department of Linguistics and Modern English Language.

Clark, R., Fairclough, N., Ivanič, R. and Martin-Jones, M. (1990a) 'Critical Language Awareness Part I: A critical review of three current approaches to language awareness', *Language and Education* 4,4: 249–60.

Clark, R., Constantinou, C., Cottey, A. and Yeoh, O.C. (1990b) 'Rights and obligations in student writing', in R. Clark, N. Fairclough, R. Ivanič, N. McLeod, J. Thomas and P. Meara (eds) *British Studies in Applied Linguistics 5: Language and Power*, London: Centre for Information on Language Teaching, for the British Association for Applied Linguistics.

Clark, R., Fairclough, N., Ivanič, R., Mcleod, N., Thomas, J. and Meara, P. (eds) (1990c) *British Studies in Applied Linguistics 5: Language and Power*, London: Centre for Information on Language Teaching, for the British Association for Applied Linguistics.

Clark, R., Fairclough, N., Ivanič, R., and Martin-Jones, M. (1991) 'Critical Language Awareness Part II: Towards critical alternatives', *Language and Education* 5,1: 41–54.

Commonword (1988) Details given in *She says: Poetry by Women*, Manchester: Crocus.

Cook-Gumperz, J. (1986) 'Literacy and schooling: An unchanging question?', in J. Cook-Gumperz (ed.) *The Social Construction of Literacy*, Cambridge: Cambridge University Press.

Crystal, D. (1987) *The Cambridge Encyclopedia of Language*, Cambridge: Cambridge University Press.

Curran, J. (1991) 'Mass media and democracy: A reappraisal', in J. Curran and M. Gurevitch (eds) *Mass Media and Society*, London: Edward Arnold.

Davies, P. (1994) 'Long-term unemployment and literacy: A case-study of the Restart interview', in M. Hamilton, D. Barton and R. Ivanič (eds) *Worlds of Literacy*, Clevedon: Multilingual Matters.

Davies, P., Fitzpatrick, S., Grenko, V. and Ivanič, R. (1994) 'Literacy, strength and identity', in M. Hamilton, D. Barton and R. Ivanič (eds) *Worlds of Literacy*, Clevedon: Multilingual Matters.

Delpit, L. (1988) 'The silenced dialogue: Power and pedagogy in educating other people's children', *Harvard Educational Review*, 58,3: 280–98.

Department of Education and Science (1989) *English for Ages 5–16*, London: HMSO.

—— (1995) *The National Curriculum for English*, London: HMSO.

Ellis, A. (1993) *Reading, Writing and Dyslexia: A Cognitive Analysis (Second edition)*, Hove: Lawrence Erlbaum.

Ellsworth, E. (1989) 'Why doesn't this feel empowering? Working through repressive myths of critical pedagogy', *Harvard Educational Review*, 59,3: 297–324.

Engels, F. (1944) *The Condition of the Working Class in England*, trans. and ed. W. Henderson and W. Chaloner (1958) Oxford: Blackwell.

Fairclough, N. (1989) *Language and Power*, London: Longman.

—— (1992a) *Discourse and Social Change*, Cambridge: Polity Press.

—— (ed.) (1992b) *Critical Language Awareness*, London: Longman.

—— (1992c) 'The appropriacy of "appropriateness"', in N. Fairclough (ed.) *Critical Language Awareness*, London: Longman.

—— (1995) *Media Discourse*, London: Edward Arnold.

—— (1996) 'Discourse across disciplines: Critical Discourse Analysis in the study of social change', paper delivered as the keynote address to the Association Internationale de Linguistique Appliquée Congress, Jvaskyla, Finland, August 1996.

Fawcett, A. and Nicolson, R. (eds) (1994) *Dyslexia in Children: Multidisciplinary Perspectives*, Hemel Hempstead: Harvester Wheatsheaf.

Flower, L. (1990) 'Studying cognition in context', Introduction to L. Flower, V. Stein, J. Ackerman, M. Kantz, K. McCormick and W. Peck *Reading-to-write: Exploring a Cognitive and Social Process*, New York: Oxford University Press.

Flynn, E. (1991) 'Composition studies from a feminist perspective', in R. Bullock and J. Trimbur (eds) *The Politics of Writing Instruction: Postsecondary*, Portsmouth, NH: Heinemann.

Forgaçs, D. (1988) *A Gramsci Reader*, London: Lawrence & Wishart.

Fowler, R., Hodge, R., Kress, G. and Trew, T. (1979) *Language and Control*, London: Routledge.

Freedman, A., Pringle, I. and Yalden, J. (eds) *Learning to Write: First Language/Second Language*, London: Longman.

Freire, P. (1972) *Pedagogy of the Oppressed*, London/Harmondsworth: Penguin (Second edition, 1982).

Gardener, S. 1992, *The Long Word Club*, Lancaster: Research and Practice in Adult Literacy Publications (originally published in 1985 as *The Development of Written Language Within Adult Fresh Start and Return to Learning Programmes*, London: ILEA Language and Literacy Unit).

Gee, J. (1990) *Social Linguistics and Literacies: Ideology in Discourses*, Basingstoke: Falmer Press.

Gibson, R. (1986) *Critical Theory and Education*, London: Hodder & Stoughton.

Gifford, T., Brown, W. and Bundey, R. for Liverpool City Council (1989)

249

Loosen the Shackles: The Gifford Report, First report of the Liverpool 8 inquiry into race relations in Liverpool, London: Karia Press.

Giroux, H. (1989) *Schooling for Democracy*, London: Routledge.

Glasgow University Media Group (1985a) *War and Peace News*, Milton Keynes: Open University Press.

—— (1985b) *War and Peace Teaching/Discussion notes (with accompanying video material on the Falklands conflict)*, Glasgow: Glasgow University Press.

Glenny, M. (1986) 'Interview with Trevor Griffiths', preface to T. Griffiths *Judgement over the Dead*, London: Verso.

Goffman, E. (1959) *The Presentation of Self in Everyday Life*, London: Allen Lane (re-issued by Penguin, 1969).

—— (1981) *Forms of Talk*, Oxford: Blackwell.

Gramsci, A. (1967) *Scritti Politici (La formazione degli intellettuali)* Roma: Editori Riuniti.

—— (1971) *Selections from Prison Notebooks*, London: Lawrence & Wishart.

—— (1977) 'Socialism and culture' in *Selections from Political Writings 1910–1920*, ed. Q. Hoare, London: Lawrence & Wishart.

—— (1978) *Selections from Political Writings 1921–1926*, ed. Q. Hoare, London: Lawrence & Wishart.

Greene, S. (1991) 'Writing from sources: Authority in text and task', *Centre for the Study of Writing Technical Report* 55, Berkeley, CA: UCLA.

Gregory, G. (1984) 'Community published working class writing in context', in M. Meek and J. Millar (eds) *Changing English: Essays for Harold Rosen*, London: Heinemann.

—— (1991) 'Community publishing as self-education' in D. Barton and R. Ivanič (eds) *Writing in the Community*, Newbury Park, CA: Sage Publications.

Grice, H. (1975) 'Logic and conversation', in P. Cole and J. Morgan (eds) *Syntax and Semantics 3: Speech Acts*, New York: Academic Press.

Griffiths, T. (1972) *Occupations*, London: Faber.

—— (1974a) *The Party*, London: Faber.

—— (1974b) 'All Good Men', in T. Griffiths (1988) *Collected Plays for T.V.*, London: Faber.

—— (1976) *Comedians*, London: Faber.

—— (1977) 'Such Impossibilities', in T. Griffiths (1988) *Collected Plays for T.V.*, London: Faber.

—— (1986) *Judgement over the Dead*, broadcast as *The Last Place on Earth*, London: Verso.

—— (1987) *Fatherland*, London, Faber.

—— (1988a) *Collected Plays for T.V.*, London: Faber.

—— (1988b) 'Country' in T. Griffiths *Collected Plays for T.V.*, London: Faber.

—— (1988c) 'Through the Night' in T. Griffiths *Collected Plays for T.V.*, London: Faber.

—— (1992) *The Gulf Between Us: The Truth and Other Fictions*, London: Faber.

—— (1992/3) Unpublished taped conversation with Romy Clark

—— (1994a) *Hope in the Year 2000*, London: Faber.

—— (1994b) *Thatcher's Children*, London: Faber.
Gurevitch, M., Bennett, T., Curran, J. and Wollacott, J. (eds) *Culture, Society and the Media*, London: Methuen.
Hall, N. (1987) *The Emergence of Literacy*, London: Hodder & Stoughton.
—— (ed.) (1989) *Writing with Reason: The Emergence of Authorship in Young Children*, London: Hodder & Stoughton.
—— (1996a) 'Learning about punctuation: An introduction and overview', in N. Hall and A. Robinson (eds) *Learning about Punctuation*, Clevedon: Multilingual Matters.
—— (1996b) 'Learning to punctuate: An ecological and conceptual investigation', unpublished report to the ESRC.
Hall, N. and Ivanič, R. (1996) 'Learning to punctuate at different ages: exploring similarities and differences', paper presented at the International Reading Association Convention, New Orleans, May 1996.
Hall, N. and Robinson, A. (eds) (1996) *Learning about Punctuation*, Clevedon: Multilingual Matters.
Hall, S. (1980) 'Encoding/decoding', in S. Hall, S. Hobson, A. Lowe and P. Willis (eds) *Culture, Media, Language*, London: Hutchinson.
—— (1982) 'The rediscovery of ideology: Return of the repressed in media studies', in M. Gurevitch, T. Bennett, J. Curran and J. Wollacott (eds) *Culture, Society and the Media*, London: Methuen.
—— (1984) 'The rise of the representative/interventionist state 1880s–1920s' in G. McLennan, D. Held and S. Hall, (eds) *State and Society in Contemporary Britain*, Cambridge: Polity Press.
—— (1989) 'The meaning of New Times' in S. Hall and M. Jacques (eds) *New Times: The Changing Face of Politics in the 1990s*, London: Lawrence & Wishart.
Hall, S. and Jacques, M. (1983) *The Politics of Thatcherism*, London: Lawrence & Wishart.
Hall, S., Critchley, S., Jefferson, T., Clarke, J. and Roberts, B. (1978) *Policing the Crisis*, London: Macmillan.
Halliday, M.A.K. (1978) *Language as Social Semiotic: The Social Interpretation of Language and Meaning*, London: Edward Arnold.
—— (1985) *Spoken and Written Language*, Victoria: Deakin University Press (reprinted by Oxford University Press, 1989).
—— (1994) *An Introduction to Functional Grammar (Second edition)*, London: Edward Arnold.
Halliday, M.A.K. and Hasan, R. (1985) *Language, Context and Text: Aspects of Language in a Social-semiotic Perspective*, Victoria: Deakin University Press (reprinted by Oxford University Press, 1989).
Hamilton, M., Barton, D. and Ivanič, R. (eds) (1994) *Worlds of Literacy*, Clevedon: Multilingual Matters.
Harris, R., Schwab, I. and Whitman, L. (eds) (1990) *Language and Power*, New York: Harcourt Brace Jovanovich.
Hashimoto, I. (1987) 'Voice as juice: Some reservations about evangelic composition', *College Composition and Communication* 38,1: 70–80.
Hayes, J. and Flower, L. (1980) 'Identifying the organization of writing processes: An interdisciplinary approach', in L. Gregg and E. Steinberg (eds) *Cognitive Processes in Writing*, Hillsdale, NJ: Lawrence Erlbaum.

BIBLIOGRAPHY

——— (1983) 'Uncovering cognitive processes in writing: an introduction to protocol analysis', in P. Mosenthal, L. Tamor and S. Walmsley (eds) *Research on Writing: Principles and Methods*, New York: Longman.

Hayes, J., Schriver, K., Hill, C. and Hatch, J. (1992) 'Assessing the message and the messenger', *The Quarterly of the National Writing Project and the Center for the Study of Writing and Literacy* 14,2:15–17.

Hedge, T. (1988) *Writing*, Oxford: Oxford University Press.

Herman, E.S. and Chomsky, N. (1994) *Manufacturing Consent*, London: Vintage.

Herzberg, B. (1991) 'Composition and the politics of the curriculum' in R. Bullock and J. Trimbur (eds) *The Politics of Writing Instruction: Postsecondary*, Portsmouth, NH: Heinemann.

Hewitt, R. (1989) 'The new oracy: another critical glance', paper delivered to the British association for Applied Linguistics annual meeting, Lancaster.

Ivanič, R. (1983) 'Nouns for hire: A study of nouns with both open system and closed system characteristics', unpublished M.A. dissertation, Department of Linguistics and Modern English Language, Lancaster University.

——— (1988) 'Critical language awareness in action', *Language Issues* 2,2: 2–7 (reprinted in R. Carter (ed.) (1990) *Knowledge about Language and the Curriculum: The LINC Reader*, London: Hodder & Stoughton).

——— (1991) 'Nouns in search of a context', *I.R.A.L.* 29,2: 93–114.

——— (1993) 'The discoursal construction of writer identity: An investigation with eight mature students', unpublished Ph.D. thesis, Department of Linguistics and Modern English Language, Lancaster University.

——— (1994a) 'I is for Interpersonal: discoursal construction of writer identities and the teaching of writing', *Linguistics and Education*, 6,1: 3–15.

——— (1994b) 'Characterizations of context for describing spoken and written discourse', in S. Čmejrková, F. Daneš and E. Havlová (eds) *Writing vs. Speaking: Language, Text, Discourse, Communication*, Tübingen: Gunter Narr Verlag.

——— (1995) 'Writer identity', *Prospect: The Australian Journal of TESOL* 10,1: 1–31.

——— (1996) 'The logic of non-standard punctuation', in N. Hall and A. Robinson (eds) *Learning about Punctuation*, Clevedon: Multilingual Matters.

——— (forthcoming) *Writing and Identity: The Discoursal Construction of Identity in Academic Writing*, Amsterdam: Benjamins.

Ivanič, R. and Moss, W. (1991) 'Bringing community writing practices into education', in D. Barton and R. Ivanič (eds) *Writing in the Community*, Newbury Park, CA: Sage Publications.

Ivanič, R. and Roach. D. (1990) 'Academic writing, power and disguise', in R. Clark, N. Fairclough, R. Ivanič, N. Mcleod, J. Thomas and P. Meara (eds) *British Studies in Applied Linguistics 5: Language and Power*, London: Centre for Information on Language Teaching, for the British Association for Applied Linguistics.

Ivanič, R. and Simpson, J. (1992) 'Who's who in academic writing?' in N. Fairclough (ed.) *Critical Language Awareness*, London: Longman.

252

Ivanič, R., Aitchison, M. and Weldon, S. (1996) 'Bringing ourselves into our writing', *RaPAL Bulletin* 28/29: 2–8.

Janks, H. (ed.) (1993a) *Critical Language Awareness Series*, Johannesburg: Hodder & Stoughton and Wits University Press.

—— (1993b) 'Developing Critical Language Awareness materials for a post-apartheid South Africa', *English in Australia*, 106: 55–67.

—— (1995) 'The research and development of critical language awareness materials for use in South African secondary schools', unpublished Ph.D. thesis, Department of Linguistics and Modern English Language, Lancaster University.

—— (1996) 'Why we still need Critical Language Awareness in South Africa', Spil Plus: University of Stellenbosch.

Janks, H. and Ivanič, R. (1992) 'Critical Language Awareness and emancipatory discourse', in Fairclough, N. (ed.) *Critical Language Awareness*, London: Longman.

Johnson, K. (1996) *Language Teaching and Skill Learning*, Oxford: Blackwell.

Johnson, P. (1996) *Words and Images on the Page: Improving Children's Writing Through Design*, London: Fulton Publishers.

Johnson, S. (1755) *A Dictionary of the English Language*.

Jordan, J. (1967) 'On listening: A good way to hear', in J. Jordan (1989) *Moving Towards Home*, London: Virago.

Karach, A. and Roach, D. (1994) 'Collaborative writing, consciousness-raising and practical feminist ethics', in M. Hamilton, D. Barton and R. Ivanič (eds) *Worlds of Literacy*, Clevedon: Multilingual Matters.

Kaufer, D. and Geisler, C. (1989) 'Novelty in academic writing', *Written Communication* 6,3: 286–311.

Kirsch, G. and Roen, D. (eds) (1990) *A Sense of Audience in Written Communication*, Newbury Park: Sage Publications.

Knowles, G. (to appear in 1997) *A Critical History of the English Language*, London: Edward Arnold.

Kress, G. (1982) *Learning to Write*. London: Routledge (Second edition: 1994).

—— (1985) *Linguistic Processes in Sociocultural Practice*, Victoria: Deakin University Press (reprinted by Oxford University Press, 1989).

Kress, G. and Hodge, R. (1979) *Language as Ideology*, London: Routledge.

Kress, G. and van Leeuwen, T. (1996) *Reading Images: The Grammar of Visual Design*, London: Routledge.

Kroll, B. (1984) 'Writing for readers: Three perspectives on audience', *College Composition and Communication* 35: 154–74.

McLennan, G. (1984) 'The contours of British politics: representative democracy and social class', in G. McLennan, D. Held and S. Hall (eds) *State and Society in Contemporary Britiain*, Cambridge, Polity Press.

McNair, B. (1994) *News and Journalism in the U.K.*, London: Routledge.

Mace, J. (1992) *Talking about Literacy: Principles and Practice of Adult Literacy Education*, London: Routledge.

Mace, J. (ed.) (1995) *Literacy, Language and Community Publishing: Essays in Adult Education*, Clevedon: Multilingual Matters.

Matsuhashi, A. (1982) 'Explorations in the real-time production of written discourse', in M. Nystrand (ed.) *What Writers Know: The Language, Process and Structure of Written Discourse*, New York: Academic Press.

Miles, T. (1983) *Dyslexia: The Pattern of Difficulties*, London: Granada.

Mills, S., Pearce, L., Spaull, S. and Millard, E. (1989) *Feminist Readings / Feminists Reading*, London: Harvester Wheatsheaf.

Milroy, J. and Milroy, L. (1985) *Authority in Language: Investigating Language Prescription and Standardisation*, London: Routledge.

—— (1993) *Real English*, London: Longman.

Ministry of Defence (1983) *The Protection of Military Information: The Beach Report*, Report of the Study Group on Censorship, London: HMSO, Cmnd 9112.

Moline, S. (1996) *I See What You Mean*, Sydney: Longman.

Morley, D. and Worpole, K. (eds) (1982) *The Republic of Letters*, London: Comedia.

Moss, S. (1996) 'Standard and non-standard language in the English education system', unpublished dissertation for the course Language and Education, Department of Linguistics and Modern English Language, Lancaster University.

Moss, W. (1995) 'Controlling or empowering? Writing through a scribe in adult basic education', in J. Mace (ed.) *Literacy, Language and Community Publishing: Essays in Adult Education*, Clevedon: Multilingual Matters.

Murray, D. (1978) 'Internal revision: a process of discovery', in C. Cooper and L. Odell (eds) *Research on Composing*, Urbana, Ill.: National Council of Teachers of English.

Nash, W. (1986) *English Usage: A Guide to First Principles*, London: Routledge.

National Writing Project, The (1989) *Audiences for Writing*, London: Nelson, for The National Curriculum Council.

—— (1989–90) *The Publications of The National Writing Project (1985–1988)*, London: Nelson, for The National Curriculum Council.

New London Group, The (1996) 'A pedagogy of multiliteracies: Designing social futures', *Harvard Educational Review*, 66,1: 60–92.

Newkirk, T. (1991) 'The politics of composition research: The conspiracy against experience', in R. Bullock and J. Trimbur (eds) *The Politics of Writing Instruction: Postsecondary*, Portsmouth, NH: Heinemann.

Nystrand, M. (1986) *The Structure of Written Communication: Studies in Reciprocity Between Writers and Readers*, New York: Academic Press.

Odell, L. and Goswami, D. (eds) (1985) *Writing in Non-academic Settings*, New York: Guilford Press.

Olson, D. (1977) 'From utterance to text: the bias of language in speech and writing', *Harvard Educational Review*, 47,3: 257–81.

Ong, W. (1977) *Interfaces of the Word*, Ithaca: Cornell University Press.

—— (1982) *Orality and Literacy: The Technologising of the Word*, London: Methuen.

Paley, A. (1988) in *She Says*, Manchester: Crocus (the imprint of Commonword).

Pardoe, S. (1991) 'Knowledge about writing: A case-study of six bilingual students in a U.K. Further Education College', unpublished M.A. dissertation, Department of Linguistics and Modern English Language, Lancaster University.

—— (1994a) 'Learning to write in a new educational setting: a focus on the writer's purpose', *Centre for Language in Social Life Working Paper Series, no. 58*, Department of Linguistics and Modern English Language, Lancaster University.

—— (1994b) 'Writing in another culture: The value of students' knowledge about language in writing pedagogy', in D. Graddol and J. Swann (eds) *Evaluating Language*, Clevedon: Multilingual Matters, for The British Association for Applied Linguistics.

—— (1997) 'Writing professional science: Genre, recontextualisation and empiricism in the learning of professional and scientific writing within an M.Sc. course in E.I.A', unpublished Ph.D. thesis, Department of Linguistics and Modern English Language, Lancaster University.

Parkes, M.B. (1992) *Pause and Effect: An Introduction to the History of Punctuation in the West*, London: Scolar Press.

Perera, K. (1984) *Children's Reading and Writing: Analysing Classroom Language*, Oxford: Blackwell.

Phillips, M. (1996) *All Must Have Prizes*, London: Little Brown.

Pilger, J. (1992) *Distant Voices*, London: Vintage.

Poole, M. and Wyver, J. (1984) *Powerplays*, London: British Film Institute.

Quirk, R., Greenbaum, S., Leech, G. and Svartvik, J. (1985) *The Comprehensive Grammar of the English Language (Second edition)*, London: Longman.

Read, C. (1986) *Children's Creative Spelling*, New York: Routledge.

Reid, E. and Hudson, R. (1996) 'Children's use of spoken standard English', review and author response, *BAAL Newsletter*, 53: 18–26.

Rich, A. (1981) *Compulsory Heterosexuality and Lesbian Existence*, London: Women's Press.

Robinson, A. (1996) 'Conversations with teachers about punctuation', in N. Hall and A. Robinson (eds) *Learning about Punctuation*, Clevedon: Multilingual Matters.

Romaine, S. (1994) *Language in Society*, Oxford: Oxford University Press.

Rose, M. (1984) *Writer's Block: The Cognitive Dimension*, Carbondale: South Illinois University Press.

Scannell, P. (1992) 'Public service broadcasting and modern public life', in P. Scannell and others (eds) *Culture and Power*, London: Sage Publications.

Schank, R. and Abelson, R. (1977) *Scripts, Plans, Goals and Understanding*, Hillsdale, NJ: Lawrence Erlbaum.

Sealey, A. (1996) 'Models of language, models of childhood', paper presented at the British Association for Applied Linguistics Annual Meeting, Swansea, September 1996.

Sheridan, D. (1993) 'Writing to the archive: Mass-observation as autobiography', *Sociology* 27,1: 27–40.

—— (1996) 'Damned anecdotes and dangerous confabulations: Mass-observation as life-history', *Mass-Observation Archive Occasional Paper No 7*, Brighton: University of Sussex Library.

Sheridan, D., Bloome, D. and Street, B. (forthcoming) *Writing Ourselves: Literacy Practices and the Mass-observation Archive*, Cresskill, NJ: Hampton Press.

Skeggs, B. (ed.) (1995) *Feminist Cultural Theory*, Manchester: Manchester Universiy Press.

Smith, D. (1939) *Dear Octopus*, London: Samuel French.

Stotsky, S. (1990) 'On planning and writing plans – or beware of borrowed theories', *College Composition and Communication*, 41,1: 37–57.

Street, B. (1984) *Literacy in Theory and Practice*, Cambridge: Cambridge University Press.,

—— (ed.) (1993) *Cross-cultural Approaches to Literacy*, Cambridge: Cambridge University Press.

—— (1995) *Social Literacies: Critical Perspectives on Literacy in Development, Ethnography and Education*, London: Longman.

Stubbs, M. (1980) *Language and Literacy: The Sociolinguistics of Reading and Writing*, London: Routledge.

—— (1986) *Educational Linguistics*, Oxford: Blackwell.

—— (1987) 'An educational theory of (written) language', in T. Bloor and J. Norrish (eds) *Written Language: Papers from the Annual Meeting of the British Association for Applied Linguistics*, London: Centre for Information on Language Teaching and Research.

Stubbs, M. and Hillier, H. (eds) (1983) *Readings on Language, Schools and Classrooms (Second edition)*, London: Methuen.

Swales, J. (1990) *Genre Analysis: English in Research and Academic Settings*, Cambridge: Cambridge University Press.

Taylor, D. (1983) *Family Literacy: Young Children Learning to Read and Write*, Portsmouth, NH: Heinemann.

Thompson, G. and Ye, Y. (1991) 'Evaluation in the reporting verbs used in academic papers', *Applied Linguistics* 12,4: 365–82.

Trudgill, P. (1975) *Accent, Dialect and the School*, London: Edward Arnold.

Upward, C. (1988) 'Simplified spelling: Prospects and perspectives', *Research and Practice in Adult Literacy Bulletin No. 5*: 6–8.

Vallins, G. (1965) *Spelling (Revised edition)*, revised by D. Scragg, London: Andre Deutsch.

Vološinov, V. (1973) *Marxism and the Philosophy of Language*, trans. L. Matejka and I.R. Titunik, New York: Seminar Press.

Wallace, C. (1986) *Learning to Read in a Multicultural Society*, Oxford: Pergamon.

—— (1992a) *Reading*, Oxford: Oxford University Press.

—— (1992b) 'Critical literacy awareness in the EFL classroom', in N. Fairclough (ed.) *Critical Language Awareness*, London: Longman.

Wardhaugh, R. (1992) *An Introduction to Sociolinguistics*, Oxford: Blackwell.

Waters, A. and Waters, M. (1995) *Study Tasks in English*, Cambridge, Cambridge University Press.

Wertsch, J. (1991) *Voices of the Mind*, Hemel Hempstead: Harvester Wheatsheaf.

Westergaard, J. and Resler, H. (1976) *Class in a Capitalist Society*, Harmondsworth: Penguin.

Widdowson, H. (1983) 'New starts and different kinds of failure', in A. Freedman, I. Pringle and J. Yalden (eds) *Learning to Write: First Language/Second Language*, London: Longman.

Williams, R. (1989) 'The idea of a common culture', written in 1968, reprinted in R. Gable (ed.) *Resources of Hope*, London: Verso.

Willis, P. (1977) *Learning to Labour: How Working Class Kids Get Working Class Jobs*, Farnborough: Saxon House.

Worpole, K. (1977) *Local Publishing and Local Culture*, Hackney: Centerprise.

INDEX

INDEX